In consideration of the season and the generally high spirits, I have procured this small token in hopes that it may express my Christmas wishes to you

Merry Christmas

חֹדֶל טוֹב

Adam

I GO POGO

POGO RE-RUNS: SOME REFLECTIONS ON ELECTIONS

SELECTED FROM
THREE POGO CLASSICS

I GO POGO
THE POGO PARTY
POGO EXTRA

BY WALT KELLY

With an Introduction and Commentaries
BY BILL VAUGHAN

A FIRESIDE BOOK
PUBLISHED BY
SIMON AND SCHUSTER

A Fireside Book
Published by Simon and Schuster
Rockefeller Center, 630 Fifth Avenue
New York, New York 10020

SBN 671-21906-5
Designed by Helen Barrow
Manufactured in the United States of America

1 2 3 4 5 6 7 8 9 10

CONTENTS

INTRODUCTION

LIKE MOST *denizens of the United States, the citizens of Walt Kelly's Okefenokee Swamp don't pay much attention to politics until an election comes around. I suppose it's because politics are at their most comical when this great democracy is engaged in its most serious function, reading palms to see what hands are best suited to grasp the Helm of the Ship of State.*

There are exceptions, of course, as when some particularly noisome scandal or obscene conduct in high and public places takes our minds off our apathy. But basically we tend to reserve our political fervor for Presidential election years. Some citizens even get so worked up that they go out and vote.

Perhaps the most hilarious part of the election process is that preceding the national conventions, the searching for and packaging of candidates, the in-depth analyses by the media, the poll-taking and the switching of horses (or bugs or possums) in the middle of the stream.

At least that is the part that most stimulates the friends of Pogo. Every four years Pogo falls into the hands of his friends, with results painfully familiar to anyone who has undergone this misfortune.

This book covers the campaigns, or rather the pre-campaigns, of 1952, 1956 and 1960.

Kelly himself once wrote that there is altogether too much searching for meaning in this world. The poets insist that a poem does not mean, a poem is. *So maybe these cartoons don't mean. Maybe they just* are.

And thank God they are.

BILL VAUGHAN

PREFACE

HEIGHDY, THERE, POGO.. I BRUNG MY SISTERN LAW 'LONG TODAY-- SHE AN' THE YOUNG'UN, TOOMEY III, IS A-VISITIN' OF ME AN' THE MR.
HOWDY FOLKS..LI'L' TOOMEY III LOOK LIKE A BRIGHT TAD--- HOW OLD IS HE?
HE READY FOR THE KINDER-GARTENS--- DON'T HE GOT PERTY EYES ON HIM? SAY SOMETHIN', TOOMEY III---
JES' FINE!
MY MY
HE SPEAK UP SOMETHIN' WONDERFUL-- GONE BE HARD TO KEEP A BOY LIKE THAT OUTEN THE WHITE HOUSE.. --BYE.
STOP OVER SOME AFTERNOON, POGO, NOW.. Y'HEAR?
JES' FINE.
WULL, SISTERN LAW--- THAT'S POGO--WHAT YOU THINKS OF HIM?
HE KIND OF A BORIN' FELLA, AIN'T HE?--- ALLUS SO ALL FIRED AGREEABLE.
JES' FINE.

POGO
JE VAIS PÔ-GEAU

I GO POGO

IN *1952 Pogo first demonstrated his most enduring and endearing political asset, reluctance. The American public is traditionally believed to admire the reluctant candidate. To seek office is considered pushy. In 1952 Governor Stevenson was more reluctant than General Eisenhower, and Pogo out-reluctanced them both.*

But the General beat the Governor, so there is little indication that Pogo would have won even if he had made it to whichever Chicago convention his little band of advisers and manipulators had in mind.

Here too we get a glimpse into the suspicious, accusatory atmosphere of the early Fifties. As Sarcophagus Macabre the vulture puts it so well, "It's these things we don't understand that are dangerous."

When Pogo says, "Critters is nice, but human beans makes the best people," it may be one of the few occasions when he has tried to kid us.

DON'T WRITE.. ..DON'T WIRE!

SEE IF YOU CAN REVERSE CHARGES

WELL ... HERE WE ARE BACK AT THAT LETTER ... THAT AIRMAIL LETTER ...
NOW'S YOUR CHANCE TO TAKE TO THE WING ... WHO'S IT FOR?

THINK I'D BE A PAUL PRY TO READ THE ADDRESS?
IT SAYS "TO CHOO CHOO CURTIS, THE NATURAL BORN MAIL MAN."

WHY, IT'S FOR ME!
WHAT IS IT? WHATISITWHATIS ITWHATISITWHAT ISITWHATISIT?

OFFICIAL BUSINESS. MY WALKIN' PAPERS.
CONGRATULAT-IONS! NOW YOU DON'T HAVE TO FLY AN' CAN WALK TO DE-LIVER IT TO YOURSELF.
NOTICE OF DISMISSAL

BY JING! THE GUMMINT CAN'T FIRE ME!
BUT HERE IS THE OL' DISMISSAL NOTE.

OH HO! I HOLDS A TRUMP CARD. THE GUMMINT IS NEVER HIRED ME. I BEEN WORKIN' ON MY OWN. UN-BE-KNOWNS!
KEEPIN' IT A SECRET FROM 'EM? WHERE'S YO' GITS THE MAIL?

FELLER I KNOWS IS GOT A "IN." IT'S FIRST-CLASS STUFF HE GOT.
YOU REALIZE THIS MAKES YOU A SECRET AGENT FOR THE GUMMINT?
FIGGER THEY'LL SEND A CLUTCH OF SENATORS TO INVEST-IGATE ME?
IF THEY DOES, GIT A JOB WITH 'EM.. INVEST-IGATIN' YOU' OWN SELF ... YOU IS A EX-PERT ON YOU.
IF THE FEDERALS NEVER HIRED YOU AS A MAILMAN, HOW COULD THEY FIRE YOU?
THEY IS PERFECTED A SYSTEM.
I ISN'T FIRED AS A MAILMAN --- THEY FIRES ME OUT OF A JOB OF BEETLE ADMINISTRATOR.
BUT..
NOTICE OF DISMISSAL
YOU NEVER WAS A BEETLE ADMINISTRATOR.
THEY'S TOOKEN CARE OF THAT TOO. THIS LETTER SENT TO ME IS ACTUAL FOR THE COMMISSIONER OF TIDES IN TENNESSEE.
HARD FOR 'EM TO FIRE HIM OUTTA THE BEETLE JOB. YOU BETTER TELL THEM HE AIN'T YOU.
NO... IT WOULD ONLY CAUSE CONFUSION.

IF I UNNERSTANDS THIS RIGHTLY, THE FEDERALS DON'T KNOW YOU IS THE MAILMAN HERE-AN'-ABOUTS.
RIGHT!
BUT THEY WANTS TO FIRE YOU OUT OF THE BEETLE ADMINISTRATOR JOB WHICH YOU DON'T HAVE SO THEY SENDS YOU A LETTER FIRIN' THE COMMISSIONER OF TIDE FOR TENNESSEE?
RIGHT--- AN I NEVER HEERD OF HIM.
SO... HE'S OUTEN A JOB?
YEP, BUT HE'LL NEVER KNOW IT--- THE LETTER WAS SENT IN 1946.
Y'KNOW, I THINK THIS IS ALL ON ACCOUNT OF YOU'S HANDLIN' SUCH A CHEAP BRAND OF MAIL NOWADAYS.
RIGHT! AN' IF I WOONT BE ACCUSED OF DISLOYALTY I'D START TAKIN' FROM ANOTHER JOBBER, BRAZIL, SAY. SERVE 'EM RIGHT TO START GITTIN' LETTERS IN PORTUGESE.
HEY, CHURCHY, HOW 'BOUT COMIN' UP THE HOUSE FO' SUPPER?
DOANMINEFFIEDOO, WILEY CATT.
I GOT A OL' COUSIN CRITTUR A-VISITIN' FROM UP KENTUCKAWAY.
CAT COUSIN, WILEY?

NOPE, A BIRD!
HEY, THERE! I BRUNG HOME A TURTLE FOR SUPPER!

GOOD! I WAS WOND'RIN' WHAT WE'D HAVE.

PUT ON THE SKILLET NOW DON'T BE 'FRAID, MAMIE'S GONNA MAKE A LULA SHORTHAND BRAID
I DON'T LIKE THAT MENU YO' COUSIN IS MENTIONED AFORE.

DON'T CARE FOR SOUP?
BUT OL' COUSIN SAY HE GONE MAKE TURTLE SOUP.

HEY SARKY, COME OUT AN' MEET OL' TURTLE!
YOU SAID YOU HAD A TURTLE FO' SUPPER...

BUT I DIN'T KNOW THE COOK HAD TO BE INNERDUCED TO TH' INGREDIMINTS.
CHURCHY, MEET COUSIN SARCOPHAGUS MACABRE...
UH, WHERE HE GO?

YESSIR, POGO, I GITS THE MAIL I DELIVERS FROM A BOY WHAT---- SAY.. HERE COMES THAT BOY NOW!
WHOA, TURKLE!
IT'S OL' CHURCHY LA FEMME!

I WAS TELLIN' POGO HOW YOU WRITES ALL THE MAIL I DELIVERS 'ROUND THE SWAMP, SO COME ON OUT.

NO! I IS HIDIN' FROM A MAN BACK THAT WAY NAME OF SARCOPHAGUS MACABRE....WANTED ME TO GO INTO THE TURTLE SOUP BUSINESS WITH HIM---- HE FURNISHIN' THE POT AN' ME FURNISHIN' ME!
NO DEAL, HUH?

NOBODY'S AFTER YOU, COME ON OUT...
I DON'T WANT THAT BUZZARD TO FIND ME.... HE GOT A SWEET TOOTH FOR TURTLE SOUP!

SO YOU WRITES UP ALL THE MAIL WHAT OL' DUCK DELIVERS! YOU KNOW IT AIN'T REG'LAR U.S. AND A. TYPE OF MAIL.. MAYBE IT MEANS YOU IS BOOTLEGGIN' LETTERS.

GOSH.. IS IT AGIN THE LAW?
WELL.. UM—
HOWDY, GENTS, I'M FROM THE F.B.I. AN' I....
WHOOSH! LOOKY AT 'EM GO! HUMMPH, THIS JOB SELLIN' FOR THE FULSOME BRUSH INSTITUTE AIN'T GONNA BE NO BEDDA ROSES!
I'M SORRY WE RUN OUT ON YOU, MOUSE BUT WE'RE A MITE FRIGHTY.
YEH... I HEAR A BUZZARD HERE' BOUTS LIKES TURTLE SOUP.
HERE COMES SARCOPHAGUS MACABRE NOW!
JUST PULL YOUR HEAD INSIDE YOUR TRUNK COMPARTMENT, KIDDO.
STEP UP AN' SEE THE DANCIN' CLAM SHELL, NEIGHBOR.. A NICKEL IN THE SLOT AND HE JIGS AN' PRANCES! HURRY! HUR-REE!
GOOD THING HE WAS A LOVER OF THE ARTS... WE MADE 5..10..15... UH.. NO... ONE IS A BUTTON.
THAT'S MINE ...OFFA MY UNNERWEARS.

COUSIN SARCOPHAGUS MACABRE AN' ME IS HEERD THAT TURTLE IS BOOTLEGGIN' MAIL ... IT'S UNCONSTITUTABLE
AN' THAT'S A HANGIN' OFFENSE....! TREASON!
HANGIN'? TREASON? JES' 'CAUSE TURTLE'S BEEN A GOOD FELLA A-WRITIN' MAIL FER OL' DUCK TO DELIVER? HOW ELSE WOULD WE GIT LETTERS?

IT AIN'T THE FEDERAL WAY, SAM! JES' 'CAST A PEEPER OVER THIS REE-SIPPY FO' TURTLE SOUP.... DEE-LICIOWS!
TURTLE SOUP, MMM? Y'KNOW MAYBE THAT NO 'COUNT, UNDERHANDLED TURTLE IS DESTROYIN' OUR NATIONAL INSTITUTIONS... HANGIN' IS TOO GOOD FOR SUCH TRASH!
WELL, WE COULD HANG HIM A LIL' BIT.
RECIPES

AH, THERE, DEACON MUSHRAT! KEEP A EYE OUT FOR OL' TURTLE! HE'S A MENACE!
¡Forsooth?
AYE ... HE'S DUE TO BE HUNG FER BOOTLEGGIN' MAIL! HE WRITES IT AN' THE DUCK DELIVERS IT.
Scandalum magnatum!
OOP!

AU CLAIR DE LA LUNE MON AMI PIER-ROT...
OH, SOLIO MELIO! RAZZ MAZZ MA TAZZ
A ORGAN GRINDER!
and his monkey!
WHAT'D HE MEAN? AND HIS MONKEY?
I DUNNO... BUT THE FOX PUT A SLUG IN THE HAT AN' THE DEACON LEFT A REQUEST,
....FOR US TO LEAVE FOR PARAGUAY...

Boy Bird Watchers Arise! Churchy Lafemme is a Dangerous menace! He must be watched, watched Watched!
GOOD THING THERE'S THREE OF US.
SO US WILL SNOOP ON OL' TURTLE?
Snoop?! Goodness, what a horrid word! No, we'll make dignified intelligence reports.

IF HE'S A MENACE, US WILL BACK YOU TO THE LIMIT IF YOU WANTS TO FIGHT THE BOY.
US MAKE INTELLIGENCE REPORTS...? HAW!
Mercy, Fight?
It's not nice to fight, We merely report Turtle's Activies ~~~ others will handle him.
YOU COULD SEND HIM A POISON PEN LETTER.
UNDER SEPARATE COVER OF NIGHT.

TURTLE SAY US CAN SPY ON HIM 'LONG AS US DON'T GIT UNDER FOOTS.
HI'LO BEAU-REGARD.
I NEEDS YOU TO WRITE SOMETHIN'.
..A FITTING SENTIMENT FOR ONE OF THE FINEST DOGS I EVER KNEW....
OKAY... HOW'S THIS?
"What gentler eye, What nobler heart doth warm the Winter day Than the true blue orb And the oaken core of our beloved old Dog Tray?"
GULP! GREAT--CHOKE-- FITS TO A "T."
FOR A FRIEND, HUH? YOU WANT IT SENT?
GULK ..SOB.. NO ... IT'S FOR ME. I'LL EAT IT HERE ... SNURF.
WATCHIN' THIS TURTLE BOOTLEG MAIL AIN'T THE SAME AS WATCHIN', SAY, LADY GODIVER.
HORSE OR NO HORSE, PEEKIN' IS PEIPING.
CAPITAL! COMMUNIST CAPITAL.
YOU KNOW THAT TURTLE WRITES A LOT OF THAT MAIL DOWN UNDER-BENEATH OF THE WATER?
I'M ABOUT TO SWEAR A MIGHTY BOY BIRD WATCHERS OATH... HOW COME WE GOT THREE AN' A HALF ACES OF CLUBS?

AN' THAT PROVES HE MUST BE A MEMBER OF A UNDERWATER GROUP.
NATURALLY 'CAUSE HALF OF 'EM IS SPADES
HAUT GOÛT?
EN-GAGED IN SUBMERSIVE ACTIVITIES.
CAN'T BE SPADES ALL FIVE ACES OF SPADES IS HERE ALREADIES.
YOU KNOW, WE MUST HAVE THE DEACON'S DECK... HE MARKS 'EM ILLITERATE

BEIN' A VIGILANTE COMMITTEE TO READ WHAT THE TURTLE WRITES IS HARD ON THE EYES, POGO.
WELL, READIN' IS A DANGEREST PRACTICE, SOMETIMES.
WRITIN' IS WORSE...
LOOKY AT THAT LETTER I WROT IN SCHOOL.

I WROTE A EX-CUSE FOR BEWITCHED HERE AN' BOTHERED TELLS ME: MAKE THE TEACHER THINK WE IS GOT CLASS IN THE FAMBLY... SO.... 'STEAD OF SIGNIN' MY FATHER'S REAL NAME, LIKE A HONEST CHILE ----
I SIGNED: President Andrew Jackson --- WELL, SIR, WE WAS THROWED ALL THE WHOLE WAY TO ---
YOU SHOULD OF PICKED SOMEBODY ALIVE -- MEBBE OF ANOTHER PARTY.
THAT'S A TOUGH PARLAY.

I UNDERSTAND YOU BATS FIGGER TURTLE'S NOT SUCH A BAD FELLA----- EVEN THOUGH HE BOOTLEGS MAIL!
WELL, IF IT ISN'T CHUCKLES!
LET ME READ YOU MEMBERS OF THE VIGILANTE COMMITTEE SOMETHING HE WROTE: "The Keen and the Quing Were quirling at Quoits In the meadow behind of the mere.....

"Tho' mainly the meadow was middled with mow-- An heretical hitherto here!" THERE! DON'T THAT SOUND SNEAKY?
WELL. WE DON'T UNDERSTAND IT.
EXACTLY! IT'S THESE THINGS WE DON'T UNDERSTAND THAT ARE DANGEROUS!
GLAD YOU WARNED US... I DON'T UNDERSTAND YOU EITHER...
BY THE SAME TOKEN, I'M GOIN' OUT AN' SHOOT MY OLD GEOMETRY TEACHER

The Fox and others claim Turtle is a menace!
HE'S A TRAITOR
ALBERT, HOW COME YOU'RE AT A LADIES' AUXILIARY MEETING?
EATS. HOW COME YOU?

I'M REPORTER FOR A PAPER I MIGHT START. THESE CHARGES 'GAINST TURTLE IS SERIOUS.
WELL, I DON'T ALWAYS AGREE WITH TURTLE...
THEN YOU GOES ALONG WITH OL' FOX AN' CAT AN' SARCOPHAGUS MACABRE?
COURSE NOT... IF I CAN'T AGREE WITH MY FRIENDS, HOW YOU 'SPECT ME TO GIT 'LONG WITH MY ENEMIES?

To prove Turtle has been bootlegging Mail, let me present Dr. Kidney of the Kidney-Garden Researches, who is an expert on the Sectional Problems of the American Mails-- He has a word 'bout Turtle.
GUILTY.

PSST...OWL, IF YOU GITS A CHANCE, SLIP CHURCHY A LI'L' SUMPIN'...I BRUNG HIM IN THE BAG 'CAUSE HE WASN'T INVITED FORMAL...
DOESN'T YOU KNOW THIS IS A PROTEST MEETIN' 'GAINST YOU?
YEP, AN' I FEELS I IS SWIPIN' THESE RATIONS UNDER FALSE PRETENSES 'COZ I IS FOR ME. (MY CONSCIENCE HURT ME)

WELL, IF IT ISN'T MY COUSINS, THE BATS! NOTHIN' LIKE A LI'L' SATURDAY GAME.
WHAT'S YOU HEAR 'BOUT OL' TURTLE?
SIT IN! SIT IN!
I'LL DEAL THE CARDS OVER AGAIN.
DON'T BOTHER, I BRUNG A PACK OF MY OWN ..... THEY'RE GONNA SPRING A SPY QUEEN ON TURTLE.

IT'S HARD FANNIN' 52 ... BUT, WHAT YOU PLAYIN', FRIENDS? ... THIS SPY QUEEN SET UP REMINDS ME OF ONE TIME I'M UP IN D.C. AND ....
I GOT A GOOD PINOCHLE HAND ... HE'S PLAYIN' WHIST AN' BEWITCHED IS A POKER MAN.
THEY HAUL ME IN AN' SAY "WAS YOU EVER IN CAHOOTS WITH A LOVELY SPY QUEEN" AN' I SAY "NO, BUT I SPENT A SEASON IN RANGOON WITH A LADY BASEBALL TEAM .."
SAY, THIS IS A OLD MAID DECK I GOT ...
AW.. GO AHEAD LEAD!

"Ladies of the Vigilante Auxiliary, here's a book written by a loyal lady spy :- "I was an ex-member of the Underground." -- The material on Turtle ~
~is so secret, that the book had to be composed entirely of Blank paper.
BY TARNAL FIRE, IF HE AIN'T RIGHT!
I WAS AN EX-MEMBER OF THE UNDERGROUND

Now who is the beautiful spy queen who watched Turtle's submersive work? None other than ---------
Lucy! Lucy, the beautiful jelly fish, brought here in a jelly jar ---- wait 'til we take the lid off this!
A REAL SIGH-REEN!
It's hard to get the top off the jelly jar so's Lucy, the jelly-fish, can tell 'bout bein' a Beautiful Spy Queen --
soon's we get her outen there ----- we'll -- oop -- she's slippery ---
SHE BROKE
can this be Lucy? Looks like she's real jelly --
BIG PIECES OF RASPBERRY ALL OVER
MFF.. MOULDY!
Where'd you get that Spy Queen?
LEFT OVER FROM A PARTY.
Y'AINT S'POSE TO OPEN UP EVERYTHIN IN PUBLIC.

Finally we have a cryptic bit written by Turtle that Peeks of guilt.
"SMILE, WAVERING WINGS, ABOVE RAIN'S POUR, WHILE HOPEFULLY SINGS LOVE OF SHORN SHORE. SHORE SHORN OF LOVE SINGS HOPEFULLY WHILE, POUR RAINS ABOVE, WINGS WAVERING, SMILE."
I DON'T GIT IT.
THAT'S THE CLEVER PART. IT'S GOTTA BE READ BACKWARD.
YEP! IT GOES FROM RIGHT TO LEFT.
"Here it is backward:
"Smile, wavering wings, Above rain's pour, While hopefully sings Love of shorn shore. Shore shorn of Love Sings hopefully while pour rain's above Wings wavering smile."
THERE!
YOU KNOW, IF I DIN'T HEAR YOU READ THAT, I WOULDN'T BELIEVE MY EARS!
WELL, IT LOOKS LIKE THE EVIDENCE IS PILED UP AGIN TURTLE...
ONLY THING EVIDENT SO FAR IS THE FOX, CAT AN' BUZZARD WANTS HIM IN THE SOUP.
BUT YOU SAW THE SPY BOOK!
FULL OF BLANK PAPER!

THAT'S BECAUSE EVERYTHING IN IT WAS HUSH-HUSH! AN' THAT POEM HE WROTE --- WHOOIE! YOU CAN'T DENY THAT?!
DENY IT? IT'S JUST A NONSENSE VERSE .... FORWARD OR BACK-WARD!
WELL, YOU GOTTA ADMIT IT'S A DEVIOUS WRITER WHAT CAN MEAN NOTHING IN TWO DIRECTIONS AT THE SAME TIME.
EVER'BODY DECIDE TO HANG TURTLE?
I'M GONNA MAKE UP THEIR MINDS FOR 'EM --- A HUNG TURTLE OUT-RANKS A HUNG JURY.
AN ACT OF KIND-NESS --- SPARIN' TURTLE THAT WORRY...
DEACON! YOU FIND OL' TURTLE YET?
The others say they're havin' trouble findin' Turtle guilty --- but I can't find him nohow -- Guilty or Innocent. I better beat a dignified retreat.
HAND ME THAT OL' MUSHRAT RECIPE!

Let me in -- them varmints is out to git me 'cause I didn't deliver the Turtle into their hands ---
THERE'S CAVE ENOUGH FOR ONE MORE.
Finally I said, "This is an innocent man you're tryin' to frame --" and They said, "Always remember the next innocent man might be you!"
YOU AN INNOCENT MAN?! WHAT A BASE CANARD!
AN OUTRAGE!
YOU SHOULD OF PUNCHED HIM RIGHT IN THE EYE.
I'll have you know I can be innocent as the next man!
DEPENDS ON WHO YOU'RE NEXT TO.
THEY'D NEVER CATCH ME BEIN' INNOCENT.
NOT THESE DAYS.
MY, DON'T YOU THINK IT'S COURAGEOUS OF THE DEACON AN' ALL TO PROVE OL' TURTLE'S GUILTY?
WHAT DID THEY FINALLY PROVE HIM GUILTY OF, HON?
OH, HEE HEE! LAND, SUGAR, I BEEN SO BUSY I NEVER DID PAY THAT PART NO MIND.
THOSE AS KNOW WAS SURE HE'S GUILTY OF WHAT-EVER IT WAS, HOWEVER.
WHERE THEY'S SMOKE THEY'S FIRE, HON.

EVER'BODY'S WORD 'GAINST HIS'N. ----- FACT IS, HE NEVER SAID NOTHIN'.
NOW THEY'S OUT AFTER HIM ---- WELL, 'TAINT MY AFFAIR-I MIND MY OWN BUSINESS AN' STAY COMFY..

AN' OUT OF TROUBLE.
NUTS, HON?
WK

SEED A TURTLE, STRANGER?
WELL, IF IT ISN'T LAUGHING GAS.

WHO'S YOU TO COME GAR-BARGIN' IN CALLIN' ME STRANGER?! YOU IS STRANGER NOR ME.

WHAT'S IN THE BASKET?
THAT THERE BASKET THERE? WHY, TURTLE'S INSIDE HIDIN' FROM YOU.

VERY FUNNY----DO YOU TAKE ME FOR A FOOL?
I WOULDN'T TAKE YOU FOR NOTHIN'!

Let me hide in there too, Churchy? Them varmints is after me, too!
HELP YO'SELF, DEACON, I GOIN' OUT FOR A BATH.
I HEAR TELL TURTLE IS IN THAT BASKET OF ALBERT'S.
FINE --- I KNOW WHERE IT IS --- COME ON.
'SPOSE HE IS IN THAT BASKET?
No, he isn't! GO away!
HA! NOW WE GOT HIM! DON'T SLIP ON THESE STONES!
WHILE I WAS SLEEPIN' SOMEBODY STOLE TURTLE IN MY LUNCH BASKET ---
I SAW 'EM! IT WAS THAT OL' BUZZARD, NAME OF SARCOPHAGUS MacABRE, AN' OL' WILEY CATT.
THEY CAN'T STEAL YOU FROM UNDER MY NOSE THAT WAY!

BUT ISN'T I HERE? YEP! IT'S ME... SEE MY NAME'S ON THIS TOWEL I IS USIN'.
CHURCHY
GOOD! I WAS 'BOUT TO REVENGE YO' DEE-MISE.
BE NICE IF YOU RESCUE DEACON! IT WAS HIM THEY SWUP IN YO' BASKET.
DUNNO 'BOUT THAT; BUT TWO INNOCENT EGG SAN'WICHES WAS IN THERE, TOO!

THEY'S UP THERE GITTIN' READY TO COOK OL' DEACON!
YOU FIGGER US IS GONE BE TOO LATE?
OH, I FIGGER THEY'LL BE SOME LEFT, THO' THEY VERY LIKELY AIN'T GONNA SAVE US ANY....

OPEN UP THERE!
GO AWAY!
WHEN NEIGHBORS COME CALLIN'.. ACK POLITE!

NOW, YOU CANNIBOBBLES! I IS COMED FOR MY LUNCH WHAT YOU STOLED. AND INCIDENTLY FOR DEACON, TOO.
I AIN'T FEARED OF YO' GUN! YOU'LL TAKE DEACON OVER HIS DEAD BODY!
WAIT

RUN, RUN! OUR SATURDAY NIGHT BATH AIN'T DUE 'TIL APRIL — AN' THAT BOY IS SPORTIN' A WATER PISTOL.
WHY, SO I IS.
HALP!
GANG-WAYS!
PLOOP
PLOOP

Oh, how can I ever thank you for rescuing me from them frightful people...
DON'T YOU BITE!
SMACK
LONG AS THE LUNCH IS GONE, US MOUGHT'S WELL HEAD BACK.
You dear courageous handsome an' brave hero— Let me help you carry your—

IF YOU DON'T STOP BEIN' GRATEFUL I IS GONE POP YOU!
HEY, THERE! IS WE TOO LATE TO RESCUE TH' DEACON?
NO! ACTUAL YOU IS JUST IN TIME TO RESCUE HIM FROM HIS RESCUERS.
?
ALL THAT INVESTIGATION INTO CHURCHY'S LIFE BY DEACON WASTED... MY MY!
I DUNNO 'BOUT THAT.... WE SURE LEARNED A LOT 'BOUT OL' DEAC'!
IT'S A-ONE AN' A-TWO AN' A SEE-LIDE, BOY!
YEP --- IT DON'T PAY TO INVESTIGATE TOO MUCH ... A BOY FALLS OVERBOARD WEIGHED DOWN WITH NOTES AN' HE'S REAL GONE!
OH, HE'S DEEP!

IGNORANCE IS A BANE, MY FRIENDS.... NOW, AS FOR ME, I GOT KNOWLEDGE WHAT I HARDLY AIN'T TOUCHED YET.
SOON AS THE PLAYIN' FIELDS ARE CLEAR OF ICE LET'S CHOOSE UP SIDES .... WE CAN HANDLE OUR IGNORANCE, CAN YOU HANDLE YOUR LINE OF
IT'S A-ONE AND A RUFFLE AND A BUFFLE O' SHUFFLE

MAGNA CUM LHUDE SING CUCCU

SH! DOCTOR OWL IS EX-AMININ' OUR NEW MECHANIWOCKLE MAN...
GOOD SOUND PULSE
WHAT YOU SHOOSHIN' ME FOR -- I GOTS MUCH RIGHT IN THIS STRIP AS
IN MY CONSIDER OPINIONS I FEEL

RRING
RING
RINGY
RING
RING

HELLO? DOC OWL'S OFFICE... DOC IS TEMPORARY UN-DISPOSE.
HELLO? WHAT? HE IS?

WHAT GOOD IS THIS HUMAN BEAN YOU INVENTED?
IT SOLVES PROBLEMS. WATCH IT ADD ONE AN' ONE.

RING GG
RING RR
RING

THERE!
FOOF! I CAN ADD BETTER'N THAT.
YOU GOTTA REMEMBER, THIS MACHINE IS MERE A HUMAN BEAN ---
IT'S NOT LIKE IT WAS A MECHANICAL DOG OR OTHER KIND OF BEAST... GIVE IT A CHANCE.
YEAH, FAIR IS FAIR, YOU KNOW.

WHAT'S ALL THIS FUSS 'BOUT POLITICS, MR. TAMMANANNY? IS IT WHAT BRINGS YOU BACK TO THE SWAMP?
CONFIDENTIAL SPEAKIN' -- YES. I'M AN EMISARRY FROM THE OLD MAIN GUARD..

THE PARTY BIG-WIGS BRIEFED ME ON WHAT THEY EXPECT OF THE BIG BOY... WHAT THEY THINK THE BIG BOY'S POLICIES OUGHT TO BE --- SO I'M GONNA ASK HIM IF HE WANTS TO RUN.

WHO IS THIS BIG BOY?
WHO? HA! WHAT A QUESTION --- WHO, INDEED..

BY GOLDERN! I KNEW THERE WAS SOME LI'L' THING I FERGOT TO FIND OUT.

MR. TAMMANANNY WAS SENT 'ROUND BY POLITICOS TO SOUND OUT THE BIG BOY.
CAN'T RECALL WHO HE IS.... BUT A CANDIDATE FOR THE TOP JOB GOTTA BE SMART, HONEST AND A FEARLESS LEADER.
I WAS CUT IN ON ALL THAT STUFF AN' IS YOU NOTICED WHAT A BIG ONE I IS?
OOG! BUT WAS YOU BORN IN A LOG CABIN?
YOU MEAN A BIG TYPE OF FEARLESS LEADER LIKE ME GOTTA BE BORNED IN A BACKWOODS HUT?
OH, MY DEAR SIR, IT'S A ABSOLUTE IRREDEEMABLE VIRTUE ~ (IE: CAN'T DO WITHOUT IT.)
BY NAB! YOU HEAR THAT? MY MAM AN' PAP IS SWUNDLED ME OUTEN THE PRESIDENSITY OF THE NATURAL BORN COUNTRY!
IT WAS CLOSE THOUGH-- MIGHTY CLOSE, FRIENDS.
HOW YOU LIKE THAT? OL' TIGER SAY A MAN GOTTA BE BORN IN A LOG CABIN TO BE PRESIDENT OR ELSE...
ELSE... ?
ELSE HE SAY THE MAN GOTTA HAVE A POWER-FUL MACHINE BEHINE OF HIM--- HUNNERDS OF VOTERS AN' ......
MACHINE?

ALBERT! THAT MECHANIWOCKLE MAN WE INVENTED! YOU REALIZE WHAT IT REALLY IS?
A LADY?
IT'S THE START OF OUR OWN MACHINE! WE'LL MAKE THOUS-ANDS OF THEM LI'L' FELLERS AN' PUT 'EM ALL OUT TO VOTIN' ROUN' THE CLOCK... A TWENTY-FOUR HOUR DAY.
MAYBE EVEN A TWENNY FIVE HOUR DAY.
POGO, HAND OVER YO' CLOCK. I IS GONE MAKE A HUMAN BEAN OUTEN IT SO'S IT CAN VOTE FOR ME.
IT'S NOT OLD ENOUGH TO VOTE.
IT LOOKS OLD ENOUGH.
THAT'S JES' 'CAUSE IT'S RUN DOWN A LI'L'.
YEOW! A LI'L' ANIMAL TYPE VARMINT!
NO, IT'S A BIRD... HARMLESS NOR A CATER-PIGGLE.
CUCKOO CUCK-KOOHOO
LEMME AT IT---I'LL TEACH IT TO POP OUT AT INNOCENT PEOPLE.
IS THAT ANY WAY TO TREAT YOUR CONSTITUENCY?

THE SCENE SHIFTS (UNEASILY)

OH... I WAS CARRIED AWAY! IT'S RUINT... I FEEL LIKE I MURDERED MY OWN CHILE .... HOW WILL I EVER ANSWER TO MY CONSCIENCE?
YOU COULD PLEAD INSANITY.
AN' WE'D BACK YOU UP.
PHOO! AIN'T EITHER OF YOU GOT NO SENTIMINTS?
OWL, IF YOU AN' ALBERT IS BUILDIN' A MACHINE CANDIDATE, YOU CAN USE THIS OL' GRAN'DADDY CLOCK OF MINE.
DANDY! JES' JAMES DANDY.
CUCKOO! CUCKOO! FOUR-SEVENTY-FIVE AND ALL IS WELL!
WHOO! HE DON'T EVEN KNOW WHAT TIME IT IS.
IT'S SATURDAY, BRIGHT EYES! WANNA MAKE SOMETHIN' OUT OF IT?!
YES. MAKE IT WEDNESDAY AND I'LL SETTLE FOR THAT FOUR SEVENTY-FIVE.
WHO'S THE AUTHORITARY ON THIS STUFF? ME OR THAT GOOGLYMUSH?
I DUNNO, POGO, YOU THINK I CAN MAKE A CANDIDATE OUTEN A CLOCK WHAT GOT A RABBIT FOR A CUCKOO?
WHY NOT?

THINK THIS OUGHT TO HAVE A MUSTACHE LIKE GROVER?
OWL IS BUILDIN' A MACHINE CANDIDATE.
HOW FEARSOMELY DROLL.
EIGHTY-FOUR O'CLOCK! CUCKOO-HOO! WEATHER FORECAST: RAIN AND--

CAN'T YOU CONTAIN YOURSELF 'TIL EASTER? YOU'RE ONLY SPOSED TO STRIKE ON THE HOUR.
FOOF!
BY JING, IF YOU GET FANCY WITH ME, I'LL STRIKE EVERY FIFTEEN MINUTES AND I'LL PULL OUT EVERY CUCKOO 'TWEEN HERE AN' CAP-ITOL HILL.
DON'T ROUSE ORGANIZED TYPES.

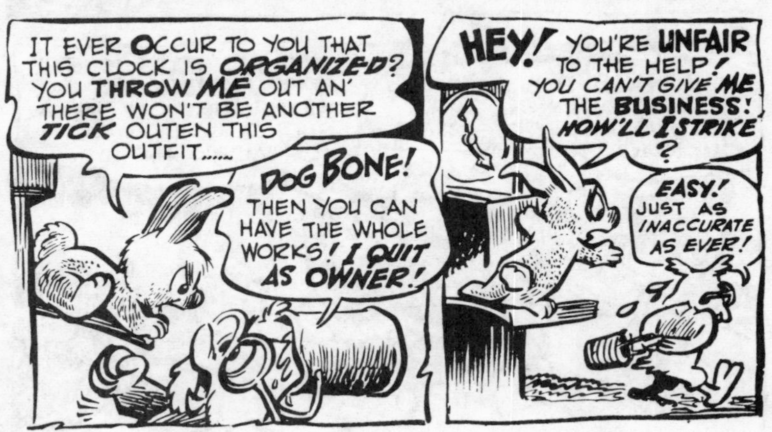
IT EVER OCCUR TO YOU THAT THIS CLOCK IS ORGANIZE-D? YOU THROW ME OUT AN' THERE WON'T BE ANOTHER TICK OUTEN THIS OUTFIT......
DOG BONE! THEN YOU CAN HAVE THE WHOLE WORKS! I QUIT AS OWNER!
HEY! YOU'RE UNFAIR TO THE HELP! YOU CAN'T GIVE ME THE BUSINESS! HOW'LL I STRIKE?
EASY! JUST AS INACCURATE AS EVER!

UNFARE
HOW COME YOU IS PICKETIN' THE GRAND OL' DADDY CLOCK, BUN RABBIT?

OWL GOT TIRED OF IT AN' GIVE IT AT ME AN', SINCE I IS THE RESIDENT CUCKOO, I IS STRIKIN' FOR A FIFTEEN MINUTE HOUR.
UNFARE
WANT SHORTER HOURS?

AN' LOWER RENTS FOR ME, THE TENANT.
BUT YOU IS LAN'LORD, TOO. WHY DON'T YOU NEGOTIATE?
UNFARE

THE LAN'LORD IS MAD AT THE TENANT AN' ISN'T SPEAKIN' TO MYSELF AN' EVEN IF THEY WAS, THE NEIGHBORS WOULD THINK I HAD TOOK LEAVE OF OUR SENSES.
TRUE... TRUE.... TEE-ROO.

OL' BUN RABBIT IS PICKETIN' THE GRAN'DADDY CLOCK AN' CONSEQUINCELY IT GOT NO CUCKOO.
THAT'S PLAIN AWFUL.
THE LI'L' BATS IS BOY BIRD WATCHERS SO MAYBE THEY C'N FIND A CUCKOO WHAT'S OUT OF WORK AN'...

WHAT!? YOU ASK US TO BREAK THE LAW?
BIRD WATCHIN' DON'T START 'TIL SPRING... YOU WANT US TO GO TO JAIL FER WATCHIN' 'EM OUT OF SEASON?
I IS GONE HAFTA LOOK FOR A CUCKOO BIRD MYSELF; WON'T YOU LI'L' BATS HELP?
YOU ASK US TO SULLY OUR BIRD WATCHERS' OATH BY WATCH-ING BIRDS OUTTA SEASON?
OH, WELL.
YOU WOULDN'T WANT US TO JEE-OPPARDIZE OUR PRISTINE POSITION WITH THE NATIONABLE SO-CIETY?
IT'S TOO MUCH TO EXPECT US UNSPOILT LI'L' FELLAS TO....
OKAY! O-KAY! YOU'RE PURE! YOU'RE PURE! I JUST THOUGHT IT MIGHT BE REWARDING TO....
REWARDING? WELL, NOW SIR! WELL-WELL-WELL!
HOW MUCH?

THE LI'L' BATS AN' ME IS ALL OUT LOOKIN' FOR A **CUCKOO BIRD.**
A COOCOO, HUH.
THE HON. ANDY LYON

Sumer is icumen in,
Lhude sing cuccu --
Groweth sed
an' bloweth med
An' springth the wude nu,
Sing cuccu!
SHOOSH

Cuccu, cuccu, wel
Singes thu, cuccu,
Na swike thu naver nu;
Sing cuccu, nu ...
Sing cuccu,
Sing cuccu,
Sing cuccu!

WE GOT US ONE!
cu?

WHO YOU?
COCCYZUS ERYTHROPHTHALMUS.
A NATURAL BORN ***CUCKOO*** *BY TRADE.*
I HEAR YOU BOYS GOT A JOB FOR ME.

YEP, YOU GOTTA GET IN A CLOCK AN' HOLLER OUT THE HOURS ....
MY HOLLER GO: ***GOWK! KULK!*** *KOW-WUK!* MOURNFUL IT IS.
YOU AIN'T FOOLIN'

CAPTAIN DAN, THE OGLIN' MAN, SAY YOU BIRDS EATS QUANTITIES OF FUZZY TENT CATER-PIGGLES.
NO WONDER YOU GO "GOWK."
IT'S THE A-MERICAN WAY.
CAP'N DAN'S ATLAS

ONLY THE EUROPEAN CUCKOO SAYS "CUCKOO." ?
I JES' HOPE I NEVER HEARS YOU STRIKE MIDNIGHT!-- MORE'N A HALF DOZEN OF THEM GOWKS AN' KOW-WUKS WOULD GIVE ME THE QUANDARIES.

EVEN IF YOU DON'T SAY: "COO-COO" GOOD, WHY NOT TAKE THE CLOCK JOB, ANYWAYS?
IT'S A NICE PUBLIC OFFICE. AN' YOU ONLY HAFTA COUNT UP TO TWELVE.
COR!

AN' EVERY HOUR ON THE HOUR, IT'S OUTSIDE WORK.
BUT US AMERICAN CUCKOOS GOES "KOW-WUK."

HIRE A EUROPEAN CUCKOO. THEM KIND GOES "COO-COO" VERY NICELY.
IS YOU IMPLYIN' THAT A RED-BLOODED A-MERICAN ISN'T THE CUCKOO THAT A EUROPEAN IS?

IT'S A ORNITHO-LOGICAL FACT.
I QUESTION THIS BIRD'S LOYALTY. HE COULD AT LEAST SPEAK AMERICAN.

AND, AFTER 16 HOURS OF PRACTICING

AS A FAVOR, I'LL PAINT THESE NUMBERS ON YO' STOMACH, TURTLE.
THANKS
US WANTS TO **SET** OUR NEW CLOCK, WHAT TIME YOU GOT?
NONE TO SPARE.
IF THE CLOCK IS ANY GOOD IT OUGHT TO HAVE TIME OF ITS OWN.

COO-COO! COO-COO! TWO O'CLOCK!
YUMP!
IF TIME-TELLIN' IS COMIN' TO ***THAT***, **I** IS SWEARIN' ***OFF!*** THIS OL' WATCH IS HAD **FIVE** O'CLOCK ON HER SINCE **1936** AN' UP TO NOW I NEVER DOUBTED IT.

THERE'S **BUN RABBIT** STILL PICKETIN' HIMSELF 'CAUSE HE'S A **TENANT** IN THE **CLOCK** OF WHICH **HE** IS **ALSO** THE ***LAN'LORD***.
UNFAIR

ENEMY OF THE LITTLE PEOPLE! **OPPRESSOR OF THE POOR!** ***BAH!***

SEEIN' AS YOU IS THE LANDLORD OF THE CLOCK US GOT A NEW CLOCKWORKS FOR YOU, SIR.
I'M ALSO THE TENANT AN' IS PICKETIN' THE GOUGIN' CAPITALISTIC LAN'LORD.
JUST BE THE LANDLORD FOR A MINUTE WHILST US PUTS IN THE WORKS.
MMM--- MOUGHT AS WELL--------- HERE, HOLE THIS A LI'L' MINUTE.
UNFAIR

NOW I'M THE LAN'LORD AN'--- HEY! IS YOU PICKETIN' THIS ESTABLISHMINT?
NO, I --
BEGONE CHURL! OFF WITH YOUR PARASITICAL PROLETARIAN VULGARITIES! A POX ON YOU! FIE!
UNFAIR
FIE?

WHAT'S YOU PICKETIN' ME FOR, POGO?
IT'S YOUR SIGN! ALL I'M DOIN' IS HOLDIN' IT FOR YOU.
UNF-ARE
A LIKELY STORY! YOU'VE THROWED A PICKET LINE UP SOS I CAN'T GIT A NEW CUCKOO FER MY CLOCK.

BUT YOU **ASKED** ME TO....
YOU WAS A **TENANT** PICKETIN' **YOU**, THE **LANDLORD**, AN' YO' SAY "**HOLE THIS!**" I'M GONE APPEAL TO THE **RENT CONTROL** OFFICER.

WON'T DO NO GOOD. *I'M THE RENT CONTROL OFFICER, TOO.* *NEITHER THE TENANT NOR THE LANDLORD TRUSTS* **ME!**
YOU IS PREJUDICED AGAINST RABBITS.
IS YOU SURE THEY NEEDS A CUCKOO?

I'D **LEAVE** THIS GRAN'FATHER CLOCK TO ITS **OWN** MISER'BLE **DEE**-**VICES** IF I COULD JUST GIT AWAY.

WHY CAN'T YOU? GO AHEAD, *LEAVE*.
I CAN'T **LOCK** UP. *CAN'T FIND THE KEY.*

WHY YOU GOTTA LOCK UP? IS THEY SOMETHIN' VALUABLE INTHERE?
YEP! *THEY IS A VERY IMPORTANT* **ITEM** IN THERE SOMEPLACE. *DON'T WANT NOBODY TO GIT IT, SO I* **GOTTA** *LOCK IT UP.*

WHAT IN THE *EVER-BELOVIN' WORLD* **IS IT?**
THE **KEY**.... THE **KEY** WHAT I CAN'T **FIND!** THE KEY TO LOCK IT UP IS WHAT'S IN THERE.

IS YOU SERIOUS WHEN YOU SAYS YOU WANTS TO LOCK UP THE CLOCK TO SAFEGUARD SOMETHIN' IN THERE AN' THE SOMETHIN' IN THERE IS THE KEY?
YEP, AN' I CAN'T FIND IT.... IT'S VERY UNBARRASS-ING.
I GOT A VERY CLEVER SUGGESTION.
TAKE OFF YO' HAT WHEN YOU ADDRESS A LADY.
I AIN'T NO HAT.
WE IS EVEN UP. I ISN'T NO LADY.
WHY NOT SET FIRE TO THE CLOCK AN' SIFT THE ASHES AN' FIND THE KEY EASY?
GREAT! THEN WE CAN FIND TH' LOCK-.....
AN' LOCK IN THE KEY ALL SAFE!
LET'S GO OVER TO MY HOUSE AN' HAVE MILK AN' COOKIES AN' FERGIT THESE PANELS
IF WE SETS FIRE TO THE CLOCK TO FIND THE KEY IN THE ASHES, HOW'LL WE PUT IT OUT?
I'LL HOLLER: FIRE!
WHERE?

NO-WHERES YET! WHAT'S YOU DOIN' IN OUR CLOCK?
IT WAS EMPTY SO I USIN' IT FOR A FIREHOUSE.... YOU TURNED IN A FALSE ALARM!
AN' THAT'S A PENAL O-FFENSE ... BUT I'LL KEEP YOU OUT OF TROUBLE BY SETTIN' ONE OF YOU ON FIRE AN'...
EVER'BODY IS NICE TO US....
IT'S JES' 'CAUSE WE IS SO CUDDABLE.
AS I WAS SAYIN', LONG AS YOU TURNED IN A FALSE ALARM. I CAN SET FIRE TO ONE OF YOU TO KEEP YOU OUT OF TROUBLE.
S'POSE I IS CONFLAGRATED, GIMME A DEMONSTRATION OF HOW YOU GONE PUT ME OUT? I WANTS THE BEST.
IF YOU WANTS THE BEST, I GIVES YOU THE TWO DOLLAR JOB.... FIRST WE SOAKS THE HOLOCAUST WITH GOOD WET WATER..
VERY NICE.
WITH THE INFERNO MO-MENTARY CHECKED, THE BRAVE SMOKE-EATER CHOPS A HOLE IN THE -.... HEY! HOLD STILL!
YEAH.. BE A SPORT.
I GOTTA GO HOME AN' TAKE MY ASBESTOS PILLS.

PEACE OF CHANGE

THE LI'L' HUMAN BEAN IS RUNNED AWAY FROM HOME.
STOP BLUBBERIN'! IT WAS ONLY MADE OF A CLOCK AN' STICKS.
WE SHOULD NEVER OF LEFT CARLSBAD! WHAT HATH THITH SWAMP WROUGHT NOW?

TICK TICK! TICK TICK
TICK TICK TICK! TICK TICK! TICK!
TINK
TICK TICK TICK
TEE-HICK
TICK

YOU HAD OUGHT TO DO SOME-THIN' FER THEM HICCUPS, JACK. LIKE PUTTIN' OVER THE HEAD A BAG OR MEBBE A DRINK OF WATER...?
OR WE CAN GIVE HIM A GOOD SCARE.
WHAT FOR A GOOD ONE? HE MERE GAVE US A BAD ONE.

LET'S TAKE THIS LI'L' HIC-CUPPIN' CRITTUR OVER TO POGO AN' SEE WHAT HE CALLS IT.
TICK TICK TICK TICK!
TICK TICK TICK

TAKE OFF YOUR HAT WHEN YOU GOES IN.
POGO

RING RING RINGY RINGY RING RING RING RING RING
DOOR BELL! DOOR BELL! I'LL GIT IT. I'LL GIT IT.
HELLO? HALLOO? SOMEBODY RING???? THAT'S FUNNY.... NOBODY'S THERE.
TICK TICK?

AS LONG AS POGO'S NOT HOME LET'S DIVIDE UP HIS COOKIES 'TIL HE GITS BACK AN' TEACH THE MECHANICAL CRITTUR A GENTEEL GAME OF SKILL.
HOO BOY!
HEE HEE

HEY, YOU'RE NOT S'POSED TO LEAVE YOUR CARDS FACE UP!
NOW, DON'T INNERFERE WITH THE STRANGER'S STYLE, FRIEND.
LACY FAIR, BOYS, LAY-SEE FAIR!

HMM.... HE SEEM TO BE EMPLOYIN' A DOUBLE WING WITH LIMITLESS SUBSTITUTIONS.
US BETTER FALL BACK AN' REE GROUP.
IT MIGHT RAIN BEFORE THE FIFTH INNING.

WELL, ONCE AGAIN IT'S PROVEN THAT NINE KINGS BEATS SIX OF A KIND.
WHAT'S HE WANT WITH OUR PANTS THOUGH?
MEBBE HE KNOWS A NAKED OCTOPOTS

YOUR FINE FEATHERED FRIEND, ALBERT, MADE A HUMAN BEAN TYPE OF BURGLAR WHAT IS LAYIN' WASTE OUR FAIR SWAMP.
LAYIN' WASTE? WHAT'S YOU MEAN?
HE SWUPPED OUR PANTS!
HIC HIC
THERE THERE.

LI'L' BEWITCHED IS SO UPSET THAT HE GITS HICCUPS AN' US HAS TO JOG HIM.
HIC HIC HIC HIC HIC HIC
WHY'S IT UPSET YOU SO MUCH?
HOW'D YOU LIKE TO STAND AROUN' WITH NO PANTS? WHAT WOULD YOU DO?
HIC HIC HIC
HIC?

THERE HE IS ... CAREFREE AN' GAY. LITTLE CARIN' IF HE MADE US LOSE OUR PANTS...
NEVER DO HE KNOW WHAT'S THE GAME ...
NOR WHOM IS PLAYIN' WHOM.
4-1

IF THE SCORE IS OVER 2-0, HE AIN'T GONE COUNT IT.
YEH, HE DOES ALL HIS FIGGERIN' ON HIS FINGER-BONES.
BUT DON'T HE GOT A NORMAL NUMBER?
WELL... NORMAL AS ALLIGATORS GO; BUT WHEN HE GITS THINKIN' WITH HIS FINGERS, HE'S ALL THUMBS.

AS ROOKERY MOTHER TO YOU BOY BIRD WATCHERS, I DEE-MANDS TO KNOW WHY YOU ISN'T OUT WATCHIN'-UP THE BIRDS THIS SPRING?
US IS A MITE CATASTROPHIED, MIZ BEAVER.
STOP PLAY-TOYIN' AROUN' AN' GIT TO WATCH-IN' BIRDS. LAW!! US'LL NOHOW GIT'EM ALL WATCHED IF YOU LALLY-GAG AN'...
BUT US IS OUTTA UNIFORM, MIZ BEAVER. US IS LOST OUR PANTS.
WHAT?! WHYN'T YOU TELL ME FIRST OFF?
YOU KNOW I ALWAYS FAINTS ON SUCH OCCASIONS.
OOOOMP!

QUICK - QUICK!
MIZ BEAVER, THE ROOKERY MOTHER OF THE BOY BIRD-WATCHERS IS FAINTED.

I'LL REE-VIVE HER WITH THE WATER IN THE BUCKET.

AWAKE! AWAKE --- FOR DAWN WHICH SCATTERED--- OOP!
SPLAMP!

I ADMITS I FERGOT TO REE-MOVE THEM FISH FROM THE BAIT-BUCKET BUT THAT CRAWFISH GITTIN' IN ON IT WAS HIS OWN IDEA.
FOO, A BEAUTIFUL GAL WASTES HER TIME GRACIN' UP THIS SWAMP.

US BATS ISN'T GOT A LEADER NOW WE LOST OUR PANTS. MIZ BEAVER FAINTS AN' DEACON DISAPPROVES.

'LONG AS YOU BOY BIRDWATCHERS IS HARD UP FOR A LEADER, I'LL SLIP INTO UNIFORM AN' LEAD A LI'L' FIELD TRIP.
WE ISN'T THAT HARD UP.
Albert

NOW OFF WE GO, MEN.
WE'RE OFF ALL RIGHT.
JUST WHAT I'M LOOKIN' FOR! A CHIMNEY.
HMM?
A STORK! A STORK! A SIGN OF GOOD LUCK.

IF YOU IS A LUCKY STORK, WHY DOES YOU PICK ME TO NEST ON?
PLEASE TILT THE CHIMNEY UPRIGHT AN' STOP COM-PLAININ'.
OH BOY! THIS IS A LUCKY SIGN.
JUST HOLD THAT WHILST I GOES FORTH FER STICKS AN' STUFF.

WHILE HE IS PICKIN' UP TRASH I IS HIKIN' TO LAPLAND.
WHOA! YOU IS COURTIN' DEE-SASTER.
A STORK NESTIN' ON YO' CHIMNEY IS LUCKY.. BUT CHASIN' HIM OFF IS SURE DEATH.
OR WORSE
THINK IT OVER AN' KEEP YO' FLUE OPEN.

AS ROOKERY-MOTHER TO YOU BOY BIRD WATCHERS, I DE-MANDS YOU FINDS YO' PANTS AN'.. SAY, WHAT AILS OL' GLOOMY-GLUM?
HE IS FALLED INTO GOOD LUCK.
LAW! LOOKS LIKE HE GOT A CASE OF THE FRITTURS... WELL, I CAN'T DO ALL TH' BIRD-GAZIN' MYSELF..

WELL, WE IS DOIN' OUR PART, WE IS WATCHIN' A BIRD RIGHT NOW.... OL' STORK!
ORK!
WHAT'S-A-MATTER WITH THE FAT OLD PARTY? SHE RUN OFF WHEN SHE SEE ME COMIN' IN WITH A LOAD OF STICKS FER THE NEST.

SO, YOU LI'L' BATS IS HELPIN' THE STORK BUILD HIS NEST IN ALBERT'S HAT?
YEP!
IT'S GOOD LUCK TO HAVE A STORK.
GOOD LUCK FOR WHO?
FER A MOMMA STORK.

D'YOU REALIZE THAT EVERY TIME THIS STORK LAYS AN EGG, YOU WILL GET BOPPED ON THE CUPOLA?
WELL ---- THEY'LL BE FRESH.

WILL IT BE POLITE FOR HIM TO LAY EGGS ON ME?
YOU CAN BET THAT IF HE DOES, HE WON'T BE NO GENTLEMAN.
OH, YOU CAN LAY TO THAT.

SO YOU LI'L' BATS IS GONNA WATCH BIRDS AT NIGHT 'CAUSE YOU IS STILL PANTS-LESS?
YEP! IT'LL BE BETTER IN THE DARK. US IS TOO EM-BARRASSED DAYTIMES.

BUT IF IT'S DARK..

HOW CAN THEY..... ??
KNOCK

BACK SO SOON? I KNEW YOU COULDN'T WATCH NOTHIN' IN THE DARK.

RIGHT! AN' NOTHIN' COULDN'T WATCH US! SO WE SWUPPED BACK OUR PANTS!

IS YOU ME OR IS I YOU? I CAN'T REMEMBER WHO WORE WHICH PANTS.
NO, I'M HIM.

DON'T LOOK SO GLUM, CHUM! NEED I REMIND YOU THAT IT'S LUCKY TO HAVE A STORK IN YOUR CHIMNEY?
YOU DON'T GOTTA REMIND ME .... YOU GOTTA CONVINCE ME.
YOU'LL BE GLAD TO KNOW THAT I HAVE A SURPRISE FOR YOU.
A SURPRISE?
TEE HEE! LOOK!
HOO BOY! THAT WILL GO GOOD WITH SAUSAGE, AN...
SIR!
DON'T LIKE SAUSAGE?
US COWBIRDS COULD USE A NEST, CONFRERE.
IS THAT THERE A NEST OR A GARBAGE CAN, COMPEER?
WELL, STILL HARBOURIN' THAT STORK, EH?
I'M TRAPPED IN FORTY FATHOM AN' CAN'T FIND THE ESCAPE HATCH.

IF I HAD THIS TO DO OVER AGAIN I WOULDN'T CONSIDER IT A-TALL.

WELL, THAT'S LIFE -- A FLEETING SHADOW, DARKSOME SEEN, AS IN A REAR-VIEW MIRROR.
IF THAT'S ADVICE YOU CAN SORT IT OUT YOUR-SELF.

LOOKS TO ME LIKE THERE'S ROOM ENOUGH IN THAT NEST FOR ALL, COMPEER COWBIRD
WITHOUT DOUBT, CONFRERE COWBIRD.
JUST BECAUSE I BUILT A STORK NEST IN YO' CHIMNEY AN' BRUNG YOU GOOD LUCK, YOU DON'T HAFTA REE-TIRE.
MMPH

I NEED A BABYSITTER. I GOTTA DO A LI'L' SHOPPIN'
AIN'T IT EARLY, MIZ STORK?

NO, IT AIN'T EARLY. SIT EASY AN' IF ANYTHIN' HATCHES GIVE ME A HOLLER.
IS YOU SURE IT'S GOOD LUCK FER ME TO HAVE MORE STORKS?

IF YOU DON'T MIND US SAYIN' SO, COMPEER, YOU IS A MIGHTY FUNNY-LOOKIN' BIRD A-SETTIN' ON THAT NEST.
SAME TO YOU, ONLY TWICE. WHAT IS YOU ANYHOWS?
US IS COWBIRDS, COMPEER...
DOVES IS WHAT! THAT IS TO SAY WE'RE DOVES, COMPEER.

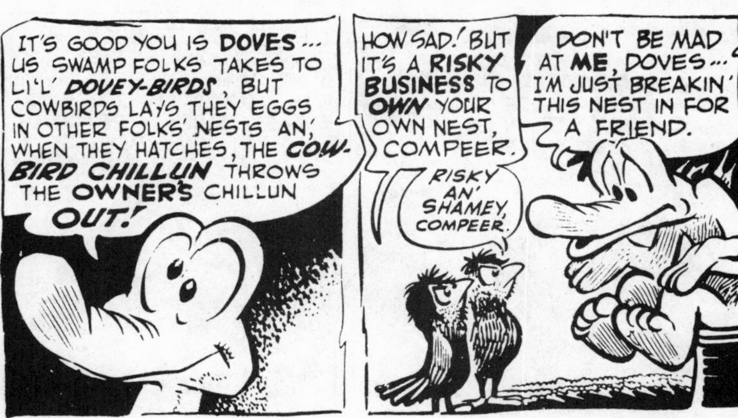

IT'S GOOD YOU IS DOVES... US SWAMP FOLKS TAKES TO LI'L' DOVEY-BIRDS, BUT COWBIRDS LAYS THEY EGGS IN OTHER FOLKS' NESTS AN,' WHEN THEY HATCHES, THE COW-BIRD CHILLUN THROWS THE OWNER'S CHILLUN OUT!
HOW SAD! BUT IT'S A RISKY BUSINESS TO OWN YOUR OWN NEST, COMPEER.
RISKY AN' SHAMEY, COMPEER.
DON'T BE MAD AT ME, DOVES... I'M JUST BREAKIN' THIS NEST IN FOR A FRIEND.

Boy Bird Watchers, Arise! I have sandwiches packed by yonder tree.... 'Tis time we were a-watching, fellows!
WE BEEN AT IT, PEERLESS LEADER.
WE FOUND SUCH A BIG ONE, DEAC, THAT BY WATCHIN' IT WE CAN GET ALL OUR BIRD-WATCHIN' DONE TO ONCE.

What?!? You'd watch Miz Stork? That Champion of Tradition, Emblem of Motherhood, enjoying a dignified lunch? She needs no watching!

TRUTHFULLY, WE'S JES' WATCHIN' THE LUNCH, SIR.
HAPPENS TO BE YOUR'N, SIR.
GOO?

YOU SHOULNTNA TOLD ALBERT US COWBIRDS WAS DOVES... WHOEVER HEARD OF BLACK DOVES? AN' 'SIDES I BEEN A COW-BIRD ALL MY LIFE.

UTTER DEVIATIONISM! AS A COWBIRD YOU WAS CHASED TOO! IS YOU BEEN CHASED SINCE WE BEEN DOVES? AS DOVES WE IS MESSENGERS OF PEACE AN' OUR FIRST PEACE MESSAGE IS "LAY OFF THE COWBIRDS"

PEACE AN' EQUAL RIGHTS FOR COW-BIRDS IS THE WORD FROM US UNSELFISH DOVES.
RIGHT! ROBINS GOT A RIGHT TO LAY EGGS IN NESTS WHAT ROBINS MAKE.

SO US DOVES DEFENDS THE RIGHTS OF COW-BIRDS TO LAY EGGS IN NESTS ---
... WHAT ROBINS MAKES! IMPERIOUS DISCRIMINATION MUST END!! PEACE!
PEACE!

IS YOU TWO DOVES WILLIN' TO. TAKE A JOB BABY-SITTIN' FOR MIZ STORK?
WE DON'T BELIEVE IN MYTHOLOGICAL MATERNAL MYSTICALITY. BUT WE'LL DO IT.
COMFY?
YOUR VICTORIAN VOCABULARY IS A STIGMA-SYMBOL OF BENIGHTED PATERNALISTIC INFANTILISM.

I DUNNO WHAT YOU IS TALKIN' 'BOUT BUT 'LONG AS YOU KEEP THEM EGGS WARM I IS HAPPY.

WE'LL WARM 'EM UP GOOD, EH, COMPEER? A POX... A PROLETARIAN POX ON ABSENTEE LANDLORDISM.

Behold fellows, birds to watch! What say you they are? Dr. Moom's piebald blitherskates?
THEM IS LESSER PIP-SQUEAKS AN' THEY CAN WATCH THEM-SELVES
PHOO SOME BIRDS!
WIPE THE EGG OFF YOUR MOUTH, COMPEER, THE HEAD OF AN AUTONOMOUS OUTDOOR FACTIONAL CENTER OF IDENTIFICATIONISM APPROACHES.

Well -- what might we have here?
WE'RE DOVES! FUNDAMENTALLY CONSTRUCTIVIST PRINCIPALS IN A PACIFISTIC ACTIVATION OF WORLD SCOPE ...

BY JING! YOU STEP OUTSIDE AN' SAY THAT!
HA! YOU NUGATORY NULLIFIDIAN.
RIGHT.

HA!
WHO SAY HA? WHO?
NOT ME. I IS SLEEPIN'

NAB DAG IT, MIZ STORK, YOU IS A PEEPLIN' TOM!
IS YOU THE SAME ALLIGATOR AS LAS' WEEK?

'COURSE! I IS EVEN THE SAME ONE I WAS LAST MONTH--- HAVE THE COURTESIES TO CLOSE DOWN YO' EYE LIDS!
YOU IS S'POSE TO BE BABY-SITTIN' MY EGGS.

YO' EGGS GOT LUMPY SO I QUIT.
YOU AIN'T TRUSTWORTHY
HIS
IT AIN'T ONE OF HIS FIRST-LINE VIRTUES AT THAT.

I SWEAR, MIZ STORK, YO' EGGS IS BEIN' WATCHED BY TWO DOVEY-BIRDS
YOU GOT A FLIMMERY EYE AN' A HONEY-POT TONGUE, ALBERT.
HEY, MR. TAMMANANNY, DID YOU FIND A CANDIDATE TO RUN FOR THE PRESIDENSITY?
MM

THE JOB BEEN SOUNDIN' SO TOUGH LATELY, IT LOOK LIKE NOBODY IN THE SWAMP IS SO INNOCENT AN' NAIVE AS TO BE DUPE ENOUGH TO ----

OH, I DUNNO, MR. TIGER, OUR SWAMP GOT INNOCENCE ENOUGH FOR ANY JOB.

THE CANDIDATURE

☆☆POGO☆☆ IN PERSON !!!
STUPENDOUS NEWS!
WONDROUS WORDS!
*P*O*G*O* Will
RUN!!
OH, H'LO MR. BRIDGEPORT.
When I heard, I DROPPED ALL!
The CIRCUS SEASON WEEPS ITS INFANT PLEADING to NO AVAIL!
{Let me carry that for you, candidate.}
3 (three) COUNT THEM (three) 3 CHEERS!

I, P.T. BRIDGEPORT, at GREAT personal EXPENSE and SACRIFICE will guide your EVERY STEP!
I SAID TO REGINALD HERE, "BREWSTER, DEAR CHAP," I SAID, "I....
BOLINGBROKE, my boy, at least have the decency to cease that ☆IN-FERN-AL☆ drumming when I'm talking about YOU!
THERE'S A GOOD LAD, HEWLITT!
I GOTTA GIT MY DRUMMIN' DONE, Y'KNOW.

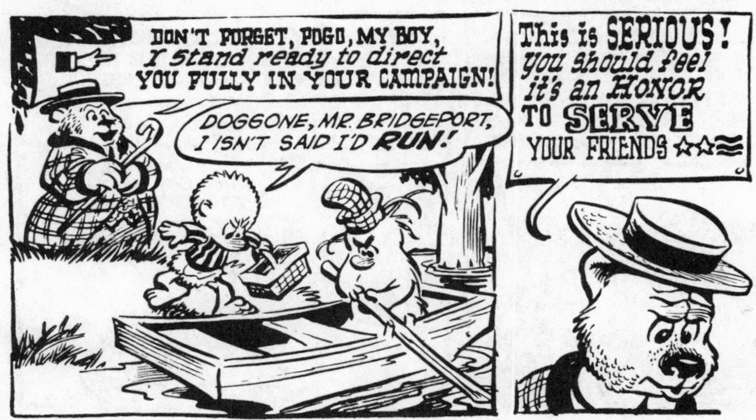
DON'T FORGET, POGO, MY BOY, I stand ready to direct YOU FULLY IN YOUR CAMPAIGN!
DOGGONE, MR. BRIDGEPORT, I ISN'T SAID I'D RUN!
This is SERIOUS! You should feel it's an HONOR TO SERVE YOUR FRIENDS ☆☆

Rest assured, Pogo, dear lad, your friends RETURN THE Feeling?!! It is !! RE-CIP-RO-CAL!!
WHATS YOU MEAN? THEY'D BE HONORED TO SERVE ME?
HOW'S THAT, SON?
NO, HE MEANS THEY'D GO 'LONG WITH YOU ---- THEY'D AGREE IT WAS A HONOR FOR YOU TO SERVE YOUR FRIENDS.

WE DOVES ARE A HARD CORE PACIFIC GROUP IN AMICABLE OCCUPATIONAL DUTY BOUND TO THE BASIC TENETS OF MATERNO-DOMICILICAL FUNCTION.
"Must be Doves! Did you ever hear such high-tone talk?
AN' SO BRAINY AN' INCOMPREHENSIBOBBLE
"Behold, Pogo! Doves have nested! What a Happy Omen for your candidature
IS I?

THESE DOVES LOOKS LIKE COWBIRDS; SOUNDS LIKE COWBIRDS AN' IS SETTIN' IN SOMEBODY ELSE'S NEST ON COWBIRD EGGS JUST LIKE COWBIRDS.

TARNATION! THE CANDIDATE KNOWS EVER'THIN'. HE KIN COUNTER-DICT US BIRD EXPERTS --- HE KIN INSULT THE MATERNO-DOMICKOWICKAL FUNCTION LIKE WHAT THE DOVES SAY... WHAT ELSE DO HE KNOW?
I KNOWS THE BEST BIRD BRAINS IN THE COUNTRY IS A-GIN ME.

Do you chaps realize that Pogo has lashed out at "Motherhood and Peace? He says the doves what is baby-sittin' for "Miz Stork is Cowbirds!"

WE TOOK THAT UP WITH THEM CHIMNEY-COLORED DOVES TOO... SHOWED 'EM COWBIRD PICTURES IN THE BIRD BOOK LOOKED LIKE 'EM... THEY SAID: "DON'T GIVE IT A DEVIATIONAL THOUGHT."
IT'S THE WATER

They are above such non-sense, I'll wager a pretty--
BLESS THEIR HEARTS.

YEP! THEY IS ABOVE AN' BEE-YOND! THEY TOOK THE OLD BOOK AN' SET FIRE TO IT... NOW THEY IS WRITIN' A BRANG NEW ONE..... SOMETHIN' TO CONFORM TO THE FACTS.
HARD A-LEE HARD A-PORT AN HARD AVAST.
IT'S THE WATER

AS ROOKERY-MOTHER TO THE BOY BIRD WATCHERS I IS BEEN BUSY HELPIN' THE DEACON PROTECT THE DOVES WHAT BEEN GUARDIN' YOUR NEST...
I'M EVER SO GRATEFUL TO YOU GIRLS.
Mmmp
POGO BEEN SPREADIN' PURE POISON 'BOUT HOW YOU IS HARBOURIN' COWBIRDS!
MY LAND! I NEVER DID!
Scandalous

THERE THEY IS, MOTHER STORK...
YEEP! THEM DOVES IS COWBIRDS!
AN INFORMER! A QUEASY CLASS-RIDDEN INHIBITIONIST!
PSSST... DON'T THROW THAT.. IT'S ONE OF OURS.

AHA! I see they are chasing the COWBIRDS!
WHEN THEY ASKED ME I TOLE 'EM AN' I TOLE 'EM... "THEY ISN'T DOVES!" I TOLE 'EM.
As a candidate you should answer controversial questions with "No Comment"
BUT I HAD COMMENT SO I GUV IT.

you must word answers so that you don't SPOIL the Questions.
BUT THE PUBLIC WANTS TO KNOW WHERE A MAN STANDS!
THEN HE SHOULD SAY: "DUE to incalculable potentials apparently inherent pro and con in aspects of the to-be determinationism of current trends I regret that..
ANYBODY LEFT LISTENIN' WOULD OF STOPPED BY THAT TIME.

HOT DOG! NOW THEM COWBIRDS IS GONE, I CAN GIT MY HAT BACK AN' EMPTY THAT RATTY NEST OUTEN IT.

Desist --- begone! Unhand that Symbol of Mother and Fireside! We Bird Watchers will not allow Miz Stork's home to again be despoiled.

MIZ STORK BUILT THAT NEST IN MY HAT FOR WHICH SHE HAD NO MORE OF A RIGHT TO DO IT THAN THEM COWBIRDS HAD TO TAKE IT OVER OFF'N HER WITHOUT SHE SAY SO AND I...
You'll touch this--

--over my dead body.
I'SE WILLIN' ----- ANY WAY YOU SAY. STAY THERE WHILST I GITS A FLYSWATTER.

HEY, POGO! THE TALK IN THE SALONS AROUND FORT MUDGE IS THAT YOUR HAT'S IN THE RING.
DON'T MENTION HATS, MOUSE.
YEAH! OL' DEACON IS GUV MY HAT TO MIZ STORK WITH-OUT SO MUCH AS A BAYOU-LEAVE.
WHAT IN THE WORLD DOES SHE WANT WITH YOUR HAT?
SHE BUILT A NEST IN IT.

ABANDON IT THEN.... ONCE A PARTY IS NESTED, NEVER DISTURB IT... I MIND ONE TIME ME AN' LUCKY JACK LARKIN BUILT US A NEST OF SCRAPS IN THE DERBY OF A EMINENT BANK PRES. ... WELL, SIR... WE JUST GOT..
A FAVORABLE GAME GOIN' WHEN THE PREXY GRABS HIS LID AN' GOES TO LUNCH. WE WAS ALL HAULED IN FOR ABSCONDIMENT... SEEMS WE'D TORE UP LARGE BILLS FOR THE NEST .. THE PRES. WAS A GOOD MAN TO BE IN THE POKEY WITH .. HE ..
HEY!

TAMMANANNY, A GROSS BLOW has befallen POGO'S CANDIDATURE
HE'S MADE A SPEECH?

NO, he was mixed up with some COWBIRDS! The Deacon claims it blackens POGO'S name
SOMEONE MUST ENDORSE POGO'S CHAR-ACTER!

YES! It will take a man of PROVEN MERIT! A CITIZEN WHO TOWERS ABOVE THE CROWD. ★★ A FIGURE ADMIRED and BELOVED by ALL!!!
IT'LL BE HARD TO GET SUCH A MAN TO SPEAK UP AND RISK HIS OWN GOOD NAME.
SAY NOT SO!! These are TIMES for STALWARCY & PLUCK One noble soul must risk it I, P.T. BRIDGEPORT WILL SPEAK FOR POGO!!
YOU SURE THAT FIGURE IS UNIVERSALLY ADMIRED?

WE SEE MR. P.T. BRIDGEPORT STRIDIN' MAN-FUL OFF.... WHAT'S UP?
DEACON'S BEEN SMIRCHIN' UP OL' POGO'S NAME...SO P.T. IS GONNA TELL 'EM A MOUTHFUL.

FRIENDS, I am here to

THEM COWBIRDS LEFT THEIR OWN EGGS IN MY NEST.

S'MATTER, SWALLOW YOUR TONGUE?
not My Tongue, NO!
HMMPH.. SOME MOUTHFUL.
I NEVER DID HOLD WITH BEARS

WELL, I GUESS WE WON'T BE VOTIN' FOR POGO!
GONNA WRITE IN YOUR OWN SELFS?

'COURSE NOT!' IT WOULDN'T BE FAIR TO PRECIPITATE A LAND-SLIDE. BUT POGO'S CAMPAIGN MANAGER IS HAD IT PROVED TO HIM THAT THERE'S A GROUND SWELL OF OPINION AGAINST POGO.
HOW PROVED?

HE GOT UP TO SPEAK FOR THE CANDIDATE AN' GOT THROWN AT WITH EGGS' THAT SHOWS POGO IS WASHED UP. THE PUBLIC IS SPOKE! FAIR MINDED AN' SQUARE ... UN-M
-- HEADED?

WELL, BULLY FOR YOU, BOYS. KEEP FINGERIN' THE PULSE OF THE GRASS ROOTS ... BUT TRY TO HOLD OFF WRITIN' IN YOUR OWN NAMES. IT'LL BE TOUGH BECAUSE CONSTANT PROOF OF OTHER CANDIDATES' CRIMINAL WAYS WILL ARISE ...

US'LL BE FIRM AN' REFRAIN 'CAUSE IT WOULDN'T BE SPORTIN'...

THRU ELECTION DAY?

YOU CAN STOP MAKIN' THEM MACHINE VOTERS .... IT'S TIME WE WAS ALL BEIN' GOOD FRIENDS WITH P.T.BRIDGEPORT.

WHY, THAT BIG OL' BLOWHEAD! HE'S A REAL FIRST OF MAY CIRCUS CIPHER --- A RUBE IN DISGUISE --- A SAWDUST FOGHORN--- WHAT'S HE GOT TO BE FRIENDS WITH?

M M

A BIG BAG OF MONEY.
LEMME HELP YOU CARRY THAT TO THE DEAR DEAR OLD PARTY! WHO'S SENDIN' THIS DIRTY OLD MONEY TO THE SWEET EVER-LOVIN' CHAP? HE'S GONE NEED A HAND COUNTIN' IT.
STOP SHOVIN'. AIN'T NO SPECIAL DEE-LIVERY STAMP ON IT.

LET'S JES' LOOK AT THE MONEY WHAT BEEN SENT TO P.T. BRIDGEPORT... HE WON'TMISSALI'L'BITIF WE.. HEEKOOHAHA
STOP THAT! THIS MAIL MIGHT BE FOURTH CLASS BUT...
U.S. MAIL
THE BAG COULD OF BEEN DAMAGED IN TRANSIT. HEEHEEHO HOHOOHA HAHOHEE!
I HAD A FRIEND TRIED THAT ONCE AN' HE WOUND UP IN THE BIG ARENA PLAYIN' A 20 YEAR GAME OF ROCK HOCKEY.

20 YEARS ?
THE KIND OF GIDDY FRIENDS YOU HAVE, PROB'LY NEED LESSONS LIKE THAT.... CHUG-CHUG, STOP HOLDIN' US UP! GIT GOIN' FOR P.T. BRIDGEPORT'S PLACE.
HOLD UP! IT'S AGIN REGULATIONS TO RUSH FOURTH CLASS MAIL.

DON'T FERGIT TO REMIND P.T. NOW, THAT THIS BAG OF MONEY WAS HEAVY AN' HE COULD SHOW HIS APPRECIATION BY.. HEEHO HAHOHEEHAHEE
U.S. MAIL
WE WAS WONDERIN', MR. BRIDGEPORT, (SEEIN' AS WE BRUNG THAT BAGFUL) IF WE COULD DIP IN AN.. AW HAW
HEE HOO HAHA HA!...
A REASONABLE REQUEST. Take all you wish!
WOW, ALL?

of COURSE, OWL! HELP YOUR'SELF TO BUTTONS!
BUTTONS ?

AYE -- aren't they BEAUTIES? POGO BUTTONS for --- his CANDIDATURE ------ ------ EMBLAZONED = I GO POGO!

EVERYBODY in the Swamp IS GOING FOR POGO Fro PRESIDENT!!! EVERYBODY ★ EVERYBODY
EV-AR-EE-BOD-DEE --

'CEPT POGO.

DID YOU SEE THE BUTTONS THAT OL' P.T. BRIDGEPORT IS GIVIN' OUT?
"Mmm- Campaign buttons- For Pogo? What you wearin' em for?

THEY WAS FREE.
GO POGO

There must be some way that we dignified few opposed to P.T. Bridgeport's gang can make use of these buttons.....
I MADE USE OF MINE!
A BUTTON COMED OFF'N MY UNDERWEARS BUT I HOLTS 'EM UP WITH MY GOOD OL' POGO BADGE --- GOTTA GIT HOME 'CAUSE IT'S LUMPY.
SEE, A WHOLE FOLK SENTIMENT IS BEIN' BUILT UP!
Gentlemen, a few dignified citizens would let bygones be gone if Pogo would be OUR candidate.
YOU WIN THAT ONE.
THAT'S ONE EACH THEN.
SHH.. WE IS SEEIN' WHO KIN DREAM 'BOUT TH' BIGGEST CAT·FISH.
We oppose the P.T. Bridgeport gang - If Pogo would come out on the side of Right -- i.e. OUR side --- Fighting--
YOU'D FERGIT POGO WAS "MIXED UP WITH COWBIRDS"? DEACON, DID YOU EVER SEE TWO DOGS FIGHTIN' OVER A BONE?
"Naturally
---YOU EVER SEE THE BONE FIGHT?

RIGHT ON THE BUTTON

YES, Gunther, YES!! NOW LISTEN To The SPEECH
WHILE YOU'RE DOIN' THAT, I'LL PRACTICE MY NEW CONCESSION.
Fearless
HONESTY
Is the Sacred
VOTER
Loyalty
PEANUTS!

GREAT NEWS, POGO!! CHURCHY has written a SONG for your CAMPAIGN!
IS I GOT A CAMPAIGN?

OH, ONCE THE OPPOSITION WAS COMPLETALLY OPPOSED TO ALL THE SUPPOSITIONS THAT WAS GEN'RALLY SUPPOSED; AN' NOW THE SUPERSTITIONS THAT WERE THO'T TO BE IMPOSED ARE SEEN BY COMPOSITION TO BE SLIGHTLY DECOMPOSED.!
THERE !!!!

It's a BANNER of BRAVERY-- a FLAG OF FREEDOM FLUNG TO THE WINDS of HEAVEN ----- A TRUMPET OF TRIUMPH Wafting a veritable vibrato-bravura of words writ in tears meaning ~uh m--uh--mm- meaning ~~
GO POGO

What does it mean, Turtle?
WHAT?
STOP BUNKO

FRIENDS! I WELCOME Each and Every ONE to this Monster Rally!!
STOP BUNKO
SO FAR, ONLY ONE MONSTER.

I GIVE YOU Brother OWL, who has a FEW WORDS to say on behalf of the CANDIDATE
ANOTHER ONE
AN', BY JING, THEY AIN'T GIVIN' THAT ONE TO ME!

A little less impulsive Shoving, friend, WOULD-
I THOUGHT YOU HAD A BROADER PLATFORM!
THE MONSTERS ARE RALLYING.

It might be of interest
you to become AWARE,
that this UNSEEMLY
REFLECTS NO CREDIT ON THE
IF YOU WOULD CLOSE THAT BIG BAZOO AND LET ME
PEANUTS!
APTLY WORDED!
THERE'S AS EARY A MONSTER AS ANY PARTY EVER SPAWNED.

YOU INVITED ME TO THE ROSTRUM TO MAKE A SPEECH AND BY WILLY DINGO I'M A-GONNA MAKE IT.
SIR, don't be so CROWDY!
STOP BUNKO
I'M HERE WITH A NEW CAMPAIGN SONG.

A PLATFORM OUGHTA BE BIG ENUFF FER TH' WHOLE PARTY.
This AIN'T NO PARTY! IT'S a unruly RALLY REALLY!
AHEM!

I'M PUTTIN' MY FOOT DOWN!
THERE'S ONE NAME TONIGHT, ONE STAR THAT SPANGLES BRIGHT, ONE HEART WHOSE STRIPE IS WHITE AND WIDELY RED AND RIGHT.....
BOOM
POGO
IT'S
PEANUTS!
YES
PEANUTS!
OH,
PEANUTS FOR ALL!
COUSIN COWBIRD, MINE COMPEER, WE'VE BEEN HARRIED AND HUNTED TOO LONG!
RIGHT! IT IS TIME WE FIGHTERS FOR THE GOOD LIFE REVEALED THE POWER OF OUR HAND.
LET US THROW UP A BARRICADE AGAINST THE GRINDING HEELS OF EXPLOITATION!
AYE! WE'LL BE HEROES IN THE RANKS, SOLDIERS FOR EQUALITY!

WILL WE TURN TAIL LIKE COWARDLY DOGS OF PROPERTY?
NO!
WILL WE BEG FOR ALMS?
NO!
WHAT WILL WE DO? CRAWL?
NO!
WILL WE BE STRONG IN THE MIGHT OF OUR RIGHT?
YES! YES! WE'LL HIDE IN HERE.
POGO

SO! THIS IS THE HOME OF POGO-PALATIAL AND GROSS IN ITS MERCENARY MUNDANITY!
STUFFED WITH THE FRUIT OF OUR NATURAL RESOURCES ALL EXCISED FROM THE PUBLIC ESTATE!

BLED FROM STORES WITH MONEY EARNED UNDER A DECADENT CASH AN' CARRY SYSTEM
HE THRIVES ONLY UNDER THE THRALLDOM OF THRIFT! A SHIFTY DEVICE!
COOKIE

AND HOW DOES HE PROTECT THESE RIGHTFUL TREASURES OF WE HARASSED HORDES? HE LEAVES HIS DOOR OPEN!
BENIGHTED FRATERNALISM! A CLEAR CASE.

YES, A SUBVERSION OF THE BASIC TENETS OF PUBLIC PROPERTY PRIVACY.
IRRESPONSIBILISM! HE ACTS AS IF HE DIDN'T CARE WHO WANDERED IN HERE.

DON'T SEEM LIKE POGO IS HOME, SO I'LL LEAVE THESE "I GO POGO" BADGES OUT HERE.
POGO

HMMPH! POGO'S HAD ANOTHER DELIVERY OF GROCERIES.
AND ABOUT TIME... LOOKS LIKE A FLIMSY BOURGEOIS BAG OF BEANS.

POUR ON POGO'S KETCHUP HEAVY... I LIKES 'EM TASTEFUL!

OW! THESE AIN'T BEANS! THEY'RE CAMPAIGN PINS!
THAT SNEAKY POGO! MISREPRESENTIN' THESE AS BEANS.

YOO HOO!
YOWP! WHAT'S YOU?

'LONG AS YOU IS RUNNIN' FOR PRESIDENT, I IS GONE BE YO' MILITARY AIDE. US WILL BOWL OVER THE OPPOSITION.

LIKE SO!
BRAM

I DUNNO ... SEEM LIKE MILITARY AIDES IS MORE SHOT AT THAN BY.

AS YO' MILITARY AIDE, POGO, I OUGHTA LOOK AT YO' CABINET AN' SEE WHO GONE BE IN IT.

WE IS!
YEOW.
COW BIRDS!

MY SAKES! HOW'S YOU GONE GIT YO' LEG OUT?
I GOT A IDEA!
IT'S STUCK.

I'LL JUST PULL THE CORD AN' THE CHARGE WILL BLOW THE ....
STOP! DO YOU WANTA DEEFEN US ALL BY FIRIN' THAT THING INDOORS?

'LONG AS WE IS CONFINED HERE WHILST YOU IS STUCK IN THE CANNON, ME AN' MY COUSIN COWBIRD WILL DO ALL THE COOKIN'....
UNTIL SOMEBODY COMPLAINS 'BOUT THE FOOD--- THEN HE GOTTA COOK.

WE'LL GIT HIM TO COMPLAIN EARLY. WE'LL SERVE HIM THE "I GO POGO" BUTTONS WE COOKED UP, THINKIN' THEY WAS BEANS.

AAKK!
THIS BLAGSTAG, DOGBONED, FOGBOUND GOOK TASTES LIKE RUSTY OL' CAMPAIGN BUTTONS.
GOOD, THOUGH!

DON'T LIKE HAVIN' THEM COWBIRDS STAYIN' HERE. I DEE-SPISES 'EM FOR ALLUS SPONGIN' OFF OTHERS ---- BUT SOUTHERN HOSPITALITY RULES.
THEY'S WORSE TROUBLES ---- YO' FOOT BEIN' STUCK IN A CANNON FR INSTINCT.
GUESS WE CAN SNEAK IN AN' BORRY SUGAR NOW --- THEY'S SLEEPIN'

I KEEPS TRACK OF ALL I BORROWS ... --- I OWES POGO 17,615 POUNDS NOW.... 'TAINT LIKE I WAS CHEATIN' HIM OUTEN IT.
MY DREAMS ARE BAD ENOUGH ... GO AWAY.

It was all I could do to spoon the sugar out over them no-good cowbirds! Imagine the Candidate having such Mountebankery in his Cabinet!!
DISGUSTIN'! IF ANYBODY ELSE HAD SUGAR, I WOULDN'T TAKE OFF'N POGO.
POGO

COULD MEBBE YOU **FOTCH** ME A COOKIE AN' A GLASS OF ***MILK*** SEEIN' AS I IS YO' ***MILITARY* AIDE,** PRES. ?
I ISN'T BEEN ELECTED TO TH' ***PRESIDENSITY*** YET.....

SORRY, POGO! US **COWBIRDS** GOT HERE FIRST AN' YO' COOKIES ***BAD*** AS THEY IS ... ***IS* GONE.**
COOKIES

ALBERT'S GONE HAFTA SETTLE FOR A **GLASS** OF **MILK.**

GIT A-WAY! DOESN'T YOU RESPECK THE ***BATHIN'*** PRIVACY OF A HOUSE GUEST?

YOU FIGGER IF I GITS **ELECTED** TO SOMETHIN' I KIN MAKE ***HOSPITALITY*** A FEDERABLE ***O***-FFENSE ?

I see you're wearing an "I GO POGO" button, Porky.
I SEE YOU IS, TOO.

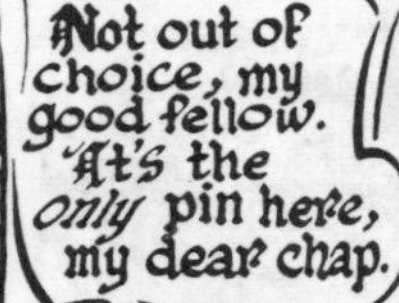
Not out of choice, my good fellow. It's the *only* pin here, my dear chap.

EVEN THO' IT'S **CROOKED,** IT'S THE ***ONE*** WHEEL IN TOWN, HUH? *AN' I'M NOT* ***NO***-BODY'S CHAP.... DEAR OR OTHER.

Eh? Do you know this Pogo has COWBIRDS in his cabinet? Strange bedfellows, I must say.......
POGO SLEEPIN' IN HIS OWN CUPBOARD? WELL, YOU BEEN INTO IT ENOUGH; BORRY-FYIN' AN' ALL.
WHAT'S THE DIFFERMINTS IF THEM OUT-LANDERS EAT POGO OUTEN HOUSE AN' HOME OR YOU DOES ?
Why, I'm a Friend of Pogo! Where's your sense of commun-ity Spirit?

FOLKS KEEP ASKIN' WHAT YOU STANDS FOR WHEN YOU STANDS FOR COWBIRDS.
NOT MUCH LONGER-- I IS GONE DO SOME-THIN'...

POGO SAY HE GONE SET FIRE TO HIS HOUSE.
NOT WHILST HE GIVIN' US HAVEN HE CAN'T---- WE IS ILL!

SO IS I ... MOOM OVER!

IF YOU'LL FORGIVE ME FER SAYIN' SO, PORKYPINES GOT THEIR POINTS.
YEP, IF I WARN'T A-TTACHED TO MYSELF, I WOULDN'T SLEEP WITH ME EITHER.

LEFT AT THE POST

HERE, borrow mine and remember ☞ Throwing ONE'S HAT INTO THE RING REQUIRES ☆☆ STANCE ☆☆ and STAMINA
6-17

STANCE AN' STAMINA PLAYED THE OLD PALACE WITH ME IN---
PROPERTY DEPT.

BAM!
-- 19-OUGHT-22.
DIST BY POST HALL SYNDICATE.

THEY DON'T MAKE THESE BOATERS LIKE THEY USE TO.
YOU LOAD THAT FOWLING PIECE WITH COLD OATMEAL from now on--- I might of been IN THAT!
COPR 1952 WALT KELLY

AND THEN:

GOT ANY OL' PLANK? THE CRITTURS IS A-BUILDERIN' YOU A PLATFORM--- LEAST US KIN DO IS COUNTERBUTE.
6-23
DIST. BY POST-HALL SYNDICATE.

PIECE OF MY PORCH DO?
SURE, THEY WAS A PORCH PLANK IN THE LAST PLATFORM.
POGO

WITHOUT BEING SUCKED INTO THE MAELSTROM OF JUVENILE FOLKWAYS.... IT WOULD AID OUR PEACEFUL AIMS OF WORLDWIDE PARTICIPATORY PROGRESS IF WE HAD A PLATFORM.

WE COULD JOIN THEIR MUDDY MINDED MELANGENOUS MEE-NAGERY AND THEN FORM A SPLINTER PARTY...

WHEE...

COPR 1952 WALT KELLY

ME AN' BEMILDRED IS GONE LAUNCH POGO'S PLATFORM BY CRACKIN' A BOTTLE OF GHASTLY WATER ON ITS BROW.
GOOD, 'CAUSE I IS READIED-UP A CAMPAIGN SONG CALLED "THE THIRD RAIL THEME."
"The Party of the first Part And the party of the next Are partly participled In a parsley-covered text..
6-25
DIST. BY POST-HALL SYNDICATE

"Were you partial to a Party That has parceled out its parts With the Party that was Second In your polly-tickle heart?
"Then parlay all your losings On a horse that's running dark... With lights-out you may triple In a homer in the park."

HEY, YOU DON'T LAUNCH A PLATFORM THAT WAY.
I KNOW... I MISSED HIM.
COPR. 1962 WALT KELLY

AND THEN:

SO, YOU IS MAKIN' SAN'WICHES FOR THE TRIP TO CHICAGO?
YEP! OL' ALBERT GITS HONGRIFIED!

'TIL HE GOT MAD AN' KICKED THE CANNON TO PIECES WHAT WERE STUCK ON HIS FOOT, IT DIN'T LOOK LIKE HE'D GO.
GOTTA FIND OWL. HE'S IN CHARGE OF THE A-RRANGE MINTS.

GOT A LI'L' SOMETHIN FOR YOU TO.....
PUL-LEASE, MISTER CANDIDATE! NO MORE FAVORS FOR NO-BODY... I IS A BUSY MAN--- WHATEVER YOU GOT, FOR-GET IT.
IF YOU'LL LISTEN TO MY CAMPAIGN SONGS, I'LL HELP YOU EAT THEM SAN'WICHES.....
YOU IS DECENT, CHURCHY.
DIST. BY POST-HALL SYNDICATE
COPR 1952 WALT KELLY

POGO! WE CAME TO SEE THE PLAT-FORM THEY MADE FOR YOU.
SHH... TURTLE IS GONE SING SOME MORE OF THE CAMPAIGN SONG HE WROT, "THE THIRD RAIL THEME."
LUNCH
7-1
"Promulge the prating prim
Of the prudent PromiSOR,
For the Premise of the Promise
Was the PrimogenitOR
Of the Primalaceous Program
With the Presbyopic DOOR!"

IT'S ALMOST UNPOSSIBOBBLE TO EAT AND REE-CITE AT THE SAME TIME.
THAT IS ALL-READY OCCURRED TO US.
NOTE IT has ★★WET★PLANKS And DRY!
EXCELLENT, P.T., EX-CELL-LENT!
LUNCH
DIST BY POST-HALL SYNDICATE
COPR 1952 WALT KELLY

YOU FOLKS GOT TIME TO SEE WHAT I GOT RINGED UP FOR CHICAGO SO'S US KIN NOMINATE OUR CANDIDATE?
THESE TWO IS BUSY WRITIN' POLITICAL PROMISES WITH BOTH HANDS... WHAT'S YOU GOT?
I'LL PULL IT OVER SO'S YOU CAN SEE .... IT'S A PORTABLE...
6-27
DIST. BY POST-HALL SYNDICATE

---SMOKE-FILLED ROOM! I STOKES THE STOVE WITH OL' SEE-GAR BUTTS AN'...
SHOO-BOY! A MAN COULD SMOKE A HOG IN A LI'L' ROOM LIKE THAT.
I DUNNO... SOME OF THEM CANDIDATES DON'T CURE EASY.
COPR 1952 WALT KELLY

MY PORTABLE SMOKE-FILLED ROOM IS BOUND TO GIT YO' CANDIDATE NOMINATED.
EVERYBODY WHO IS Anybody IS GOING.
EVEN SOME WHO ISN'T.
IS CHICAGO IN INDIANA OR MASSACHUSETTS?
OHIO.
MOE, AS I LIVE AN' BREATHE.... HOW'S THE MOTHIN' GAME?
BAD--I FOLLOWS THE WORD; LAYS EGGS ON CROWS; THE CATERPIGGLES HATCH OUT AN' GIT SHOOK OFF. I'M GOIN' INTO ANOTHER LINE.
7-3
DIST BY POST HALL SYNDICATE.

YOU LOCKS ALL THE POLITICIANS INSIDE AND TURN ON THE SMOKE.
YOU USE CROWS?
CROWS.
I'M FOR BI-PARTISAN FOREIGN RELATIONS.
AN' WHEN YOU MENTIONS YO' MAN---?
THEY IS IN TEARS
A FOREIGN RELATION OF MINE WENT WITH ALL THE PARTIES ONE YEAR. NAME OF MABEL.
WAY I HEERD, IT'S CLOTHES YOU USE.
OH, CLOTHES? I'LL GIVE 'EM A TRY.
COPR 1952 WALT KELLY

BOY! OFF TO CHICAGO AT LAST--- WAIT'LL WE UNVEIL OUR CANDIDATE, MISTER, POGO POSSUM.. HA!
WOW! I GO POGO!
OWL! I GOT A FEELIN' WE IS LEFT SOMETHIN' BEHIND.
HEAR! HEAR!!
HOO BOY!
THE CRIMSON
7-4

CAN'T THINK OF NOTHIN'.... LESSEN IT'S A SACK OF I GO POGO PINS.
AN' WE WOULDN'T GO WITHOUT ALL OUR BUTTONS.
NO GO?
BUTTONS
ZZZZ
COPR 1952 WALT KELLY
DIST. BY POST-HALL SYNDICATE

FREE TO GET READY and SORE TO GO

GET THE BALL, PLEASE, GET THE BALL!

GET THE BALL? UH... MM? WONDER... WONDER WHO'S PLAYIN'?

HERE'S YOUR BALL.. UM - WELL... GOSH!
THERE'S A GOOD CHAP! GRAB A FLYSWATTER AN' JOIN IN A GAME OF BADMINTON.
I'M PLAYIN' GOOD-MINTON... AN' THAT'S A BIRD.

WHY SO IT IS! A COWBIRD.... HE LOOKS A LITTLE PEAKIED.
WELL, THROW IT AWAY THEN... THEY COMMON ENOUGH.
DISGUSTING SO! THERE'S ONE.

AARGH HE DEVIATED.
ORDERS
I'LL SET YOU DOWN CAREFUL.... OW
YOU CAPITALIST! WEARIN' A HAT.

HA! YOU'VE GOT ONE ON YOU.
I HAVE NOT.
YOU HAVE TOO!
I HAVE NOT!

OH, I SHALL SMITE YOU TO A SMITHEREEN!
THIS WILL ONLY LEAD TO BLOWS, I WARN YOU.

BY THOR! YOU WILL GET A NASTY LETTER FROM MY LAWYER IN THE MORNING.

LOOK! LOOK! ONE OF THEM THERE IS GETTIN' AWAY!
LOOK! LOOK! ONE OF THEM THERE IS GETTIN' A WAY.

SHEER ME-TOO ISM! WHY DON'T YOU USE YOUR OWN HEAD?
YOURS IS GOT BIG ENOUGH FOR BOTH OF US.

ONE OF WHAT WHERE IS GETTIN' AWAY?
ONE OF THE GINGER-BREAD BOYS IS RUN OFF. WE MUST GIVE CHASE.

YOU CAN RUN AN' RUN AS FATS AS YOU CAN .. BUT YOU CAN'T CATCH ME, I'M A GINGER-BREAD MAN.
COME BACK, YOU TRAITOR .... COME BACK
MIGHT AS WELL USE THE SAME BALLOONS.
WHOO! I'M A LI'L' WINDED.
GLAD TO MEET YOU! I'M A LI'L' ELEPHANT.
THERE'S NO SUCH THINGAS A LITTLE ELEPHANT.
WHY WAS THAT GINGERBREAD BOY RUNNIN' OFF?
HE WAS DESERTIN'
WE WAS GOIN' TO SHIP HIM TO THE ARMY OF THE REALM --- BUT HE QUIT --- IT MAKES ME MAD.
ME TOO
THE ARMY OF THE WHOM? THEY LIKES GINGERBREAD BOYS?
THEY ARE GINGERBREAD BOYS ... NOW COWBIRDS WILL GET THIS ONE.

AND THEY, LIKE AS NOT, WILL CONVERT HIM.
CONVERT HIM?
YES, INTO FOOD.
BUT WE MUST NOT DWELL ON GINGERBREAD BOYS WHO'D SOLDIERS BE.
OUT OF SIGHT...OUT OF MIND.
THEY'RE OUT OF SIGHT... WE'RE OUT OF MIND? WHY NOT SAVE THE GINGERBREAD BOY?
BECAUSE WE ARE BUSY PLAYIN' NATIONAL PASTIMES ...HIGH-LOW TARIFF AN' THE GAME...
AN' NEXT WE IS GONE PLAY AT JACKSTRAWS. MEBBE I'LL GIT TO WIN.
PIG! YOU WON TWENTY-FOUR YEARS AGO.
NOT SO'S IT REALLY COUNTED, REALLY.
SAY!
YOU THERE! HOW'D YOU LIKE TO PLAY?
PLAY WHAT?

GINGER BREAD BOY!
GIVE US A TASTE.
SHAKE HIM UP! IT'LL GET THE FLAVOR ROUSED.
SHAKE HIM UP.. WAKE HIM UP...
WAKE UP, UNCLE POGO! WAKE UP!
GOSH.... RACKETY-COON CHILE, I MUST OF WAS DREAMIN'.
ISN'T YOU GONE GO AN' GIT ELECTED PRESIDENT?
WELL, I DUNNO... I'LL GO 'LONG AN' VOTE FOR EVERYBODY IN SIGHT... THAT WAY WE'LL GIT A GOOD ONE... Y'KNOW, CHILE, CRITTERS IS NICE, BUT HUMAN BEANS STILL MAKES THE BEST PEOPLE.
NOW, YOU GOT NO CALL TO BE TALKIN' CRANKY JES' 'CAUSE YOU IS FRESH WOKE.

The POGO PARTY

IT WAS NOT UNTIL *after the 1968 election that "selling the President" became a household phrase. So if, as some insist, there are undertoads of meaning and even prescience below the surface of the swamp, we might consider Howland Owl, crying in 1956, "We got to* SELL *our man." To which Churchy LaFemme responds, "It's agin the law to sell, give away or allowed to be consumed on the premises anybody what's a citizen of these here states."*

This was a year when Pogo was up against an incumbent. He himself remained characteristically recumbent while the Committee to Re-Run the Possum indulged in such dirty tricks as trying to arrange a crowd-pleasing marriage with Mam'selle Hepzibah, who was equally determined not to be First Lady.

The razor-sharp correspondent from Newslife *magazine hit home with anyone who had ever had contact with those vast publishing monoliths that first decide what the story is and then send out a Task Force to confirm it.*

MIND THE MOON

WELL, MEBBE SO, BUT THIS SETTIN' AROUN' DOIN' NOTHIN' AIN'T GOIN' GET US NOWHERES.
SURE--- WE KIN SET AROUND DOIN' NOTHIN' IN THE BOAT, AN' WHO KNOWS, A FISH MAY LEAP ABOARD!

I BEEN STUDYIN' THE PLATFORM YOU OUTLINED ---- IT GOT A LOT OF SOUND PRINCIPLES IN IT.
PLATFORM-? WHAT PLATFORM?
FAY BLANCHARD
WHEN YOU SAYS YOU WON'T RUN IF NOMINATED AND WON'T SERVE IF ELECTED---
THE S.S FAY BLA

COMIN' RIGHT OUT LIKE THAT-- TELLIN' WHAT YOU WON'T DO, OUGHT TO GIT YOU A LOT OF VOTES -- PEOPLE KIN COUNT ON PROMISES LIKE THAT-- WHAT ELSE WOULDN'T YOU DO, DO YOU S'POSE?
HEY!
OH--I WOULDN'T WANNA SAY.
OL' FAY (HIS BOAT)
THE ROCHESTER ROCKET

HEAR 'BOUT MR. TAMANANNY AN' OL' P.T. BRIDGEPORT? THEY'S DECIDED TO QUIT SHOW BUSINESS.
QUIT IT ENTIRELY?
TORONTO
OL' DUNC

YEP--QUITTIN' IT ENTIRELY-- GOIN' INTO A LINE COMPLETELY DEE-VORCED FROM IT-- NAMELY THE TEEVY.
CHANGE IS RAMPANT.
THE HON. DUNC HALLIDAY

HOW COME RAMPANT?
POGO GOT A CAMPAIGN PLATFORM FULL OF PROMISE IN CASE HE EVER GIT CAUGHT IN ANOTHER ELECTION---- IF NOMINATED HE WON'T RUN, IF ELECTED, HE WON'T SERVE.
THE S.S. HALLIDAY

THAT'S NOT ZACKLY A CHANGE- WE'S HAD PUBLIC OFFICIALS IN OUR TIME WHAT DEE-LIVERED THAT AN' NEVER EVEN PROMISED IT.
DUNC HALLIDAY

WHAT WE NEEDS IS SOMEBODY HONEST... HE DON'T PROMISE ANYTHIN'. AN' HE LIVES UP TO IT!
THE DIRTY DOG!
THERE GOES ONE NOW! COME HERE, YOU UNWASHED PUP! YOU IS NEEDED A BATH SINCE 19 OUGHT 36.
OL' DUNC HALLIDAY

PEOPLE CONTINUES TO WANT TO KNOW IS YOU GONE RUN FOR THE PRESIDENSITY AGAIN--- ---SEEM LIKE THEY IS A BIG DEE-MAND FOR THAT SORTA THING.

IF YOU IS... IT MIGHT BE A GOOD THING TO SAY SO -- IT WOULDN'T HURT TO GIT A EARLY START.

THEN, AFORE ANY OF THE OTHERS IS READY, YOU COULD FORGE OFF AHEAD ON YO'OWN... RUN THE EE-LECTION A YEAR EARLY, SAY, AN'

--GIT ALL EE-LECTED UP AN' 'STABLISHED IN OFFICE WHILST THE OTHERS IS ASLEEP... THING TO DO IS KEEP THE OPPOSITION OFF-BALANCE.

IF YOU WANTS TO GIT ELECTED YOU GOTTA THINK UP SOMETHIN' TO SAY AFTER YOU IS IN OFFICE SO'S HISTORY BOOKS'LL HAVE A BIG MEMORABLE HOMILY TO PESTER KIDS INTO MEMORIZIN' EVEN IF THEY DON'T KNOW WHY YOU SAID IT--- SOMETHING LIKE---

DOG-----

GONE!

I JUST THUNK OF THE THING YOU CAN SAY WHEN YOU IS EE-LECTED.

"YOU CAN BELIEVE IN SOME OF THE PEOPLE MOST OF THE TIME AND IN MOST OF THE PEOPLE SOME OF THE TIME ....

"BUT YOU'LL NEVER BELIEVE ALL OF THE PEOPLE YOU CAN BELIEVE IN -

"ALL OF THE TIME."

AND RUNE THE RHINE

THIS YEAR AIN'T ONLY FER WHEN WE CHOOSES A PRESIDENT IT'S FER WHEN WE CHOOSES THE TWO GENTS WHAT GONE RUN.

HOT DOG! THAT'S RIGHT! ALL YEAR WE'S GONE HAVE HOOTIN' AN' HOLLOWIN' AN' ROMPIN' AROUN' -- PARADES AN' SCREAMIN' AN' FIGHTIN' AN' SAM'WICHES AN' B'LOONS.

YEP--- TWO BIG CONVENTIONS AN' LOTS OF SPEECHES AN' ROLL CALLS AN' NAME CALLIN' -- THEN WHEN WE GITS THE TWO FELLAS PICKED OUT, OFF THEY GOES FIGHTIN' AROUN' THE COUNTRY.

YESSIR! IT MAKE YOU PROUD TO BE A CITIZEN --- 'CEPTIN' OF COURSE THE FUN GOTTA END SOMETIME -- ONE OF 'EM ALLUS GITS ELECTED FINELY.
A SHAME TOO, BLUB.
EASY ON THAT COFFEE -- I GOTTA SHAVE.
HIS
SOAP

WHAT WE OUGHT TO HAVE IS PRESIDENTAL ELECTIONS EVER' YEAR LIKE THE WORLD SERIES.
BUT IT TAKES A LOT OF WORRYIN' AN' SCHEMIN' AN' SPEECHIN' AN' THINKIN'.

WHAT OF IT? WE KIN WORRY ABOUT ANYTHING.
TRUE TRUE -- AN' WE KIN SCHEME.
AN' WE KIN MAKE ANY KIND SPEECHES.

AN' WHEN IT COMES TO THINKIN' WHY, SHUCKS --UH-YES-- WELL--HUM-HOO-HA--
WELL, ANYWAYS WE KIN WORRY GOOD--
AN' SCHEME AN' SPEECHIFY.
LET'S GIT INTO POLITICS.
TROUBLE WITH PRESIDENTAL EE-LECTIONS IS THEY COMES UP ONLY EVERY FOUR YEARS
SAME GOES FOR GALS PREE-POSIN' TO MEN ON LEAP YEARS.. YET IT REMAINS A POPULAR SPORT.
IF US DOES BECOME PRESIDENTAL POLITICIANS--US WILL CHANGE THAT-- WE'LL HAVE A NEW ELECTION EVERY YEAR.
HEY! GIT YO' FEET OUTEN THAT FRYIN' PAN!
DON'T WORRY.. 'TAIN'T HOT.
'COURSE BEIN' A CANDIDATE IS A BIG SACKERFICE-- HOWEVER IF HE'LL ACCEPT, I KNOWS JES' THE MAN.
ME TOO.
SO DOES I.
DON'T TELL ME YOU FELLAS IS FOR ME, TOO.
DON'T WORRY! I WOULDN'T THINK OF TELLIN' YOU THAT.
OH I IS FOR YOU, GOOD ENOUGH BUT NOT FER NO JOB. .. I IS JES FOR YOU.

I THUNK YOU BOYS WOULD WELCOME MY CANDIDATURE WITH SCREAMS OF PURE JOY.
IF YOU VOTES FOR YOU, I WILL VOTE FOR ME.
TO SAY NOTHIN' OF ME, TOO.
REMEMBER THE OLD HOMILY: A VOTE FOR ME IS A VOTE FOR YOU.
A VOTE FOR ME IS A VOTE FOR ME, WAY I LOOKS AT IT.
COMERE.

NO SECRETS!
IT'S EARLY TO START MAKIN' DEALS BUT LET'S BE REALISTIC... LONG AS HE'S VOTIN' FOR HIM.. WE'LL JOIN FORCES.. I'LL VOTE FOR YOU AN' YOU VOTE FOR ME! THAT WAY WE'LL BEAT HIS EARS OFF.
GREAT!
US GOT TWICE AS MANY VOTES LINED UP AS YOU.. THE NOMINATION'S IN THE BAG... REE-MEMBER! IN UNION THERE IS STRENGTH!

ALL RIGHT, LET'S PUT YO' VOTIN' THEORIES TO THE TEST OF BONE AN' SINEW - DROP YO' BALLOTS HEREIN.
REMEMBER, NOW.. PSST-PST.
NO LOITERIN' NEAR THE POLLS!
REMEMBER, LONG AS HE VOTES FOR HIM, WE BEATS HIM OUT BY VOTIN' FOR EACH OTHER.. MAN! JES' WAIT! HEE HEE

VERY WELL, THE VOTE'S ALL IN... LESSEE.. ONE SAYS "ONE VOTE FOR ME" 'NOTHER ONE SAYS "ONE VOTE FOR ME" 'NOTHER SAYS "ONE VOTE FOR ME."
WHAT?!

I BE DOGGED! EITHER WE IS GOT A THREEWAY TIE OR ONE OF US IS LANDSLID HIS WAY INTO OFFICE IN ONE FELL SWOON.
OR SOME RAG-A-BONED BODY IS A CHINCHY CHICKEN-HEADED DOUBLE CROSSER.

WHEN I STOPS AN' REALIZES THAT YOU TWO GANGED UP ON ME AN' TRIED TO CHEAT ME OUTEN THE NOMINATION FER THE PRESIDENSITY I IS OVERCOME WITH FAMILY LOATHING.
ME TOO.

YOU TOO? WHY, YOU WAS PART OF THE PLOT.. PART OF THE EVIL SCHEME.. HOW KIN YOU BE OVERCOME WITH FAMILY LOATHING? AIN'T YOU GOT NO PRIDE? IN YOUR OWN KNAVERY?
I GOT PRIDE TO BURN.

NO MATTER HOW I SHUFFLE MY HAND IT STILL COMES OUT WITH TWO CARDS OVER!
SOMEBODY DEALT ME A PIECE OF BREAD AN' JAM 'STEAD OF A CARD.
IT'S SO DIRTY IT LOOKS LIKE A ACE OF SPADES --PLAY IT.
YOU IS FREE TO EAT IT AN' DRAW A NEW CARD.
PHUMPH!
YOU'S LUCKY! YOU GOT PEANER BUTTER ON PUMPERNICKEL THAT TIME.

THIS IS THE YEAR WHEN THE **PEOPLE SPEAKS**···**AND** AS A REVERED MEMBER OF THE PEOPLE, **HERE I GO!**
WHERE?
WHERE WHAT?
YEAH, WEAR WHAT?
I DIN'T SAY **NOTHIN'** BUT SINCE YOU **ASKS**, WHY NOT WEAR YOUR **OPEN TOED SEQUINS** WITH THE **OVERHEAD DECOLLETAGE?**

WELL, FRIENDS ·· ***HEEDLESS OF UNCOUTH INTERRUPTIONS I PRESSES ON***·· IT WILL BE MY AIM WHEN IN OFFICE TO REDUCE ALL EXPENSES AN' **MAXIMIZE** THE **MINIMUM**.
HE DON'T MEAN MORE'N **HALF** WHAT HE SAYS.

AND ***FURTHER* MORE** I PROMISES TWICE AS MUCH.
EVEN IF HE ONLY MEANS ***HALF***- ··**HE** PROMISES AS MUCH AS **ANYBODY**.
NOW IF WE COULD FIGGER **WHAT** HE'S RUNNIN' **FOR**.

FEAR BEFORE

OH I KNEW IT WOULD HAPPEN-- THE MINUTE MY BACK WAS TURNT.
WHAT DIRE JUGGERNAUT OF DOOM IS DAMPED YO' DAY?
THIS HERE 1956 CALENDAR... GOT 3 FRIDAY-THE-THIRTEENTHS IN IT, ALL OF WHOM FALLS ON FRIDAY!
WHERE ELSE YOU WANT 'EM? OTHER DAYS IS BUSY BEIN' TUESDAY AN' MONDAY AN' ALL --COULDN'T DOUBLE UP TOO GOOD.
COULD OF SQUOZE IT INTO A SUNDAY AFTERNOON... NOT MUCH GOIN' ON THEN.
WHY DON'T YOU WRITE UP YO' OWN CALENDAR IF YOU DON'T LIKE THE WAY THIS'N 'S BEIN' RUN?
BY JING! IF I KNOWED WHAT COMES AFTER JULY I'D DO IT.
JAN

IF I STARTED A DIFFER'NT CALENDAR MEBBE I COULD GIT THE WHOLE WORLD TAKIN' OFF'N ME.
S'POSE YOU GOT ONLY HALF... WHAT DO GOOD'S THAT?

JUST THINK IF HALF THE WORLD TOOK OFF'N ME AN' THE OTHER HALF STUCK TO THE OLD CALENDAR IT WOULD MEAN PEACE IN OUR TIME.
PEACE? HOW COME?

SIMPLE! WHEN HEADS OF STATE MAKES A DATE TO MEET FOR A PEACE TALK--KABOOM! HALF OF 'EM DON'T SHOW UP! 'CAUSE THEY GOT A DIFFER'NT IDEA AS TO WHAT THE REAL DATE WAS-- SO WE'RE SAFELY THRU THAT ONE AN' THEN THE NEXT TIME--UH WHAT?
I SAYS GRUNDOON ET THE BAIT.

MY SAKES! HE DID? WHAT WAS IT?
I DON'T REE-MEMBER. ...AN' FROM THE LOOK ON THE TAD'S FACE I THINK WE BETTER NOT ASK...

THINK OF IT ... IF I ARRANGE A NEW CALENDAR WE CAN HAVE A WHOLE MONTH OF CHRISTMAS.

EASY DOES IT--REMEMBER, THE CHILD GOT A STOMACH FULL OF FISH BAIT AN' IS LIKELY FEELIN' KINDA PASTY--
OH I IS. IS-IS

IF GRUNDOON ET ALL THE BAIT HOW'S YOU GONE CATCH ANY FISH..?
OH CATCHIN' 'EM AIN'T THE ONLY REASON WE COME FOR...

SOMETIMES WE'D JES' AS LEAVE PLAIN FISH AN' NOT MESS AROUND WITH CATCHIN' ANYTHING.
YONDER IS MY FAV'RITE SECRET UN-FISHIN' HOLE --I KIN GUARANTEE YOU WON'T GIT A BITE FROM A SKEETER EVEN.

S'POSE I DID GIT UP A NEW CALENDAR AN' PUT IN A WHOLE MONTH OF CHRISTMAS.. THAT'D SUIT MOST FOLKS RIGHT DOWN TO THE GROUND WOULDN'T IT?
WULL..

IT'D MORE SUIT MOST FOLKS UP A TREE.... TWELVE DAYS OF CHRISTMAS JES' ABOUT CLEARED THE COUNTRY OF PEAR TREES AN' THIRTY DAYS WOULD.UH..

WULL.. IT MIGHT RID THE COUNTRY OF FATHERS AN' MOTHERS.
HOW ABOUT A WHOLE MONTH OF FOURTH OF JULY? WE COULD HAVE IT DURIN' FEBRUARY WHEN THINGS IS DULL.
I DUNNO.. THE WAY PEOPLE DRIVES CARS ON FOURTH OF JULY THAT WOULD RID THIS COUNTRY OF FOLKS ENTIRELY AN' NOTHIN'D BE LEFT BUT TURTLES AN' 'POSSUMS.
SO..?

WHAT'D BE WRONG WITH A WORLD MADE UP OF 'POSSUMS AN' TURTLES?
I GOT A LOT OF FRIENDS WHAT'S TURTLES.

AN' I LIKE TO BE WITH 'EM --S'POSE ONE BUNCH SAYS THE OTHERS IS INFERIOR AN' GOTTA GO LIVE IN LABRADOR...? HOW'S I EVER GONNA SEE MY TURTLE FRIENDS? --SEPARATED THAT WAY?
MIND THE TAD.

LABRADOR, HUH?

DON'T WORRY, POGO... WE WOULD MAKE A SPECIAL CASE OUT'N YOU... YOU WOULDN'T HAFTA GO TO LABRADOR.

DOGGONE! YOU GOT ME SO BUSY TALKIN' I NEVER NOTICED WE BREEZED RIGHT THRU FRIDAY THE 13 WITHOUT EVEN SLOWIN' FOR THE INTERSECTION.
YUP--NOT EVEN A RED LIGHT TO STOP YOU.

GRS!
GRS?

YUP..GRS..GRUNDOON GIVE THE FISH CALL.. SOME USES DUCK AN' MOOSE CALLS..GRUNDOON CALLS FISH... SORRY FELLAS, GRUNDOON JES' FOOLIN' AROUN'.

WE DON'T EVEN GOT BAIT OR HOOKS.
IF YOU AIN'T READY FOR BUSINESS YOU MOUGHT STOP WASTIN' OUR TIME -

KIND OF A CALENDAR I'M GONNA MAKE IS THE KIND WHAT TELLS WHAT THE FUTURE HOLDS
HOW YOU GONE KNOW THAT?

EASY! I JES' LOOKS ON MY CALENDAR... SAY I IS WANT TO SEE WHAT HAPPENS AUG. 15.
ALL RIGHT S'POSE YOU WANTS TO KNOW 'BOUT AUG. 15.. WHO PUTS THAT DOWN?
JAN

WHY, I PUTS IT DOWN---WHATEVER IS FORECASTED IS DONE BY ME... WHO'S IN CHARGE ANYWAY-? SO I SEES AUGUST FIFTEEN GONNA BE FINE 'CAUSE IT'S MY BIRTHDAY.
THOUGHT IT WAS IN MAY?

HEE-HO! IT IS TO LAUGH--! WITH ME RUNNIN' THE CALENDAR I MIGHT WIND UP WITH PROB'LY A DOZEN BIRTHDAYS EV'RY YEAR.
BULLY! THO' IN TEN YEARS YOU'D BE 120 YEARS OLDER.

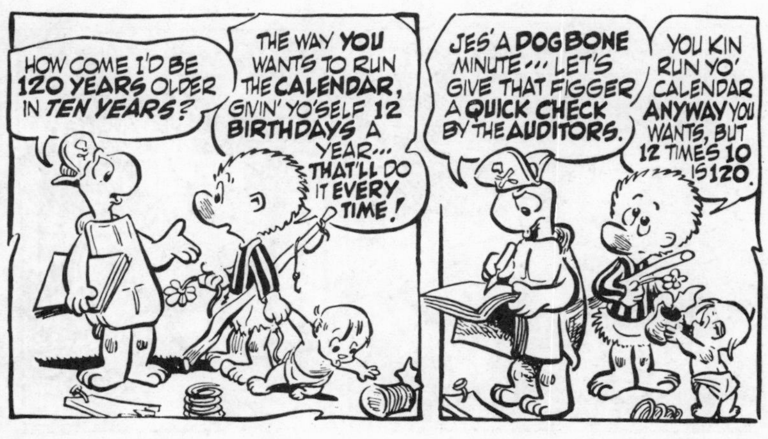
HOW COME I'D BE **120 YEARS** OLDER IN ***TEN YEARS***?
THE WAY **YOU** WANTS TO RUN THE **CALENDAR**, GIVIN' YO'SELF **12 BIRTHDAYS** A YEAR... **THAT'LL** DO IT **EVERY TIME**!
JES' A **DOGBONE** MINUTE... LET'S GIVE THAT FIGGER A **QUICK CHECK** BY THE **AUDITORS**.
YOU KIN RUN YO' CALENDAR **ANYWAY** YOU WANTS, BUT **12** TIMES **10** IS **120**.

BY JING IT 'PEARS LIKE YOU ***MOUGHT*** BE RIGHT-- IN THAT CASE IN **FIFTY YEARS** MORE I'D BE **600** YEARS OLDER... AN' IN A HUNDERD I'D BE OVER **1200**.. COUNTIN' WHAT I GOT ***NOW***...
SURE.. **OLD** AFORE YOUR **TIME**.
MY FRIENDS WOULD OF ALL **PASSED ON** --WHAT WILL ***THEY*** DO WITHOUT ME?
YONDER'S **POGO**- **HE** WOULD OF MADE A **GOOD CANDIDATE**, BUT SEEM LIKE HE'S BECOME A **JUNK COLLECTOR**.

FER A MINUTE THERE, POGO, YOU HAD US **WORRIED**.. WE FIGGERED YOU'D BECAME A **JUNKMAN**.. BUT WE SEE IT'S THE **TAD** WHO'S COLLECTIN' ALL THE ODDMENTS-- --HOW'D YOU LIKE TO BE **PRESIDENT**?

PRESIDENT OF **WHAT**?
THE WHOLE **SHEBANG**.. FAR AS THE EYE KIN SEE.. **COAST** TO **COAST**.

WELL --UH-- IT'S HARD TO SAY.
THAT'S QUITE A OFFER YOU MADE THERE-- WHO DO YOU REPRESENT?
A POWERFUL MINORITY-- US -- THREE SOLID VOTES.
THREE VOTES? THAT DON'T HARDLY CONSTITUTE NO TIDAL WAVE OF POPULAR SUPPORT.
THE WAY WE VOTES, IT DOES--WE VOTES EARLY, OFTEN AN' LOUDER'N ANYBODY..

HOW COME THEM BATS STARTS ALL THE TALK AGAIN 'BOUT ME RUNNIN' FOR PRESIDENT AGAIN! FAR AS I'M CONCERNED, US 'POSSUMS GOT A PRESIDENT.
IT'S A OL' AMERICAN FESTIVAL.. A FOLK-WAY SORTA... EVERY ONCE AN' A WHILE WE BUST OUT AN' EE-LECT SOMEBODY... FIRST OF ALL HAVIN' A LOTTA FUN WITH SPEECHES AN' HOOTIN' AN' ALL THAT STUFF.
LAND! I DON'T GOT NOTHIN' TO SAY.

YOU CAN STILL MAKE A SPEECH CAN'T YOU..? HAVIN' NOTHIN' TO SAY AIN'T STOPPED ANYBODY YET... JUST FEED 'EM UP ON SUGAR AN' SPICE AN' ALL WHAT'S NICE.
GRS GRS
AFTER ALL, ONE DON'T KETCH FISH ON BARE HOOKS.

THE FOUR BY FIVE

LOOK.. LET'S BE PRACTICAL... I'M MAKIN' UP MY CALENDAR FOR THIS YEAR... NO FRIDAY-THE-THIRTEENTHS IN IT...
ALSO I PREEDICKS THINGS.
SUCH AS..?
SUCH AS THE S.S. PRESIDENT, A STEAM-SHIP, LEFT NEW YORK IN 1841 AN' WAS NEVER SEED AGAIN... ALL ON A FRIDAY-THE-THIRTEENTH WHAT COME ON A TUESDAY..
THAT AIN'T THE FUTURE!.. THAT'S THE PAST.

IF YOU WANTS TO PREE-DICK THINGS YOU GOTTA SAY YESTERDAY WHAT'S GONNA HAPPEN TOMORROW..
THAT'S WHY I WANTS YOU TO RUN FOR PRESIDENT --- THEN FER EE-LECTION DAY I KIN PUT DOWN "POGO ELECTED 1956"
PHOO.. EVEN IF A MAN RUNS YOU CAN'T SAY HE'S GONNA WIN.. HE COULD LOSE.
LOSE!? GO TO ALL THAT TROUBLE AN' THEN LOSE? CALL THIS A FREE COUNTRY?!

HERE'S ANOTHER THING OUTEN MY LI'L' BOOK... WOULD IT BE OKAY TO PREE-DICK THAT THE SWALLOWS WILL COME BACK TO CAPISTRANO ON MARCH 19?
IF YOU B'LEEVES IT.. YES.
GOOD.. THEN I KIN PREE-DICK THAT... ALSO THE BLIZZARD OF 1888 ENDS ON MARCH 14.
WHAT!?.. THAT'S A DIFFER'NT THING!

THE SWALLOWS ALLUS COMES BACK THE SAME DAY EVER' YEAR... RIGHT? THEY COME BACK ANY OTHER DAY?
NOT USUALLY. NO.

RIGHT.. THEN THE BLIZZARD OF 1888 ALLUS ENDS ON MARCH 14... SAME'S THE SWALLOWS ON MARCH 19... NEVER HEARD OF THE BLIZZARD ENDIN' ANY OTHER DAY IN ALL THESE YEARS .. INTO THE CALENDAR IT GO.
HOW'S THE GRASSHOPPIN' GAME?
JUMPY

WHAT'S GRUNDOON UP TO?
'PEARS LIKE HE THINKS HE'S A GRASSHOPPER.

SOMEBODY BETTER TELL HIM HE AIN'T AFORE HE CHANGES INTO A CHRYSALIS AN' PASSES ON INTO THE BUTTERFLY BUSINESS.. YOU AIN'T NO GRASSHOPPER, GRUNDOON!
YOU'S THINKIN' OF CATER-PIGGLES.

SO I IS...! MY MISTAKE, SON,..STOP CRYIN'... YOU CAN BE A GRASS-HOPPER.. NO HARM NO HARM.
YOU'RE A BUTTER BRAIN, OWL.
OKAY! OKAY!..O-KAY! YOU'RE A GRASS-HOPPER
THE IDEA! A GROWED MAN MAKIN' A CHILE CRY BY CALLIN' HIM NAMES!
OWL AIN'T ACTUAL FULL-GROWED MIZ. BEAVER.

IF, AS YOU SAY, OWL AIN'T FULL-GROWED, MR. LA FEMME, I HATE TO SEE HIM WHEN HE'S AS BIG A DUNDERHEAD AS HE GONNA BE!
BUT BUT BUT BUT BUT BUT BUT BUT
YO' MOTORS RUNNIN', OWL.
YOU AIN'T MY PAL NO MORE WHYN'T YOU TELL HER I DIN'T CALL THE CHILE NAMES? ALL'S I DID WAS TELL HIM WHAT HE WANTED TO BE ... A GRASSHOPPER.
FIE
I SWORE OFF BEIN' YOUR PAL FOR NEW YEARS! BESIDES YOU MADE HER TAKE GRUNDOON THE GROUN'CHUCK AWAY JES' WHEN I AN' HIM WAS GONNA DO A EXPEARMINT.
FAW.
I CAN DO ANYTHING A CHILE KIN DO... I'LL ASSIST YOU INSTEAD.
GOOD! I WAS GONE SEE IF GROUN'CHUCKS IS REALLY FEARED OF THEIR SHADOWS.. SO, CRAWL INTO A HOLE UNTIL NEXT THURSDAY-
HO AN' HUM
DOES YOU MEAN TO IMPLY THAT I GOTTA CRAWL INTO A HOLE AN' ACT LIKE A GROUN' CHUCK?
YOU SAID YOU COULD DO ANYTHING GRUNDOON KIN.
FOOF! JES' TO SEE HOW MANY WEEKS MORE OF WINTER WE GETS..
YOU PROMISED! BESIDES I NEEDS THE INFORMATION FOR THE CALENDAR I IS FIXIN'.

NOW WHAT'S I DO?
IMAGINE I IS A SHADOW AN' YOU IS A GROUN'CHUCK -- SEE KIN YOU STAND ME ... BOO!
BOO
YOUR SELF!
YOWP!
LAND! ONLY CASE OF A GROUN' CHUCK SCARIN' HIS SHADOW! RUN! WE GONNA GIT A BLOOZZARD!

IF YO' IS GONNA HELP OUT BY BEIN' A GROUN'CHUCK FOR THIS EXPEARMINT YOU CAN'T HOLLER "BOO" AT YO' OWN SHADOW.
THAT'S UNFAIR.

ALL RIGHT -- S'POSE IT'S GROUND-HOG DAY .. YOU, AS A BONA FIDE GROUN'CHUCK OR GROUN'HOG, IS CRAWLIN' OUTEN YO' BURROW .. AN' HERE, I, YO' SHADOW COMES ALONG
LA LA LA LA
I DON'T FEEL VERY GROUN' HOGGY
WOOF! WOOF!

WOOF WOOF? HOW CAN YOU SAY WOOF WOOF? OOP!
WOOF WOOF WATCH IT! WOOF WOOF WOOF
GROUN'HOGS DON'T BARK! YOU GOT YO' RULES MIXED.
AN' SHADOWS DON'T FALL OVER THEIR MASTERS EITHER -- YOU, SIR, IS MORE A OSTRICH.

ALL RIGHT NOW TRY IT AGAIN -- I'LL POP OUT FROM AHIND THE TREE AN' HOLLER BOO... YOU SEE IF YO' SHADOW SCARES YOU.
I'LL CRUNCH DOWN.

BLESS MY SOUL -- A READY-DUG HOLE TO BURY THESE GARBAGE SLOPS IN --

BOO!
MY NANNY! BUT YOU GUVVED ME A START, CHURCHY.

I'SE GLAD OF THAT, MR. 'COON, 'CAUSE WE'SE GONE NEED ONE.
ROWR!!

PUFF PUFF PUFF PUFF PUFF PUFF PUFF PUFF PUFF PUFF PUFF PUFF
YOU SAID IT.

OWL GITTIN' MAD AN' CHASIN' US, SURE WORED ME OUT, DIN'T YOU?
HIM CHASIN' OF US DIN'T SO MUCH TIRE ME AS US RUNNIN' AWAY FROM HIM DID
PUFF

AN' ALL FOR WHAT..? ALL'S I DO WAS ACCIDENTAL DUMP SLOPS ON. HIM..
SURE 'TAIN'T LIKE 'TWERE ON PURPOSE.. ..UH.. LOOK!
IT'S GRUNDOON! HE'S.. HE'S..
A FATHER!
THAT'S HIS NEW BORNED BABY SISTER!

SO THAT'S WHAT ARRIVED ON GROUNDHOG DAY! A NEW BRAN' NEW BABY SISTER FOR GRUNDOON TO PLAY WITH!
YUP.. WE'S MOUGHTY PROUD OUT OUR WAY.
AN' GRUNDOON IS PROUDEST OF ALL--HE PROUDER'N A PIG WITH A PURPLE POCKABOOK.

A SEEGAR! WELL, THANKEE, GRUNDOON.
HE DOIN' THINGS UP IN STYLE.
DON'T LIGHT IT! WHEN WE LEAVES THE TAD TAKES IT BACK.... HE ONLY GOT THE ONE AN' IT'S RUBBER.

I BE MOUGHTY OBLIGED TO YOU MISTER LA FEMME IF YOU KIN BABY-SIT THE NEW TAD A SPELL.
IT'D BE A PLEASURE MIZ GROUN' CHUCK... WHAT'S HER NAME?

WE AIN'T REALLY THOUGHT OF NOTHIN' YET 'CEPT HONEY BUNNY DUCKY DOWNY SWEETIE CHICKEN PIE LI'L' EVERLOVIN' JELLY BEAN.
THAT'S NICE.

AIN'T THAT MORE OF A BOY'S NAME, THOUGH?
NOT IF YOU SPELLS IT WITH A FINAL "E".

C'MON, SON, WE GOTTA GIT YOUR HAIR CUT ... IT GOT A LI'L' LONG.
COOCHIE COO LI'L' HONEY BUNNY DUCKY DOWNY SWEETIE CHICKEN PIE LI'L' EVERLOVIN' JELLY BEAN.. COOCHIE COO LI'L HONEY BUNNY DUCKY DOWNY SWEETIE CHICKEN PIE LI'L' EVERLOVIN' JELLY BEAN COOCHIE COO

UM.... IS THAT DOOD IT? IS YOU GONE TO SLEEP LIKE A GOOD FELLA? IS YOU?
Z Z Z

IS YOU?!

FIVE BY FOUR

THERE AIN'T HARDLY NOTHIN' CUTER NOR A SLEEPIN' BABY TAD LESSEN IT'S A PORK CHOP.. ..WHAT YOU NEEDS IS A GOOD ROUSIN' LOOLABYE...

TWIGGLE TWIGGLE LILY STARCH! HOWIE RUMBLE WODDY YARCH, UPPA BUVVA HIGH OHIO LIKE A DIME ON A PIANO

AWNING RODEO MANDO-LAYEE-- WETTER FLY AN' FIDGEY SPLAY ANNIE DON'T COMMA PLIKE TUNDRA OTTER CHEYENNE CROWS TOUPEE!
QUIET!
SHHH..... DON'T WAKE UP THE CHILE.

MA BUNNY LICE SODA DEVOTION! MAY BOONEY LIFE SAVER D.C.! McBONIFACE ROVER COMMOTION, OH, BRICKBAT MAHONEY TOOMEY!
THE S.S. IRIS WOOLFE
IT MOUGHT BE A MAIDEN CAUGHT IN DIRE PEARLS.
WHOM, HOW MANY RAGE, WEARY BEER IN THE CANTALOUPE AGE, AUNT SELMA IS HURT AMIDST CORSICAN WURT AN' ---
CHURCHY! WHAT'S WRONG?!
SHHHH!
YOU'LL WAKE THE CHILE WHAT I IS JES' LOOLABYED INTO DREAM LAND.

WELL, WE WILL BE DOGNABBED! A REAL LIVE NEW BORN BRAN' NEW BABY TAD CHILE ··· LOOKS JES' LIKE YOU, TOO
WHAT!?
DO I LOOK LIKE A GROUN' HOG?
NO, YOU LOOKS MORE LIKE A PLATE OF COLD ROBBY.

WELL I AIN'T NO GROUN'HOG.
'TAIN'T NOTHIN' TO BE SHAMED OF.. YOU'S DID YO' BEST.
THIS MUS' BE MIZ GROUN'CHUCKS NEW TAD... WHAT'S THEY CALL HER?
HONEY BUNNY DUCKY DOWNY SWEETIE CHICKEN PIE LI'L' EVER LOVIN' JELLY BEAN... ...THAT'S JES' SO FAR..
MAN.. THEY GONNA HAFTA START CALLIN' HER TWENNY MINUTES AFORE SUPPER, IF SHE GONE GIT THERE IN TIME FOR DESSERT.

WELL, I'SE MOUGHTY PROUD SAMES AS EVER'BODY 'BOUT THE NEW TAD BUT MIZ GROUN'CHUCK OUGHT TO THINK UP A NEW NAME.
WHAT'S THE MATTER WITH "HONEY BUNNY DUCKY DOWNY SWEETIE CHICKEN PIE LI'L' EVERLOVIN' JELLY BEAN"--?
OL' GAIL SMITH ESQ
THE POOR CHILE GONNA BE BOW-LEGGED CARRYIN' ALL THEM ETCETERIES... SHE NEED SOMETHIN' SHORT LIKE SAM, PETE, BILL OR POSSIBLY, MERV.
STOP DRAGGIN' YO' TAIL.

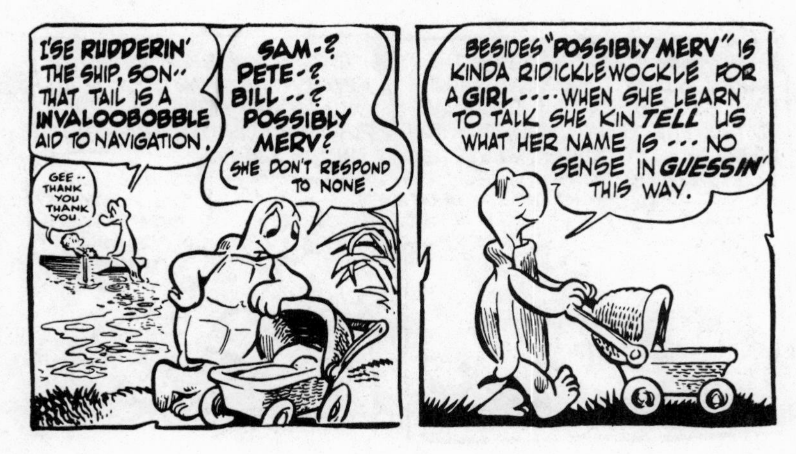
I'SE RUDDERIN' THE SHIP, SON.. THAT TAIL IS A INVALOOBOBBLE AID TO NAVIGATION.
GEE.. THANK YOU THANK YOU.
SAM-? PETE-? BILL..? POSSIBLY MERV?
(SHE DON'T RESPOND TO NONE.
BESIDES "POSSIBLY MERV" IS KINDA RIDICKLEWOCKLE FOR A GIRL.... WHEN SHE LEARN TO TALK SHE KIN TELL US WHAT HER NAME IS... NO SENSE IN GUESSIN' THIS WAY.

WHAT A WAY TO START THE WEEK... FRIDAY THE THIRTEENTH COMES ON A MONDAY!
NOTHIN' BUT BAD LUCK, BAD LUCK, BAD LUCK ALL THE WHOLE WEEK.... I FORESEES DOOM!
I AIN'T GONE MOVE. I GOT MY RIGHTS.
DOOM DOOM DOOM DOOM
I GOT MY RIGHTS! MY GUARANTEED PERSONIAL RIGHTS. DON'T GOTTA GIT OUTTA THE WAY.... DOOM OR NO DOOM.
WATCH WHERE YOU'RE GOIN'... IT'S A VERY UNLUCKY WEEK IN WHICH TO BE TOOK DEAD.
I GOT RIGHTS.
HAPPY VALLEY-TIME DAY, BUN RAB, THO' TO TELL THE TRUTH, HARD LUCK ABOUNDS IN ALL DI-RECTIONS.
IT'S THE WEATHER.. THE RAW GITS INTO MY VERTIGO AN' BLIGHTS MY LUCUBRATION SOMP'N FIERCE.
YEP... THE WEEK STARTED ON FRIDAY-THE-THIRTEENTH ALL ON ACCOUNT SOME DUNDERHEAD PUT THE CALENDAR TOGETHER IN THE DARK.
WHAT'S IN THE PUSHCART, SON? WHAT' YOU SELLIN'?

CALENDARS IS MY NEW LINE .... I IS PUTTIN' OUT A JAMES DANDY OF A REE-VISED ONE ....
LESSEE.. OOP! HAHOO
OH, I AIN'T GOT NONE FOR SALE, YET.
WHAT BIT ME ON THE SCHNOZZ THEN? IS YOU CARRYIN' A CON-CEALED OLD TYRANNOSAUR?

EE
NOW YOU MENTIONS IT I FERGETS JES' WHO IS IN THE PUSH CART.. ... SEEM TO ME I WAS BABY-SITTIN' SOME TAD.
CARE-FUL!
NOTHIN' TO BE FEARED OF ... JES' LOOK IN, SMILE AN' SAY WAHOOHO!
ALL'S I SAID WAS : OW! WHICH WAS VERY SERVICEABLE INDEED.

IT BIT ME ON THE NOSE, TOO.
SEEM TO ME IT'S A PERTY FORWARD TAD, BITIN' STRANGERS.
YEAH, 'AT'S GITTIN' DOG-BONED IN-TIMATE..
WISHT IT'D OF BIT ME SOMEWHERES ELSE ... WOULDN'T WANT ITS MA TO CONSTRUE MY POSE AS A OPINION.

IS YOU RECALLED YET WHOSE TAD YOU IS BABY-SITTIN'?
ON ACCOUNT OF ITS FAMBLY HERITAGE, I RECALLS.
WHOSE?
IT TAKES AFTER GRUNDOON FER BITIN'.. ---IT'S MIZ GROUN'CHUCKS TAD.
NEXT TIME IT BITES ME I IS GONE BITE IT BACK...
NOSSIR! NOT WHILE I IS TAKIN' CARE OF IT.
I'M GONNA SAVE THE MONEY I MAKES FROM BABY-SITTIN' MIZ GROUN'CHUCKS CHILE AN'..
--GO INTO THE CALENDAR BUSINESS... WANT TO GO ALONG?
YES, WAIT FER ME... WAIT FER ME!

WAIT FER ME WAIT FER..
OH... H'LO MIZ GROUN'CHUCK.
WAIT FER ME WAIT FERMEWA ITFERMEW AITFERM EWAITFE RMEWAIT FER ME.

'AT'S THE LIMIT, CHURCHY! I LEAVES YOU GUARDIN' THE NEW PRICELESS PEARL AN' YOU ACTS LIKE A APACHE.
I NEVER! I GIVE THE SCADER RIDES DOWNHILL AN' SUNG SONGS AT HER.
LIKE WHAT? LIKE B. THOVEN'S FUNEREAL MARCH? SEE, SHE'S CRYIN' AN' FIGHTIN' GOOTCHIE GOO BOOTIE BOO
SHE DIN'T CRY WHEN I WAS HEADMAN! LANGRIDGE LIKE YOU IS USIN'...NO WONDER!

WHAT KINDA LANGRIDGE DID YOU USE, MISTER SMART POT?
SONGS LIKE "OLE FOLKS AT HOME." WADE ON A POND A SWAN HE ROVER FARF FARFA WEIGH DAYS WORMY HARDY STERN AN' OVER STAIRWAY KEYHOLE FLOATS DAY..
STOPPED DIN'T SHE?
YEP.. BUT I DON'T LIKE THAT STUNNED AN' GLASSY STARE.

I DUNNO HOW YOU'S DOOD IT, CHURCHY, BUT BY SINGIN' SUWANNEE RIVER IN TURTLE TALK YOU IS QUIETIFIED THE CHILE.

LISTEN TO "CARRY ME BACK TO OL' VIRGINNY" CARAMEL BAG TWOFOLD McGINTY TEAR SWEAR TEA GARDEN ANNA CORNER TAKER SCROLL

EE-NOUGH!

IF I IS TOLE THIS TEDDY BEAR ONCE I IS TOLE IT TWO HUNNERD TIMES... EASY DOES IT OR YOU'LL WAKE UP THE CHILE!

THE SIX ALIVE

LET'S EVER'BODY CALM DOWN... LET'S EVER'BODY CALM DOWN, AN' MAKE OUT LIKE WE AIN'T LOST NO TEMPER!
SHALL I ACCOMPANY YOU ON THE KITTLE DRUM?

WHEN I SAYS THE FIRST LADY MIGHT BE SOON DOIN' YO' LAUNDRY, I DIN'T MEAN MIZ DAVIS.
I THUNK YOU MUST OF WAS FOOLIN'.
MIZ DAVIS AIN'T FIRST LADY NO MORE ANYWAYS..
MY SAKES! SHE GET DEFEATED?

TO BE EGG-ZACK SHE NEVER GOT EE-LECTED.
WELL, NOW, THAT'S TOO BAD...THAT WHY SHE GOT TO TAKE IN WASHIN'?
NO FIRST LADY NEVER GITS EE-LECTED!
THEN WHAT GOOD DID IT DO TO GIVE WOMEN A VOTE IF THEY DON'T GIT TO ELECT THEIRSELFS?

I DON'T HAVE TO HANG AROUND HERE TO TALK LIKE A IDIOT! I KIN TALK LIKE A IDIOT BY MYSELF.
OH, RUB A DUB DUB!
WHAT, PRAY TELL IS A DUB-DUB?

SMELL TO ME LIKE YOU LADIES IS PREE-PARIN' A BREW FIT FOR THE GODS ... AN' I GOT A SWEET TOOTH FER SUCH.
BUT YOU AIN'T NO GOD, PRAISE BE.
NO, BUT I HAPPENS TO REPRESENT POGO IN HIS QUEST FOR A FIRST LADY. LIVIN' IN THE WHITE HOUSE AN' ALL LIKE THAT THERE AIN'T TO BE SNEEZED AT.
I DIN'T SO MUCH AS SAY KA-CHOO

ME, I AM NO UNDERSTOOD THESE BUSINESS. LIKE AS FOUR YEAR AGOES I ASK WHOM IS THESE SECOND, THIRD, FIFTH LADY AND-CETERA?
IT DON'T WORK LIKE THAT! YOU MAKES IT SOUN' LIKE WE WAS CHOOSIN' UP A BASKETBALL TEAM.
THAT'S WHAT I AM MEAN ----- MARRIAGE IS A DIFFERENT SPORT --- A TWO HANDED GAME OF SOLITAIRE.

MM-M... mmM AN'MMmmmM
IF MISTER OWL REPERSENDS POGO YOU MOUGHT THINK IT OVER, MISS MA'M'SELLE.
EHEU!
DON'T FERGIT.... IT'S LEAP YEAR. THAT AN' THE CONTEST FER THE PRESIDENSITY DON'T COME TOGETHER FER NOTHIN'.
M

AN', IF POGO BECOMES THE PRESIDENT, YOU COULD BE HIS FIRST LADY.
SUCH A GAME! IT SEEM TO ME THESE IS JOKE, HA-HA.
SO I AM FIRST LADY... THEN, POOF! M'SIEUR POGO BECOME THE ADDICT.... AN' LIKE EATING THE PEANUTS... SECOND, THIRD, FOURS, SEVENS COME ELEVENS...
THAT'S DEMOCRACY .... A CHANCE FER ALL.

HEY! HEY! WATCH WHAT YOU'RE DOIN'... YOU IS ACCIDENTAL POURIN' THE GORP ONTO ME!
FRANKFULLY, MADAME BEAVERS, I AM NO COMPREHEND WHY THERE IS FIRST LADY...
WULL, SHE'S A LI'L' BIT LIKE A QUEEN IN A WAY... SHE'S THE FIRST LADY OF THE LAND... THE ONE MOST HONORED...
MM

THEN, IF M'SIEUR POGO ASK FOR MY HAND AN' IF I AM ACCEPT AN' IF WE ARE MARRY AN' IF POGO DE-CIDE TO RUN AN' IF HE IS NOMIN-ATED AN' IF HE WIN, THEN, LA-LA....
SURE...YOU'LL BE FIRST LADY...NOTHIN' TO IT!
AH... LE PAYS OUVERT AU TALENT.

YEP, THIS IS THE LAND OF OPERA-TOONITY... NO TWO WAYS 'BOUT IT... WHEN A GAL STARTS GITTIN' MARRIED UP, THEY IS NO WAY TELLIN' WHERE IT'LL END.
I MIND WHEN I AN' THE MISTER TOOK THE PLEDGE. LAND, WHAT A SCORE WE PILED UP AT THE PARTY AFORE THE WEDDIN'... HOOTIN' AND HOLLOWIN' WAS A DIME A DOZEN.

WE WAS HAPPY AS LOX SWIMMIN' UPSTREAM... WOMEN WAS FAINTIN' AN' THEY WASN'T A DRY EYE IN THE HOUSE, MOSTLY 'CAUSE THE SHERIFF'S DEE-PUTIES MOVED IN WITH TEAR GAS... I CAN STILL HEAR MY LOVER BOY CALLIN'...
HELP!
YOU MAKE IT VERY REAL, MADAME BEAVER...

YEP, WHEN THE SHERIFF'S POSSE MOVED INTO OUR WEDDIN' PARTY IN A MOP-UP OPERATION I QUICK SEIZED A FORWARD POSITION AT THE DOOR AN' HEARN MY MAN A-CALLIN'...
HELP?
(THIS HERE REE-SIPPY KEEPS BOOBLIN' UP.) WELL, I WAS ALL DOLLED UP IN A SKEETER NETTIN' POTOSO-A-SAMARE WITH TUCKER AN' HOLSTER AN' REACHED FOR MY HARQUEBUS....
WHOOSH! WHOOTS! I CLEART THE PLACE LIKE I WAS SCUTTLIN' A OYSTER! AN' IN THEM DAYS I WAS A PERFECK THIRTY-SIX!
ALORS! WHAT WERE THESE MEASUREMENT.?
THIRTY-SIX, THIRTY-SIX, AN' THIRTY-SIX.
FORMEE-DOUBLE PARFAIT!
Y'KNOW WHAT TODAY IS? IT'S LEAP DAY! THE DAY I GOT HOLT OF THE MISTER AN' PER-POSED TO HIM AN' HE SAID..
HELP?
HE SAY NOTHING ELSES EVER TIMES?
THIS DING STUFF KEEP ON A-RAISIN' AN' A-BLUBBLIN' -- MUST OF GOT SOME FOREIGN BODY INTO THE REE-SIPPY.

I AIN'T NEITHER!

I'SE STOOD ENOUGH! TRAPPED INTO YO' CAKE! UNLAMENTED AN' UN-NOTICED! AN' NOW YOU CALLS ME A FOREIGN BODY.. I WHOM AM A HUNNERD AN' TWENTY PROOF AMERICAN PHAW!

DON'T YOU RECOGNIZE A TRUE CITIZEN WHEN YOU SEES ONE? I AIN'T NO FOREIGN BODY!
RECOGNIZE YOU? I DON'T EVEN KNOW YOU.

WHAT IS YOU, A STRANGER, DOIN' IN MY CAKE BATTER?
I AIN'T NO STRANGER I IS HOWLAN' OWL.

HOWLAN' OWL?! LAN' KNOWS YOU'S UGLE ENOUGH.. MR. OWL, YOU IS CAUGHT YO'SELF A CASE OF THE UGLIES WHAT'S FIT TO CURDLE A WHOLE HERD OF CATTLE.

IF I AIN'T WELCOME, I'LL LEAVE... BATTERED BUT UNBOWED.
WHEN I WAS A GAL COMIN' OUT OF A CAKE WAS A HIGH-TONE SPORT BUT NO MORE... BATTER UP, OWL!
NON NON

GOOD DAY!
WELL, THAT, MORE OR LESS, TAKES THE CAKE.
WHAT ARE LEFTS WOULD MOST BE OF OWL FLAVOR ANYHOWS.
MY JAPE ABOUT "BATTER UP" REMINDS ME OF THE YEAR I SPENT IN THE NATIONABLE LEAGUE --HAD A FIGHT TWO THREE TIMES A DAY.

FIT WITH EVERY UMPIRE IN THE GAME ... WHAT A SEASON! HIT FOUR HUNDERD AS I RECALL.
HOT ALORS! HOME RUNS?

NO THE SAME THINGS I GUESS?
NO... UM-PIRES!

NOW THAT OWL'S WALKED OFF COVERED WITH OUR CAKE BATTER THERE AIN'T NO SENSE IN CONTINUIN' TO STIR ..
TELL ME MORE OF THE WEDDINGS.

WELL .. WE WAS TO BE MARRIED NEXT DAY SO NATURALLY I GOT TO THE PREACHERS REAL BRIGHT AN' EARLY .. WE WAITED AN' WAITED AN' WAITED AN' WAITED -
FOR THE PREACHER?

NAW .. FER MY MISTER .. THAT WEEVIL NEVER DID SHOW UP .. SO I WAS A WIDDER EVEN AFORE THE WEDDIN' SO TO SPEAK AN' BEEN A WIDDER EVER SINCE.
HE WAS DEAD?
CEMENT

DON'T B'LEEVE SO .. BUT HE BE DEAD IFFEN HE DO SHOW UP ... SAY! WE ACCIDENTAL PUT CEMENT IN THAT CAKE 'STEAD OF FLOUR .. GOOD THING WE NEVER FINISHED IT.
CEMENT

YEH ... IT WOULD OF BEEN HEAVY.
AND TOUGH -- PERHAP WE BREAK THE CHOPPERS WHEN WE CHEW HIM?

SAKES ALIVE

H'LO OWL, YOU BEEN SICK? YOU LOOK A LI'L PALE.
NO! AN' I AIN'T PALE, NEITHER.
DOES YOU FEEL BAD? FRANKLY, I IS NEVER SEED YOU LOOK WORSE.
SAME TO YOU. ANY FOOL KIN SEE WHAT'S WRONG.

NOT ME THO' .. YOU LOOKS LIKE YOU NEEDS SOME NEW CLOTHES. WHAT'S COME OVER YOU?
CAKE BATTER!
CAKE BATTER? IT DON'T HARDLY BECOME YOU.. YOU LOOKS BETTER IN KETCHUP LIKE YOU USUAL WEARS TO DINNER ... OR PORK GRAVY .. TURN AROUND, LEMME SEE HOW IT FITS IN BACK.
I CAN'T TURN.. I IS FROZE STIFF.

MY SAKES, OWL! YOU IS RIGHT.. THE CAKE BATTER IS SOLID.. YOU IS FRIZ.
UNLESS I IS CHIPPED FREE I IS DOOMED... MEBBE HAFTA STAY HERE FOR COUPLE THOUSAND YEARS.
PULL MY ARM FREE IF YOU KIN.. MY NOSE ITCHES... I'D SURE ADMIRE TO SCRATCH IT IF I COULD..
MMMPH!
PHOOF...! THAT'S AS FUR AS I KIN GIT IT... YOU IS A CONGEALED MESS.
SCRATCH MY NOSE AFORE I GOES MAD!
OOG..OOSH..OOM AH.. HOO HA A LI'L' HIGHER .AH..
WHAT WORRIES ME IS HOW YOU'LL MAKE A LIVIN' FROM NOW ON.... 'COURSE YOU COULD GIT A JOB WAITIN' FOR STREET CARS FOR BUSY FOLKS.

MY MOUTH IS FREEZIN' SHUT, TOO... CAN'T TALK NO MORE
C'MERE, WOODPECKER CHILE... WANNA JOB?
QUEERP.
PECK AWAY, SON.. TRY AN' CHIP HIM FREE WHILST I GITS A KETTLE OF SCALDIN' WATER TO MELT HIM DOWN.

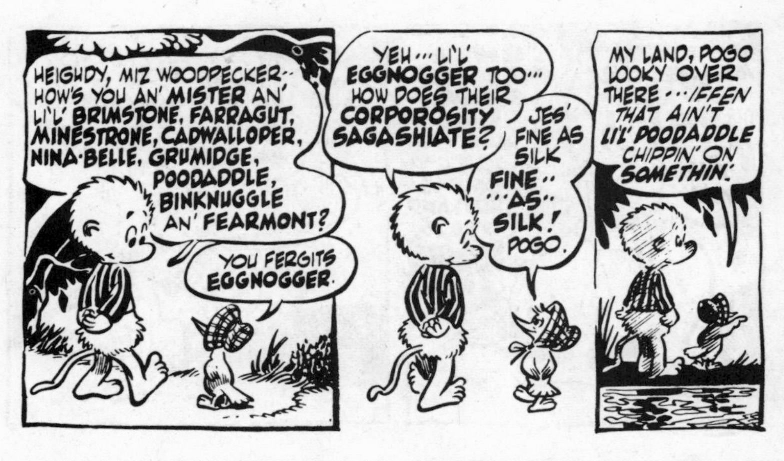
HEIGHDY, MIZ WOODPECKER-- HOW'S YOU AN' MISTER AN' LI'L' BRIMSTONE, FARRAGUT, MINESTRONE, CADWALLOPER, NINA-BELLE, GRUMIDGE, POODADDLE, BINKNUGGLE AN' FEARMONT?
YOU FERGITS EGGNOGGER.
YEH ... LI'L' EGGNOGGER TOO... HOW DOES THEIR CORPOROSITY SAGASHIATE?
JES' FINE AS SILK
FINE.. ...AS.. SILK! POGO.
MY LAND, POGO LOOKY OVER THERE ... IFFEN THAT AIN'T LI'L' POODADDLE CHIPPIN' ON SOMETHIN'.

IT'S A STATUE! A STATUE WHAT LOOKS A LI'L' BITTY LIKE OL' HOWLAND OWL!
THE TAD IS DONE IT HISSELF! HE'S A GENIUS! A CHILE PRODIGALLY! A UNSUNG SCULPTOR! IT LOOK JES' EXACT LIKE MR. OWL ... UGLIES AN' ALL.
QUEERP.

GEE WHIZ! IMAGINE A BABY BIRD, ONLY FOUR DAYS OLD, PECKIN' OUT A STATUE!
OH, LI'L' POODADDLE! YO' MAMMY IS PROUDER'N' A PURPLE PIG.
GIDDYAP! GIDDYAP!
ALBERT! LOOKY HERE, YOU NEVER SAW NOTHIN' LIKE THIS AFORE.

WHAT IS IT? QUICK! I'M A BUSY MAN... A BUSY MAN!
A STATUE OF OWL...CARVED OUT BY LI'L' OL' POODADDLE, THE 4 DAY BIRD.
YOU FLEA BUGS GO ON HOME.. WE'LL PLAY COWBOY TOMORROW --SOMETHIN' IMPORTANT IS COME UP
OKAY, WHEN'S THE NEXT DOG GO BY?
I IMAGINE MIZ WOODPECKER WOULD ADMIRE TO HAVE A HAND TOTIN' THE STATUE HOME...LONG'S WE'RE HERE, ALBERT.
OH, I SURE WOULD, GENTMINTS.
NOTHIN' TO IT, MA'M ... YOU GIT AROUND THERE, POGO.. I'LL H'IST THIS SIDE. NOW, ONE. TWO - THREE - ALLEZ - OOP!
WHOOIE! THIS STATUE OF OWL WHAT LI'L' POODADDLE CARVED OUT IS HEAVY EVEN WITH TWO OF US CARRYIN'...
LETTIN' HIM GO ON LIKE THAT AIN'T FAIR, ALBERT.
YER RIGHT, MA'M ... HEY POGO..COME BACK! YOU IS GOIN' THE WRONG WAY!

HEIGHDY, PORKYPINE.. RUN A BIT WITH ME.. I IS GITTIN' LONESOME.
WHERE'S YOU RUSHIN' TO..? TO A TEA PARTY?
NOPE.. I IS GOIN' TO POUR SCALDIN' WATER ON OL' HOWLAN' OWL.
A ERRAND OF MERCY, NO DOUBT. HE'S LUCKY HE KNOWS YOU.
YUP... IT'S THE ONLY CURE HE'S GOT LEFT FOR WHAT AILS HIM! HE GOT STIFF.
WHOOSH! THAT'S QUITE A CURE.. NEVER HEARD OF THAT ONE... WHAT'D HE GIT STIFF FROM?
TOO MUCH OF MIZ BEAVER'S CAKE BATTER.
THE FEDERALS KNOW ABOUT THIS?
FASTER! FASTER! FASTER!
HUFF! PUFF! WE KIN.. PUFF... TAKE A SHORT-CUT 'ROUND THAT LAGOON ...WOOF.
WON'T DO NO GOOD... PUFF

WHY NOT..!? IT'LL GIT YOU. HUFF THERE QUICKER. PUFF. PUF
ORDIN. PUFF NARILY. ..YES

'CEPT .. I CAN'T REMEMBER WHERE I'M GOIN'.

THIS MUS' BE THE PLACE I LEFT OWL... YEP.. I 'MEMBERS NOW.

WHOOSH... AFTER ALL THAT RUNNIN'.. HE AIN'T HERE?
NOPE..SIT DOWN.. AN' REST..YOU MUST BE WORED OUT.

OH I IS.. ..IS IS.
WELL, WHAT'S YOU TEARIN' OFF LIKE THAT FOR?

MAN, I IS SO TIRED I CAN'T WAIT TO GIT HOME TO BED... I'SE READY TO DROP.

AND TWO IS TEN

THERE! I IS DELIVERED THE STATUE OF OWL AT YO' VERY DOORSTEP WITH NO HELP FROM THAT SLACK PACKIN' GOL' BRICKIN' POGO!
OOP! WHERE'D YOU COME FROM, POGO?
YOU ACCIDENTAL CARRIED ME HERE... 'LONG WITH THE MONUMINT.
I DID? OH H'LO PORKYPINE.
Y'ALL HEAR 'BOUT OWL? ..CHURCHY SAY HE FROZE STIFF AN' NOW IS GONE.
GONE?
GOSH - LI'L' POODADDLE PECKED OUT THIS MEMORIAL STATUE OF OWL JES' IN TIME.
MUS' BE ABSTRACK ART-- IT DON'T LOOK LIKE OWL TO ME.
NO.. IT'S CONCRETE... ALL ACCORDIN' TO HOW YOU LOOK AT IT.
IF POODADDLE KEEP AGOIN' THAT WAY, HE GONNA MAKE A NAME FER HISSELF.
OFF HAND, I'D SAY THAT SCAPER GOT JES' 'BOUT ALL THE NAME HE KIN HOLD.
BEIN' WHITE LIKE THAT, I GUESS YOU MIGHT SAY IT'S VANILLA ABSTRACT. HO HO?
NOT IN FRONT OF THE CHILE I WOULDNT.

WHAT'S ALL **THIS** I HEARS 'BOUT YOU **RUNNIN'** **FER THE PRESIDENSITY** AGAIN?
AIN'T **SAID** I WOULD... THE JOB GOT A **COUPLE DRAWBACKS**
WULL.. **THIS** MOUGHT BE A GOOD TIME TO SOUND OUT **PUBLIC OPINION**.. YOU KIN ***UNVEIL OWL'S STATUE*** AN' MAKE A SPEECH AN' SEND UP A ***TRIAL BALLOON.***
I ***LOVES*** BALLOON RIDES ... I'LL DO IT.

FIRST YOU **SAYS** WHAT A **GOOD PUBLIC SERVANT** OWL WAS... ***EE***-NUMERATE HIS **GOOD QUALITIES** ..F'RINSTANCE.. **NO. 1**.. UH.. **NO. 1**. ..UH.. WELL.. HMM.. LESSEE NOW---
WULL, HE HAS A **PERTY BROWN** EYE ON HIM.
THAT'S NOT MUCH BUT.. **ANYWAYS**.. **NUMBER 2**, ..HE.. UH.. WELL.. HM.. NO. 2, HE.. ALSO.. UH.. MM.. **NO. 2**, HE ALSO...
TO BE FAIR, HE GOT **MORE THAN ONE EYE!** NO. 2, HE ALSO GOT **ANOTHER** PERTY BROWN EYE! HOW 'BOUT ***THAT?***
IT'S TOO BAD A FELLER LIKE **OWL** AIN'T A **OPPONENT**... HE DON'T LEND HISSELF TO BEIN' ***FOR*** HIM.. I KIN THINK OF THINGS **AGIN HIM** BY THE **BARREL**.
WELL, HE ALLUS GOT A READY ANSWER.
WRONG, BUT READY.
OH.. HE GOT A ANSWER FER ***EVERYTHIN'*** ..'CEPT QUESTIONS.
I FIGGER THAT STATUE OF OWL AIN'T **ABSTRACK** AFTER ALL.

YOU FIGGER IT'S CONCRETE, HUH ..?
IT'S CONCRETE ALLRIGHT. I GUV IT A KICK AN' MOS' SPRAINT MY TOE... ..IT'S A POW'FUL LOT LIKE OWL.
IF IT DIN'T KICK YOU BACK, IT AIN'T LIKE OWL ATALL.
US PORKYPINES DON'T GIT KICKED MUCH, SOMEHOW.
THE WOODPECKER FAMBLY ALL DECIDED TO WORK ON THE STATUE ... SAY IT TASTES GOOD ... BUT THEY'S GOIN' DOWN TOO FINE.
THEY'S CHIPPIN' AWAY.
YOU IS RIGHT, PORKY! THEY IS GOIN' TOO FAR!
IT'S LOST A CERTAIN "JENNY SAY QUOITS".. WHY DON'T YOU BIRDS QUIT?
NOW NOW

YOU'RE SPOILIN' IT! IT DON'T LOOK NOTHIN' LIKE OWL NOW.
THEY MEANS WELL.
IT'S TOO SORTA LOPSIDED.... IT GOT A KINDA DEAD LOOK ABOUT IT! IT AIN'T LIFELIKE.
WOWF! I IS TOO LIFELIKE! EVERYBODY OFF!

POOR SPORT!
ALL OUR WORK FOR NOTHIN'.
I IS GLAD TO SEE YOU LOOKIN' LIKE YO' OLD SELF AGAIN.
YEP... I IS PERTY CRUSTY.

WELL...IT'S A PITY.. POOR MIZ WOODPECKER THUNK HER LI'L' BOY, POODADDLE, WAS A SCULPTOR... THUNK YOU WAS A STATUE.
JES' 'CAUSE I WAS ALL FRIZ UP WITH CAKE BATTER AN' HE WAS CHIPPIN' ME FREE.
I MUST SAY YOU LOOKED LIKE A GREEK GOD THERE FER A SPELL ...A LUMPY ONE.
OL' CHURCHY WENT FER HOT WATER TO MELT THE STUFF OFF ME...WONDER WHAT BECOME OF HIM?

GITTIN' SO YOU CAN'T TRUST NOBOD.....
EEYOWP!
THERE YOU IS, SIR.
YOU BUNGLEBRAIN! DIN'T YOU SEE I WAS OUT OF THE BATTER? DON'T YOU KNOW I CAN'T STAND HOT WATER?
THAT'S WHY I BRUNG HOT TEA... MEBBE YOU PREFER COFFEE?

TWO ARRIVE

'LONG AS THIS IS LEAP YEAR, DEARIE, THEY AIN'T NOTHIN' TO PERVENT YOU FROM GOIN' OVER AN' WOOIN' POGO WITH A BANJO YERSELF 'STEAD OF WAITIN' FOR HIM.
WHY SHOULD I WOO POGO WITH THESE BANJOSEPH? IF HE ARE GENTLEMANS HE NO DOUBTS WILL WOO HIMSELF ME.
HE MOUGHTN'T BE NO GENTLEMAN.
THAT'S WHY YOU NEED A BANJO --THEN IF HE TRIES TO GIT AWAY, YOU RING RING THE BANJO RIGHT 'ROUN' HIS RASCAL NECK ... LIKE OL' JACK KRAMER SERVIN' A VOLLEY.
BUT -- IF I AM CATCH THESE FELLOW I WILL BE FIRST LADY IF HE IS ELECT ... MAYBE I DON'T LIKE.
YOU'RE JES' TRYIN' TO CHEAT ME OUT OF VISITIN' YOU AT THE WHITE HOUSE.

LIKE IT ER NOT, I'M PACKIN' YOU A CLUTCH OF PEANER BUTTER SAN'WICHES TO TAKE OVER TO POGO.
HE IS HUNGRY?

NOPE.. FAR'S I KNOW.. BUT THE WAY TO A MAN'S HEART IS THRU THE SOFT UNDERBELLY.. .. SOMEDAY, WHEN YOU IS MIZ PRESIDENT POGO, YOU'LL THANK ME.
BUT.. BUT.

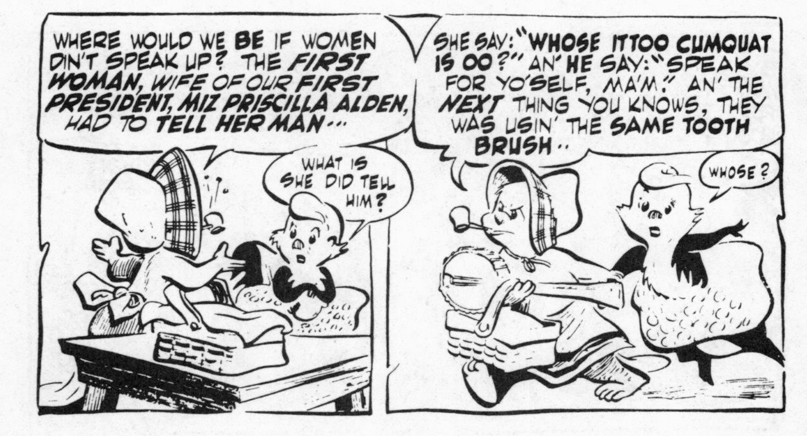
WHERE WOULD WE BE IF WOMEN DIN'T SPEAK UP? THE FIRST WOMAN, WIFE OF OUR FIRST PRESIDENT, MIZ PRISCILLA ALDEN, HAD TO TELL HER MAN...
WHAT IS SHE DID TELL HIM?
SHE SAY: "WHOSE ITTOO CUMQUAT IS OO?" AN' HE SAY: "SPEAK FOR YO'SELF, MA'M." AN' THE NEXT THING YOU KNOWS, THEY WAS USIN' THE SAME TOOTH BRUSH..
WHOSE?

C'MON! C'MON! YOU DON'T GIT MARRIED EVERY DAY.
CORRECT! IT IS BAD HABIT TO GET INTO... NON! NON! MA'M'SELLE IS STAY HERE.

IF YOU DON'T LEAP-YEAR AT POGO AN' GIT TO BE FIRST LADY, I'LL DO IT FOR YOU.
HOW YOU GO AT THESE JOB, MADAME BEAVER?

I HAULS OUT THE OL' BANJIO AN' RIPS OFF A LOVE SONG : "OH, MAMIE MINDED MAMA 'TIL ONE DAY IN SINGAPORE A SAILOR MAN FROM TURKESTAN COME KNOCKIN' AT THE DOOR."
ENUF!
WANGABLANGABLA

DONCHA WANNA HEAR THE REST? I KNOWS IT ALL..
NO..GO WOO POGO..I WILL BE VER' SAFE ...AN' PLEASE TO NOT POINT THESE WEAPON AT ME...SOMETIMES SHE ARE LOADED.

BY DOGNAB! IF MISS MA'M'SELLE WON'T GO POP THE QUESTION AT POGO I'LL DO IT FOR HER.
MIZ BEAVER

I GOT A FEW DOOS AN' DADS OF FINERY LEF'OVER FROM MY FLAPPER FRIPPERIES.. AN' WITH A VEIL ON, POGO WON'T KNOW ME FROM MISS MA'M'SELLE HEPZIBAH.

DOGGONE! IT'S MORTAL HARD TO SEE WITH THIS VEIL ON.
WHOOSH! KEEL MY HAULS!

MIZ BEAVER! MIZ BEAVER! LEMME IN! HOLP! HOLP! A HORRIBLE MONSTER IS WALLOWIN' IN YO' POOL.
BLOOB

MIZ BEAVER! MIZ BEAVER! LEMME IN! A UGLY AN' FIERCE MONSTER IS OUT HERE ... MIZ BEAVER!
SOME SOUL IS A-CALLIN' ME!

HERE I COME!
NO! NO!

HELP
(THAT POOR CRITTUR MUS' NEED A HAND) HOLD ON, SON!

YEOW!
COME BACK! WAIT!

POGO
HALP! IT'S A-GITTIN' ME!
HOLE ON! YOU DING FOOL!

POGO
WAP

IT DISAPPEARED!

POGO
WELL··MIGHT OF BEEN IT WAS A HALLUCIONATION ··GUESS I'LL GO IN AN' SEE WHAT'S COOKIN' IN POGO'S PLACE.

YOO HOO! GUESS WHO I IS, HONEY BUNCH... I PREEPOSES MARRIAGE.
THAT'S NICE·· FROM WHOM TO WHO?

IT'S ME! MISS MA'M'SELLE HEPZIBAH, THE FOREIGN AN' FRENCH BEAUTY.. KISS ME, POGO.
UNNA-CUSTOM AS I IS, I IS ON MY WAY AN' ALL PUCKERED.

SMACK SMACK YOU'RE A LIVIN' DOLL! SMACK!
YOO HOO?

DOGGONE IT! YOU AIN'T KISSIN' ME, POGO, YOU IS KISSIN' THE MIRROR!
NOW THAT YOU MENTIONS IT···I AIN'T EVEN POGO!

FOUR GOTTEN MEN

WHAT KIND OF A FIERCE SUPER-NATURAL SPIRIT WAS THIS OVER'T MY PLACE ?
IT LOOK LIKE IT COME FROM MARS AN' YET IT DIN'T ... IT LOOKED FAMILLER BUT UNKNOWED!
DID IT HAVE HORNS?

BLOWIN' OR REINDEER TYPE ?
REIN-DEERS DON'T HAVE HORNS .. THEY GOT LI'L' BELLS.

I S'POSE FIGHTIN' GHOSTS IS LIKE ALL ELSE ... IF YOU CAN'T LICK 'EM ... JOIN 'EM.

NOTHIN' DOIN'... ONLY OVER MY DEAD BODY.

I CAN'T SLEEP HERE... I AIN'T GOT NO NIGHT SHIRT.
BUT THEY'S A GHOST OVER AT YOUR PLACE .. ..YOU CAN'T SLEEP THERE EITHER.

WELL, I CAN'T SLEEP NOWHERES WITHOUT NO NIGHT SHIRT.
WHY NOT NIP HOME, GIT ONE, AN' HUSTLE BACK.

A GOOD IDEA... DON'T GO TO SLEEP WITHOUT ME.
BRING BACK SOME COOKIES.
THERE'S SOMETHING STUPID ABOUT THAT IDEA BUT I DUNNO JES' WHAT.
MEBBE HE AIN'T GOT ONE CLEAN -- TO WEAR -- OUT VISITIN' THAT IS.

I MISSES OL' POG' ---WAS KINDA HOPIN' HE'D WHUP UP A BATCH OF COCOA AN' CRULLIES.
ME TOO--'THOUGH ALL THE STUFF TO WORK WITH IS OVER'T POGO'S.
DOES YOU BORRY EVER'-THING FROM POGO?... NOTHIN' IN HERE BUT FISH-HOOKS.
WHAT ELSE WOULD YOU KEEP IN THE BREAD BOX? LET'S MAKE SOME TEA.

OUTEN WHAT? YOU AIN'T GOT NO TEA.
OUTEN SUGAR AN' WATER.... THEM'S ALL WE GOT... POT LUCK, OL' BOY.
I PUT A WHOLE POUND IN... YOU MOUGHT FIND IT A LI'L STRONG.... --ONE LUMP OR TWO, OL' TOP?
NO THANKS, I'LL DRINK IT STRAIGHT... GOTTA WATCH MY FIGGER YOU KNOW.

IT'S PERTY RISKY SNEAKIN' UP ON MY HOUSE --- I ALLUS KEEPS A LOADED LEMON MERINGUE PIE UNDERNEATH THE COVERS.

I'LL SLEEP IN POGO'S NEW WASH 'STEAD OF RUMPLIN' HIS BED, LONGS HE AIN'T COME HOME.... WOZZAT!

I'LL POKE THIS FORKY STICK IN AN' SNUTCH A NIGHT-SHIRT OUTEN MY LAUNDRY BASKET.. .. WOON'T WANNA DISTURB THAT GHOST.

WOWF! THEY'S A-COMIN' FOR ME!

IT'S A POORADE! A PAST-MIDNIGHT PARADE WITH A FLAG.
DID YOU SEED WHAT I SAWN POGO?
NO BUT I HEERD WHAT YOU HEARN, MIZ BEAVER.

TITHE ME KNOTS

WHILE WE IS SETTIN' 'ROUN' WORRYIN' 'BOUT POGO, THE HEARTLESS WRETCH, I IS GONE FILL IN MY INKUM TAX.
GOOD, I'LL HELP.

HOW COULD YOU HELP ME? IT SAYS HERE: FORM 1040 HOW TO FILL IN
ONE WAY I KIN HELP IS TO POINT OUT THAT YOU GOT THE BOOK UPSIDE DOWN.

THAT'S THE GUMMINT FOR YOU EVERY TIME! HERE I MUST IS... WHERE IT SAYS SINGLE PERSON WITH DEE-PENDENT MAMA... MA'M' IS MORE FIERCE... SHE GOT A INDEPENDENCY ON HER LIKE A FROZE HAWG!
WELL.. DOES YOU SUPPORT YO' MAMA?

SUPPORT HER?... I CAN'T EVEN LIFT HER... WHAT'S THIS HERE...? MARRIED COUPLES GITS A BIG CUT-RATE SERVICE... I IS GONE BE A MARRIED COUPLE.
YOU CAN'T! THERE'S ONLY ONE OF YOU.

BEST THING TO DO ON THIS INKUM TAX IS CLAIM I IS A MARRIED TYPE HUSBAN' WITH TWO CHILLUN..
THAT'S DISHONEST! YOU IS EGG-ZAGGER-ATIN'.

NOT MUCH... I COULD SAY I GOT TWO WIVES AN' NINE CHILDREN.
THEY'D COME LOOKIN'... AN' ASK FOR 'EM.

I'D SAY THEY HAD PASSED ON.. I'D SAY I WAS A WIDDERER.. ..I'D CRY AN' WAIL AN' CARRY ON SOMETHIN' FIERCE.
YOU'D BE ACCUSED OF MURDER AN' HUNG.
WHAT!? ME HANGED!? JES' FOR A LI'L' INNOCENT CHEATIN' ON MY INCOME TAX?
IF YOU DON'T LIKE OUR RULES, MOVE TO FRANCE.

I THINK YOU IS ALL WRONG 'BOUT THEM HANGIN' ME FOR SAYIN' I IS A WIDDERER ON THE INKUM TAX... IT SAY HERE: IF WIFE DIED DURIN' YEAR THE NUMBER OF HER EXEMPTIONS IS DEETERMINED AS OF DATE OF DEATH.

NOW YOU SEE WHAT THAT MEANS, DON'T YOU?
WHAT?!
OF COURSE.

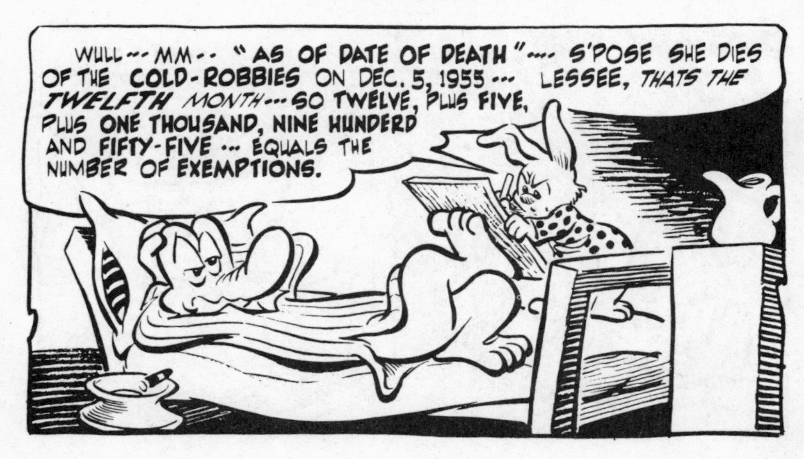
WULL--MM-- "AS OF DATE OF DEATH"---- S'POSE SHE DIES OF THE COLD-ROBBIES ON DEC. 5, 1955--- LESSEE, THATS THE TWELFTH MONTH--- SO TWELVE, PLUS FIVE, PLUS ONE THOUSAND, NINE HUNDERD AND FIFTY-FIVE--- EQUALS THE NUMBER OF EXEMPTIONS.

THAT'D BE ONE THOUSAND, NINE HUNDERD AND SEVENTY-TWO EXEMPTIONS AT, SAY, $600 APIECE... UM... YOU COULD HAVE AT LEAST ONE MILLION, ONE HUNDERD AND EIGHTY-THREE THOUSAND, TWO HUNDERD DOLLARS TAKEN OFFA THE TOP OF YO' TAX! A VERY TIDY SAVING...

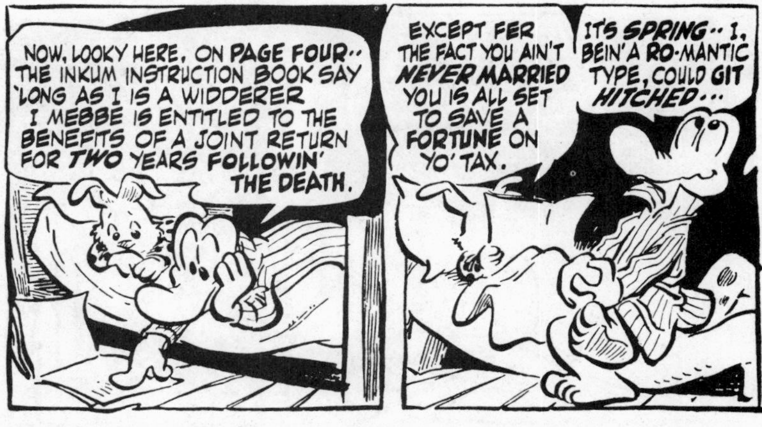
NOW, LOOKY HERE, ON PAGE FOUR.. THE INKUM INSTRUCTION BOOK SAY 'LONG AS I IS A WIDDERER I MEBBE IS ENTITLED TO THE BENEFITS OF A JOINT RETURN FOR TWO YEARS FOLLOWIN' THE DEATH.
EXCEPT FER THE FACT YOU AIN'T NEVER MARRIED YOU IS ALL SET TO SAVE A FORTUNE ON YO' TAX.
IT'S SPRING.. I, BEIN' A RO-MANTIC TYPE, COULD GIT HITCHED...

TROUBLE IS YOU'D HAFTA MARRY SOMEBODY ALREADY DEAD.. ANOTHER SNEAKY ITEM IS WHEN THEY SAYS: "BENEFIT OF A JOINT RETURN FOR TWO YEARS...."
YOU DON'T WANT THE 'BENEFIT' OF NOBODY LIKE THAT MAKIN' "RETURNS" OVER TWO YEARS, DO YOU...? COMIN' BACK WAILIN' AN' GROANIN'---PROB'LY CLANKIN' CHAINS AN' ALL?...
BY JING, I KNOWED THEY WAS A CATCH.

ACTUALLY, ALBERT, THE WAY TO FIGGER YO' INKUM TAX IS TO BE AS HONEST AS THE LAW ALLOWS.
I ALLUS FIGGERED GITTIN' IT IN ON TIME WAS THE BIG I-DEE ... THAT'S WHY I IS WORKIN' MY HEAD TO THE BONE.
YOU IS A SINGLE PERSON... YOU, IT SAYS, SHOULD TEAR OFF PAGES 3 AN' 4.
GOOD! THEM'S THE PAGES WHAT BEEN GIVIN' ME ALL THE TROUBLE .. OFF THEY COMES!

NOT THEM ONES! NOT THE ONES WHAT'S NUMBERED THREE AN' FOUR... THEM'S INSTRUCTIONS... ~ THEY MEANS 3 AN' 4 OF THE FORM.
I IS HAD ENOUGH.... I DIN'T HAVE NO INKUM LAS' YEAR AN' I AIN'T GONE PAY NO TAX... SO THERE.

OF COURSE! WHY IS YOU BEEN FIGGER'N' YO' TAX ON NOTHIN'?
A CITIZEN KIN ONLY DO HIS DOODY AS HE SEES IT... BESIDES, PAYIN' TAXES IS ALL THE RAGE.

IN MORNING NUMBER

Who told you this?
A LITTLE BIRD.
hmmmm

You don't need a Phi Beta Kaplin key to know you can't beat that source ---
OH, IT'S ABSOLUTELY AUTHENTIC.

You've heard? Pogo's running.. He'll need counsel ....
INDUTABUBBLY! AND VOTES!
Exactly -- I have here, for purposes of my own, a list of the cemeteries east of the Mississippi -- You may find it of use as a - uh - m - source book..

VERY NICE AN OLD-FASHIONED APPROACH ★ BUT WE MAY NEED IT! I, SIR, INTEND TO GO NORTH and !! CAPTURE !! The CANADIAN VOTE!
Bless me -- A coup --- The Canadian Vote!
IF I MAY BE ALLOWED A MODEST COMMENT It's The BEST ★ FINEST and MOST BRILLIANT IDEA THE WORLD HAS EVER SEEN!

YOU HEARD THE BIG SECRET? POGO'S GONNA RUN FER THE PRESIDENSITY..
HE'LL NEVER BEAT CLEVELAND.. .. TOO MUCH POWER.
CLEVELAND'S RUNNIN'?
WELL THE INFIELD'S SLOW, BUT DON'T TRY TO DOUBLE 'EM UP.

I'M TALKIN' SERIOUS... NOT BASEBALL FRIVOLITIES ...OL' P.T. BRIDGEPORT'S AT THE TORONTO PRESS CLUB TO ADDRESS THE NEWSPAPER MENS AN' CAPTURE THE CANADIAN VOTE.
LONG AS YOU'RE TALKIN' SERIOUS, LET ME REMIND YOU: CLEVELAND OUTNUMBERS POGO, TOO...
I DUNNO HOW A TIGER GOT TO BE KNOWED AS A POLITICAL SYMBOL.

YOU REALLY WANT TO KNOW HOW A TIGER GOT TO BE A POLITICAL SYMBOL? IT'S ON ACCOUNT OF THE NEW YORK PUBLIC LIBERRY.
THAT AIN'T THE SAME AS TAMMANY HALL IS IT?
NO, YOU CAN DISTINGUISH 'EM WITH THE NAKED EYE... WELL I AND ANOTHER TIGER HAD JOBS OUT IN FRONT GUARDIN' THE PLACE... KEEPIN' FOLKS OUT..
KEEPIN' 'EM OUT?

NATCH! SOME BUSY-BODY DECIDED TWO STONE LIONS WOULD DO AS WELL AN' FOR LESS PAY..... WE WAS OUT OF A JOB... MY FRIEND TOOK A POSITION WITH PRINCETON UNIVERSITY ON ACCOUNT OF HAVIN' BEEN NEAR BOOKS.... AN' I GOT A JOB POSIN' FOR A ARTIST, NAME OF NAST.

HE WAS TRYIN' TO DRAW A INDIAN... REPERSENTIN' THE TAMMANY WIGWAM.. BUT THE INDIAN KEPT COMIN' OUT PERTY STRIPEY ON ACCOUNT I WAS THE MODEL... SO HE UP AN' MADE IT A PLAIN TIGER AFTER A WHILE.
THERE'S NOTHIN' PLAIN 'BOUT A TIGER.

YOU, SIR, MAY WONDER HOW I GOT OUT OF THE MODELIN' BUSINESS AN' REACHED MY PRESENT EMINENCE.
NO - DON'T KNOW AS I WONDER AT ALL.

AS A SIDELIGHT I MIGHT SAY THAT THE LIONS INSTALLED BY THE LIBERRY WERE VERY INEFFECTIVE... NEVER STOPPED NOBODY... NOW ANYBODY CAN GET IN..... NOTHING SPECIAL NOW AS A CLUB.

NAST STARTED DRAWING ELEPHANTS --A RUBBER BEAST WITH TWO TAILS... INCENSED, I WITHDREW TO DETROIT WHERE I HELPED INVENT THE AUTOMOBILE... THEN TURNED MY BRAIN TO SPORTS...

QUICKLY, I, UNDER THE NAME OF DOUBLEDAY INVENTED BASEBALL AN' CALLED MY TEAM "THE TIGERS".. THEN ...HEY! YOU'LL NEVER KNOW HOW ALL THIS COME OUT...

NIMBLE SQUATS

WELL! WELL! POGO GONNA RUN FER THE HIGHEST OFFICE AGAIN... AN', AS HIS BEST FRIEND, I WILL GET A RIPE PLUM!

COURSE THEY'S GONE BE A LOT OF DEE-MANDS ON HIS TIME.

I WON'T WANNA BARGE IN AN' DEE-MAND NOTHIN'.. ~LEAVE THAT FOR THE BUMS.

AS TIME GOES ON EVERYBODY WILL BE WANTIN' SOMETHIN' OF HIM... HE'LL BE DEE-LUGED BY JOB REQUESTS.
JOHNNY-COME-LATELIES! USIN' UP HIS GOOD SPIRITS --GITTIN' THE JOBS.
IT'S A DAGNAB SCANDAL! HE CAN'T TREAT OL' FRIENDS THIS WAY... I'LL FACE HIM WITH IT.. LOYALTY IS A PRESIDENTAL PREE-ROG-ATIVE!

BY GEORGE Y. WELLS! POGO GOTTA REMEMBER HIS OL' FRIENDS WHEN IT COME TO CABINET POSTS, POSTMASTERS AN' SUCH.
I KIN ROUTE THE MAIL GOOD AS ANYBODY... ASK ME WHAT'S THE STATE CAPITOL OF NORTH DAKOTA.
LIKE A FLASK! I REPLIES: "LINCOLN, NEWBRASKA!" RIGHT ON THE NOSE!

I'M POLITE ... DEEP-ENDABLE AN'.. OONK!
I BEG YOUR PARDON SIR ... JES' VOTE EARLY AN'..
THERE IS A SIGHT, CLIFTMON, ALBERT SAYIN' "SIR" TO A TREE.
PERSONABLY, I WOON'T KNOW'F IT WAS A LADY OR A GENT.

I S'POSE IT'S SILLY OF ME TO WORRY POGO WITH MY LI'L' TROUBLE ..I SHOULDN'T PRESS HIM ... HE KIN APPOINT ME TO THE CABINET WHEN HE'S READY.
HERE I WAS GOIN' OVER AN' TELL HIM WHAT A SCALAWAG I THINKS HE IS ..HOWEVER, MEBBE I WAS HASTY.. I'LL TELL HIM I FORGIVES HIM.
POGO

POGO
YOO HOO! POGO, OL' FRIEND... I FORGIVES YOU, OL' PAL.

YOO HOO?

HOW DO YOU LIKE THAT! THE NO-GOOD SCALAWAG AIN'T EVEN HOME...I TAKES BACK MY FORGIVES.

Good morrow, Sir-- Is the candidate at home? I'm here to help him--
YOU'D HELP HIM MORE BY NOT BEIN' HERE.

Now, now--We must all join forces--Back the candidate. Help him!
I THUNK OF HELPIN' HIM AFORE YOU DID, DEACON.

Indeed! In what way, pray tell?
BY BEIN' SECERTARY OF STATE FOR HIM OR SECERTARY OF SOMETHIN'.. THAT'S "WHAT WAY," PRAY TELL.

A puny contribution. I thought of being Vice-president for him---I'm going all out--
OH YEAH! WELL I THUNK OF THAT, TOO.

ROWR!
Ahrg!

Mr. Seminole Sam, Pogo's running -- The country needs him ----
FOR WHAT?
-- for President - and I'm for Vice --
SO AM I! ALWAYS HAVE BEEN! BUT HOW ABOUT THE CANDIDATE, IS HE FOR IT?

Who knows? As long as I have your support, I'm content ---
YOU GOT MINE -- BUT FIFTY MILLION FRENCHMEN MIGHT NOT BACK YOU.
Don't forget -- I'm relying on you --
WE'RE FOR VICE! WHAT A SLOGAN! WHY DIDN'T I THINK OF THAT?

IT'S ABOUT TIME YOU GOT HOME ... I'M ALL TIRED OUT WAITIN'.
WAITIN' FER WHAT ?

WELL, I HEARD YOU IS RUNNIN' FER PRESIDENT AN' I SAYS IF I WAS IN HIS PLACE I'D ASK MY BEST FRIEND TO BE MY VICE-PRESIDENT.... SO I RUSHED OVER TO TELL YOU...

I ACCEPTS!
BUT.. BUT..

THREE CHEERS! THE PERFECK CANDIDATE! FIRST IN WAR, FIRST IN PEACE, AND SECOND ON THE TICKET!
IS EITHER ONE OF YOU POLITICAL EXPERTS KNOW HOW TO CLEAN A FISH ?

ACUTE CUCUMBER

ONE THING I THINK ANY CAMPAIGN NEEDS, OWL, IS A BIG WAR CHEST...
I AGREES.
UH.. HOW MUCH IS IN-UH-OUR CAMPAIGN FUND? .. IF YOU-UH-DON'T MIND.
NOT ATALL NOT ATALL. LESSEE.. WE'RE JUST SHORT OF HALF A MILLION DOLLARS.
JUST SHORT OF HALF A MILLION! WHOOIE!
SHORT OF HALF A MILLION? WHO TOOK IT..?!
WE'RE RICH! AWK
GIVE IT BACK!
BOTH OF YOU DON'T UNDER-STAND ME!
GARROTTER! ASSASSIN! WOULDST IMBRUE YOUR SLOV'LY HAND IN MY SWEET AND INNOCENT BLOOD?!
LET ME AT HIM! THIEF..CUT PURSE! CANDY-SNATCHER! POOR BOX JOHN! GIVE BACK THE MONEY!
NOW BE CALM... I SAID "OUR TREASURY IS JES' SHORT OF HALF A MILLION DOLLARS.."

AN' ALL I SAID WAS "WE'RE RICH!" AN' HE LEPPED ON ME!
AN' I SAYS "SHORT OF HALF A MILLION?!" WHO GOT IT..!? HIM IS WHO!
NO!
WHAT I MEANS IS WE IS SHORT BY $499,999 AN' 96 CENTS.. ALL'S WE GOT IS FOUR CENTS.
YOU MEANS WE DIN'T LOSE THE WHOLE THING?
WHAT WE'VE GOT TO DO IS MAKE OUR CANDIDATE LOOK GOOD AN' THE OTHERS LOOK BAD.
WE COULD KEEP HIM OUT OF SIGHT.
WE'VE GOT TO USE THE OLD SAVVY, THE KNOW-HOW, THE MOXIE, THE MOTHER-WIT, ARS CELARE ARTEM!
YOU SAID IT!
THANK YOU.
I'M BEHIND HIM AT LEAST ONE HUNDERD POOR CENT.
I'M BEHIND HIM ABOUT SEVEN MILES.. WHAT'D HE SAY?
WHO KNOWS...? IT WAS IN LATIN AN' THAT IS RECOMMENDATION ENOUGH FOR ME.
WONDER WHAT LANGUAGE THE ROMANS USED FOR THE OLD 14 KARAT BAMBOOZLE?

I MEANS WE GOTTA ACT LIKE THE RED BLOODED PIONEERS WHAT INVENTED AN' DISCOVERED THE TALL CORN, THE SQUARE PEGS, THE EMPTY VISTAS OF THE TEEVY SCREEN.

WE, AS TRUE PATRIOTS, TRUE KNIGHT ERRANTS, BLUE BLOODED BOYS OF RED, WHITE AN' TRUE STRIPE, WE GOTTA PUT A BLOOM ON OUR CANDIDATE ... WE GOT TO SELL OUR MAN ..

WHY!? WHY!? WE ONLY JES' GOT HIM .... HE RUN ONCE AN' NEVER GOT TO SET OFF HIS ALARM, HE JES' STOPPED... CONSIDERIN' HOW HE WAS WOUND UP, HE WOUND UP GOOD .... JES' BARELY LAST.

BESIDES IT'S AGIN THE LAW TO SELL, GIVE AWAY OR ALLOWED TO BE CONSUMED ON THE PREMISES ANYBODY WHAT'S A CITIZEN OF THESE HERE STATES.

YOU GETS ME WRONG, TURTLE ... YOU IS TOO TURTLE-MINDED ... WHEN I SAYS WE GOTTA SELL OUR MAN, I DON'T MEAN WE GOTTA SELL HIM ... I MEAN WE GOTTA SELL HIM.

WE GOTTA RUN WITH THE BALL.. PUT OUR BOY ACROSS THE LINE... KNOCK HIM OVER THE FENCE FOR A BASES-LOADED BEER BOTTLE BLAST! WE GOT TO BLOW A NOTE OF PUREST AN' GENUINE UNSIMULATED GOLD!

A NOTE WHAT WILL ALERT THE THIRSTY BLOOD OF A BUYING PUBLIC ... AROUSE THE HUNGER OF A HUNDRED MILLION HUMBLE HEARTS ... FLAME THE FLARING PASSIONS OF THE MAN IN THE STREET! ANY QUESTIONS ?
YES ... WHAT IN THE WORLD DOES YOU PUT IN YO' WATERMILLION RHYME PREE-SERVE ...? IT'S DEE-LICORICE!

IT'S TRUE, OWL, YOUR BIG SPLASH HAS RAISED A THOUSAND RIPPLES OF THOUGHT-- -NOW, HERE'S A HANDFUL OF CORN THAT I TOSS OUT TO SEE IF A BIRD OF PARADISE WILL GIVE IT A PASSING PECK.
I'M RIFLING THIS INTO THE DARK, INTO AN OFF-SEASON SHOOTING GALLERY, MIND YOU, BUT IT HAS A CHANCE OF RINGING THE OLD BELL ... WE MAY WIN A KEWPIE DOLL WITH THIS ...

I'M NOT GOING TO FANCY THIS NUGGET UP WITH A SUNDAY SUIT ... I'LL JUST TOSS IT INTO THE FIRE, RAW, AN' SEE IF IT SPITS BACK, SEE IF IT SIMMERS INTO A BROTH OF OH BOY! OR IF IT CURLS ITS TAIL AND ...

WHAT IS YOU TALKIN' ABOUT?!
DON'T YOU DIG THE MOTHER TONGUE OR DO YOU NEED ANOTHER EAR?

THE ONLY THING ALL YOUR TALKIN' IS DID SO FAR IS CONFUSE ME AN', AS A MEMBER OF A ALREADY CONFUSED PUBLIC, I RESENTS IT... IT'S CONFUSIN'.

BEST THING SO FAR IS DEACON MUSHRAT'S SLOGAN... "WHO CARES WHO'S FOR PRESIDENT...? WHO'S FOR VICE?"

THIS BRIGHT YOUNG MAN IS TYPICAL OF ALL WHAT'S TYPICAL OF TYPICALLY TYPICAL TYPES... HE'S SLOGAN CONSCIOUS... A MEMBER IN HIGH STANDIN' OF THAT GREAT BODY OF MEN... OUR BELOVED CONSTITUENCY!

YOU MAKES ME ALL COME OVER GULPY.
WE KIN TAKE THE PULSE OF THE PUBLIC BY MERE TAKIN' A POLL OF THIS LAD'S THOUGHTS.
WITH WHAT?! A MICROSCOPE?

MEBBE YOU IS RIGHT, OWL.. TURTLE GOT THE WIDE-EYED LOOK OF THE ORNERY CITIZEN... LET'S GIVE HIM A QUICK POLL.
I GOT A POLE... WHAT I NEEDS IS BAIT.

NO, NO, FRIEND... YOU DON'T UNDER-STAND... WE IS GONE TAKE DOWN YOUR OPINIONS ON THE POLITICAL SCENE.
GOOD FOR ME.

WE FIGGER YOU IS ABOUT AS COMMON AS THE COMMON MAN KIN GIT...
IN THAT FIELD YOU IS A STICK-OUT.
GEE.
IN SHORT, WE WANTS TO QUERY A CROSS SECTION OF THE PUBLIC.
USUAL, ALBERT IS THE CROSSEST SECTION OF THE PUBLIC I KNOWS.
NOW.. BEARING IN MIND THAT ALL YOUR ANSWERS IN THIS POLL ARE MERE OPINION... UH.. WHAT'S YOUR NAME, FIRST?
CHURCHY LA FEMME.
US POLL TAKERS DON'T WANT NO HASTY TYPE ANSWERS... IS THAT YOUR CONSIDERED REPLY?
NO.. I MEAN. UH-WELL, YEAH.

THINK HARD NOW.... SUPPOSE THIS WASN'T YOUR NAME, WHAT WOULD YOUR SECOND CHOICE BE?
CHURCHY LA FEMME AGAIN.
HOLD IT.. NOT TOO FAST.
CHURCHY LA FEMMIGAN! HMMM...
AND YOUR THIRD CHOICE?
CHURCHY LA FEMME AGAIN AGAIN AN' AGAIN.
CHURCHY LA FEMMIGANAGAN NANNAGAN?

WHAT WOULD YOU LIKE TO SEE DONE ABOUT FOREIGN POLICY? 'LONG AS WE'RE TAKIN' A POLL.
I'D LIKE TO SEE IT CONTINUE.
IN OTHER WORDS, YOU'D LIKE TO SEE THEM GO RIGHT AHEAD WITH FOREIGN POLICY?
I'D LIKE TO SEE IT MOVE RIGHT ALONG.
WHAT YOU MEANS IS YOU'D BE IN FAVOR OF KEEPIN' GOIN' WITH FOREIGN POLICY...?
YES...I DON'T THINK IT SHOULD STOP.
WHAT HE'S TRYIN' TO SAY IS THAT HE THINKS FOREIGN POLICY SHOULD CONTINUE.
IN OTHER WORDS HE'D LIKE TO SEE THEM GO RIGHT AHEAD WITH IT.
YES..IT OUGHT TO MOVE RIGHT ALONG.
YOUR ANSWER TO OUR POLL QUESTION, THEN, IS THAT YOU'RE IN FAVOR OF PLENTY OF FOREIGN POLICY?
LOTS OF IT.
TO PUT IT ANOTHER WAY, YOU'RE STRONG FOR A GOOD DEAL OF FOREIGN POLICY?
YES, FOREIGN POLICY IS ONE OF MY FAVORITES.

TO BOIL IT DOWN, YOU'RE SAYING THAT YOU CAN'T HAVE TOO MUCH FOREIGN POLICY.
IF WE GOT ANY LEFT OVER WE COULD EXPORT IT AN' MAKE A BUCK.

ACTUALLY, WHAT HE'S GETTING AT THERE, IS THAT HE'S IN FAVOR OF LOTS OF FOREIGN POLICY.
BASICALLY, HE REALLY MEANS HE'S FOR PLENTY OF IT...
OR, LIKE YOU SAY, WE CAN'T HAVE TOO MUCH.

NOW, WHAT GRADE FOREIGN POLICY WOULD YOU BE IN FAVOR OF IS OUR NEXT QUESTION ON THE POLL... HIGH, LOW, MEDIUM OR RARE?
WULL, I-UM.
I FIGGER A FOREIGN POLICY LIKE AS WHEN YOU MIGHT BUY A LI'L' POLICY ON A STEAMBOAT ACCIDENT IN PATAGONIA... THEN, IF YOU IS KILLED IN A STEAM-BOAT ACCIDENT IN PATAGONIA YOU'D BE FIXED FOR LIFE AN' THAT'S A GOOD FOREIGN POLICY, I ALLUS SAY.

YOU DON'T EXPECT US TO SQUEEZE A BIG FAT ANSWER LIKE THAT ON TO OUR POLL QUESTIONNAIRE, DO YOU? MAKE IT SHORT!
VERY WELL, MY ANSWER IS NO!

THAT'S A NICE SHORT ANSWER BUT IT DON'T ANSWER THE QUESTION...
WHAT DIFFERMINTS? IT FITS THE SPACE WE GOT FOR A REPLY TO A "T"!
"NO" AIN'T GOT NO "T"!

QUIZZICAL LEARY

I DUNNO AS YOU OUGHT TO IGNORE THIS HERE POLL ME AN' SEMINOLE SAM TOOK OF CHURCHY.. KNOWIN' HOW A SPECIFIC SAMPLE UNIT OF YO' PUBLIC IS THINKIN' IS A STEP..! A BIG STEP.
WHICH WAY?

WHAT DIFFERN'TS? LONG AS YOU IS MOVIN'? .. NOW POPULATION FIGURES SHOW THAT CHURCHY IS A MERE UNDECILLIONTH OF THE VOTING POTENTIAL OF THE COUNTRY COUNTIN' TURTLES, (WHICH CHURCHY IS ONE OF), DOGS CHICKENS AN' BABY SPIDERS, THE MOST NUMEROUS SEGMENT.

BABY SPIDERS? KIN THEY VOTE? BUGS AIN'T USUALLY REGISTERED VOTERS.
SPIDERS AIN'T RIGHTLY BUGS, BEIN' AS THEY GOT TWO EXTER LEGS, WHICH, IN A ELECTION YEAR COMES IN HANDY.

YOU ASKS ME IS A BABY SPIDER OLD ENOUGH TO VOTE, AN' I REPLIES ANY SPIDER TWENTY ONE YEARS OLD IS ELIGIBLE .. IF YOU GOT 21 SPIDERS A YEAR OLD EACH THEY GITS ONE VOTE .. AN' VOTES AS A BLOC ... THEN..
ZZ

HEIGHDY THERE, HOUN' DOG, ME AN' POGO IS DISGUSTIN' HIS CHANCES OF EE-LECTION AN' I IS POINTIN' OUT TO HIM HOW IMPORTANT THE BABY SPIDER VOTE IS.
UM?

YOU MEAN THEY'RE GOIN' TO BE DELEGATES TO THE CONVENTION ... 'SPIDERS?
YEP... THEY'LL BE STANDIN' FOR POGO.

AN' MORE'N. ANYBODY THEY'LL HAVE A LEG TO STAND ON.
THAT WON'T BE YOUR PROBLEM... SEATIN' 'EM IS THE THING TO WORRY ABOUT.
SEATIN' 'EM..?! WHY CAN'T THEY STAND?..'TAIN'T LIKE THEY'D ROCK THE BOAT.
IT'S AGIN ALL PROTOCOL TO STAND..DELEGATES GOTTA HAVE SEATS... AN' HOW DOES A SPIDER SIT..? ..WHERE'S HE BEND AT..? WHICH KNEES DOES HE CROSS? WHAT DO HE SIT ON? IT'S A HEADACHE FOR ALL.

I S'POSE IT'S NONE OF MY BUSINESS BUT WHAT'S YOU DOIN'..?
YOU'RE RIGHT.. RUN ALONG, WHY DON'T YOU?..WE'RE BUSY MEN; BUSY, BUSY MEN!
WE'RE TALKIN' ABOUT HOW TO GIT YOU ELECTED.
ACTUALLY, IF YOU GOT A GOOD DOG ON YOUR SIDE IT'S LIKE BELONGING TO A GOOD LODGE..ALL CANDIDATES SHOULD HAVE DOGS WITH THEM...

LOOK, WHY DON'T YOU TAKE OUR PICTURE AND CALL IT "CHUMS".. THEN UNDERNEATH IT SAY, "NOBLE DOG, MAN'S BEST FRIEND, POSES WITH CANDIDATE."
BUT YOU IS BIGGER'N ME... MEBBE I COULD WEAR ELEVATIN' SHOES.. A MAN OUGHT TO BE TALLER'N HIS DOG.
NOT NECESSARILY.. HOWEVER I COULD CRUNCH DOWN AN' MAKE A SORT OF FACE LIKE A PEKINESE.
PHOO.

AT BOTTOM, THERE'S NO REASON WHY A MAN HAS TO BE TALLER'N HIS DOG... --LOTS OF CANDIDATES HAVE ONLY BEEN COLLAR HIGH TO THEIR BASSETT HOUND.
AND SOME OF 'EM HAD TO STAND ON TIPPY TOE TO REACH THE SPIGOT ON THE BRANDY KEG OF THEIR BABY ST. BERNARD-- --MATTER OF FACT I THINK I'LL HIRE OUT AS THE PERFECT CANDIDATE'S DOG..
THEN YOU'LL HAVE TO FIND THE PERFECT CANDIDATE.
I'LL FIX THAT ...I'LL HIRE OUT TO ALL PARTIES...WEARIN' A WIG FOR ONE, A BEARD FOR ANOTHER, AND LOOKING STRONG, SILENT AND WISE.
IN CASE OF A DEADLOCK YOU MIGHT FIND YOURSELF ELECTED PRESIDENT OF THE UNITED STATES.
ME? A DOG? NOT A CHANCE... --NOT OLD ENOUGH.

LYRICAL QUIZ

LESSEE, CHURCHY FIGGERS HE LIKES OUR MAN... CHURCHY REPERSENTS HALF THE POPULATION OF FORT MUDGE, A TYPICALLY TYPICAL TYPE OF A TOWN... ... NOW THE REST OF FORT MUDGE MIGHT NOT VOTE... LEAST NOT ALL OF IT.

WE CAN SAFELY PRESUME THAT A GOOD THIRD OF THE BALANCE, OR A SIXTH OF THE TOTAL IS UNDER AGE, NOT INTERESTED OR UNDETERMINED... ...FIGURES WILL PROVE THAT OF THE REMAINING TWO SIXTHS AT LEAST ONE QUARTER WILL BE INFIRM AND UNABLE TO REACH POLLS OR OUT OF TOWN BUYING PEACHES.

ANOTHER QUARTER, CONSTITUTING THE NOW ONE HALF, (OR ANOTHER SIXTH IN ALL) WILL REACH THE VOTING BOOTHS TOO LATE OR TOO EMPTY, BECOME DISCOURAGED, INASMUCH AS RAIN IS ONE THIRD LIKELY TO OCCUR...

THIS MEANS THAT CHURCHY REPERSENTS HALF THE VOTING PUBLIC AND WILL VOTE OUR WAY... NATIONALLY, THAT'S ROUGHLY 31,000,000 VOTES FOR OUR FELLOW... AND ONLY ONE SIXTH WILL BE IN OPPOSITION, SAY A MEASLY EIGHT POINT THREE MILLION... IT ALL MAKES A MAN STOP AN' SORTA THINK LIKE...

ALL OUR WORK FOR NAUGHT! INTERVIEWIN' THE LOWEST, COMMONEST, DENOMINATOREST CITIZEN WE COULD FIND... HA! FOR WHAT!?
BUT... BUT FIGGERS DON'T LIE.

WHEN CHURCHY SAID HE WAS AGAINST A CHANGE AND WAS FOR POGO BEIN' PRESIDENT WE OVERLOOKED ONE THING... POGO AIN'T PRESIDENT, NOW.

IF HE'S AGAINST **CHANGE**, POGO ***CAN'T*** BE PUT IN OFFICE ... OUR WORK IS WASTED...
OH, I DUNNO ... WE GOT SOME PERTY **INTERESTIN' ANSWERS** AN' **FIGURES** HERE.
DOES YOU REALIZE THAT WITH ***ANSWERS*** AN' ***CONCLUSIONS*** LIKE THESE, ALL ***WE*** GOTTA DO IS ***DREAM UP THE RIGHT SET OF QUESTIONS*** AND ***WE*** KIN GO INT BUSINESS PROVIN' CTICALLY NYTHING?

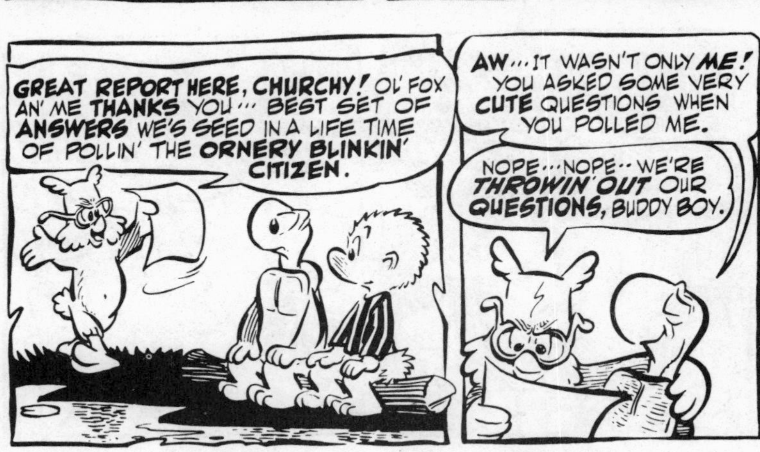
GREAT REPORT HERE, CHURCHY! OL' FOX AN' ME **THANKS** YOU ... BEST SET OF **ANSWERS** WE'S SEED IN A LIFE TIME OF POLLIN' THE **ORNERY BLINKIN' CITIZEN**.
AW ... IT WASN'T ONLY ***ME!*** YOU ASKED SOME VERY **CUTE** QUESTIONS WHEN YOU POLLED ME.
NOPE ... NOPE .. WE'RE ***THROWIN' OUT*** OUR **QUESTIONS**, BUDDY BOY.

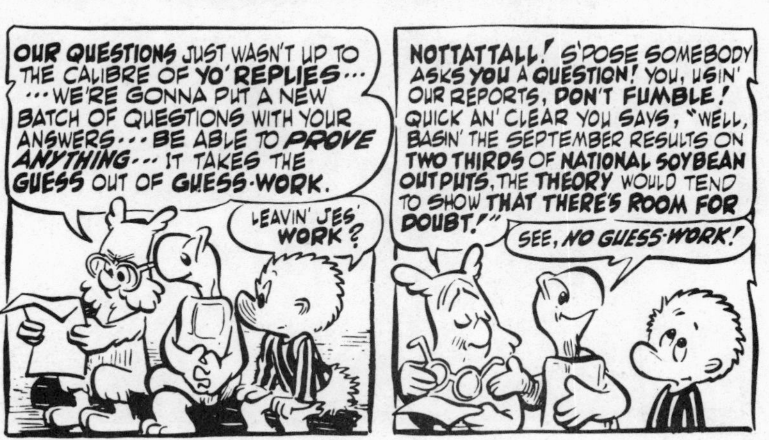
OUR QUESTIONS JUST WASN'T UP TO THE CALIBRE OF **YO' REPLIES** ... ... WE'RE GONNA PUT A NEW BATCH OF QUESTIONS WITH YOUR ANSWERS ... **BE ABLE TO *PROVE ANYTHING*** ... IT TAKES THE **GUESS** OUT OF **GUESS-WORK**.
LEAVIN' JES' **WORK**?
NOTTATTALL! S'POSE SOMEBODY ASKS **YOU** A **QUESTION!** YOU, USIN' OUR REPORTS, **DON'T FUMBLE!** QUICK AN' CLEAR YOU **SAYS**, "WELL, BASIN' THE SEPTEMBER RESULTS ON **TWO THIRDS** OF **NATIONAL SOYBEAN OUTPUTS**, THE **THEORY** WOULD TEND TO SHOW **THAT THERE'S ROOM FOR DOUBT!**"
SEE, ***NO GUESS-WORK!***

HOW DOES YO' RESEARCH POLL SERVICE WORK?
WULL, WE IS ALREADY INNERVIEWED TURTLE HERE AS THE LOWEST COMMON DENOMINATOR.. HE'S A PRIZE SAMPLIN'.
S'POSE WE WANNA KNOW HOW YOU FEELS ABOUT DOIN' AWAY WITH FEBRUARY... OR MEBBE TUESDAY...
WULL, I'D FEEL IT'D LEAVE A SORTA HOLE.
TUT-TUT-TUT-SHH! YOU DON'T ANSWER A THING! WE GOT TURTLE'S ANSWER... AS THE AVERAGEST CITIZEN WE KNOWS HOW HE FEELS... HE'S FOR IT! AN' THAT MEANS YOU, BEIN' 8/9 THS NORMAL, MORE OR LESS, YOU IS FOR IT TOO, MOSTLY.
BUT I AIN'T! I'M DEAD AGAINST THE WHOLE IDEA.
YOU TRYIN' TO TELL ME THAT FIGURES LIE? YOU TRYIN' TO BUCK A TREND & TRYIN' TO SCUTTLE THE SENTIMENT OF A NATION?
YEAH!

PHYSICAL THEORY

YOU'RE POGO?! YOU SURE? OUR RESEARCHERS SAID POGO IS A RABBIT! NEWSLIFE'S RESEARCH IS NEVER WRONG, SIR... ARE YOU A RABBIT?
NOPE, I IS A POSSUM.
HOLD IT MAC, HOLD IT.
THIS IS MAD, MAD! RABBIT, NAMED POGO, CLAIMS TO BE AN OPOSSUM... WE RESEARCHED YOU VERY THOROUGHLY... LOOK, ON MY BRIEFING SHEET IT STATES CLEARLY: RABBIT.

LOOK, MAC, CAN YOU MAYBE CROUCH DOWN A LITTLE...? ..ALL I GET IS YOUR FEET, MAC. GET LOWER, LOWER.
YOU'LL GET ME IN TROUBLE WITH THE BRASS, SIR... THEY'RE EXPECTING YOU TO BE A RABBIT.
THAT'S IT MAC, NOW DON'T POSE.. NEWSLIFE WANTS YOU AU NATUREL.
YES, LOOK NATURAL ...RABBITS LIE DOWN AT TIMES, I SUPPOSE?...HOW ABOUT HAVING A CARROT IN YOUR TEETH?

NOW, WHO ARE THESE PEOPLE OVER HERE?
THAT'S CHURCHY LA FEMME, A TURTLE BY TRADE AND HOWLAND OWL A FREE HAND OWL.
READY FOR THE INTERVIEW, CHURCHY?
YUP.
WHO DO YOU THINK WILL BE THE NEXT PRESIDENT OF THE UNITED STATES, MR. LA FEMME? AND NO PEEKIN'!

THAT'S HARD TO SAY, BUT TO COME RIGHT OUT WITH A FEARLESS AN' UNBIASED OPINION, I WOULDN'T HESITATE A MINUTE TO SAY FLATLY THAT IT'S A TOSS-UP!
YOU DON'T S'PECK TO WIN $64,000 CARRYIN' ON LIKE THAT?
NEWSLIFE WANTS ONLY WHAT'S NATURAL.. ..WHAT ARE THEY DOIN'?
THEY'S BEIN' MORE OR LESS NATURAL... OWL'S RUNNIN' A POLITICAL EXPERT PANEL SHOW AN' TURTLE'S THE GUESS EXPERT.

GOOD MORNING SIR, WE'RE FROM THE NATIONAL MAGAZINE, NEWSLIFE, AND OUR RESEARCHERS SHOW THAT POGO IS A RABBIT ... WHAT'S YOUR OPINION?
A RABBIT! HAW HAW HAW! A RABBIT!

AND WHAT WOULD YOU CALL YOURSELF? ..AN OVERGROWN LIZARD?
HOLD IT... HOLD IT.. THIS'LL BE THE BEST SHOT OF THE STORY.
PHAUGH! A OVERGROWED LIZARD! ALBERT ALLIGATOR DON'T TAKE THAT LAYIN' DOWN.

I'M MAD AT BEIN' CALLED A RABBIT BY YOU FELLOWS FROM NEWSLIFE. I'M GOIN' HOME.
I'LL GO TOO... OUR RESEARCHERS CLAIM YOU'RE MIGHTY GOOD WITH A SKILLET, MR. POGO.
HEY.
IT'S AN OUTRAGE LEAVING ME.
HEY POGO... IT'S HOUN'DOG, OL' BEAUREGARD, AND PORKYPINE LOOKIN' FOR YOU.
IT'S HIM.

IS YOU UNDER THERE, POG'?
IT'S ABOUT TIME SOMEBODY GOT THAT THING OFF ME... I TELL YOU IT'S AN OUTRAGE AND...
'TAIN'T HIM.
SORRY TO DISTURB YOU, SIR, WE IS LOOKIN' FOR POGO.
MEBBE HE'S OVER HOME.

THERE HE IS, POOR SOUL, THE WRITER FROM NEWSLIFE, WHAT'S GONE WRITE US UP WITH HIS HEAD STUCK IN A WATERIN' CAN...
HELP.

DON'T YOU WANT TO MEET TWO PERTY GALS, MIZ BEAVER AN' MISS MAM'SELLE HEPZIBAH, THE GENUINE FRENCH LADY SKUNK?

WELL, NO THANK YOU, ACCORDING TO MY RESEARCHERS REPORT HERE I'VE ALREADY MET EVERYBODY IMPORTANT.

WELL, EVERYBODY'S ENTITLED TO HIS OWN OPINION.

PHONK

WELL, IT'LL TAKE MORE THAN A POT ON MY HEAD TO STOP NEWSLIFE! THE NEWS WILL GO THROUGH!

GOOD AFTERNOON, SIR. I'M FROM THE BIG NATIONAL MAGAZINE NEWSLIFE.... THE MAGAZINE THAT THINKS.
THE MAGAZINE THAT THINKS WHAT?
YOU'LL HAVE TO WAIT ON THAT UNTIL I READ THIS DIRECTIVE HERE FROM OUR HEAD OFFICE... ...LET'S SEE..MM.. WE THINK THAT POGO IS.. MM.. THIS DIRECTIVE READS A LITTLE SPOTTY THRU THE SPRINKLER HERE.
UM

HOW CAN YOU DO ANY THINKING FROM INSIDE A WATERING CAN?
IT'S THE READING THAT BOTHERS ME ...THINKING IS SOMETHING I CAN TAKE OR LEAVE ALONE.
MUST BE GETTIN' NEAR SIGHTED... CAN'T SEEM TO GET CLOSE ENOUGH TO THIS DIRECTIVE HERE.
MAYBE YOU'RE TOO CLOSE...HAVE A PIECE OF APPLE?
OUR RESEARCH DEPARTMENT HAS TOLD ME THAT POGO IS A RABBIT... THAT'S AN INTERESTING ANGLE, DO YOU KNOW ANY OTHER BASIC FACTS ABOUT HIM?
UM... YEH.
GOOD!... WHAT ARE THEY?...KEEP THEM BRIEF...I'LL KNOW IMMEDIATELY IF THEY'RE WORTH WHILE ...SHOOT.
FRINSTANCE, I KNOW HE'S A 'POSSUM.
MM.. NO...CAN'T USE THAT... WE'VE GOT STUFF ON WHAT HE IS ALREADY... HE'S A RABBIT... THAT'S GOOD ENOUGH... ANYTHING ELSE?
BUT RABBITS GOT LONG EARS... POGO'S EARS ARE SHORT.
YEAH! WELL, THAT'S A GOOD SIDELIGHT .... IS THAT PRETTY UNUSUAL...? A SHORT-EARED RABBIT? OR WOULD YOU SAY THERE'S A LOT LIKE POGO?

ETHERICAL FIZZ

NOW ASSUME A LOOK OF PRIDE ... AS IF YOU'D REALLY CAUGHT THIS FISH ...
I DID CATCH IT.
H'LO, FRIENDS.
CANDIDATES AREN'T S'POSED TO CATCH THEIR OWN FISH ... BUT, IF YOU DID, LOOK A LITTLE PROUD.
INWARD I IS AGLOW.
MM JUST WHAT I NEEDED.

AS MAINE GO, OH, SO GO KEY LARGO, OTSEGO, FRISCO AND FARGO, PLAYIN' POSSUM ON A POGO STICK AROUND AN' SEE THE SHOW GO!
I GO, YOU GO, WHO GO POGO WIN, LOSE OR TI-KIYONDEROGO FROM DIEGO TO OSWEGO HE GO, SHE GO, WE GO POGO!
GIMME THAT CAMERA!
AAAH... IT'S OUT OF TUNE ANYWAYS.

ALL RIGHT NOW, MR. POGO, THAT'S JUST FINE ... HOLD THE SMILE, SHOW A LITTLE MORE TOOTH ... WAVE MY HAT ... LOOK ELATED ...
UH. HM.
AS MAINE GO, OH SO GO KEY LARGO OTSEGO, FRISCO AN' FARGO PLAYIN' POSSUM ON A POGO. STICK AROUND AN' SEE THE SHOW GO!
WHAT'S YOUR NAME?
PUDDIN' TAME.

GIVE US SOME MORE OF THAT, MR. TAME.
I GO, YOU GO, WHO GO POGO! WIN, LOSE OR TI-KIYONDEROGO! FROM DIEGO TO OSWEGO HE GO, SHE GO, WE GO POGO.
SONG ABOUT THE CANDIDATE HERE, I GUESS HUH?
YUP... 'BOUT POGO.

SO YOU'RE A SONG WRITER? WROTE THE CAMPAIGN SONG, HUH? DO THAT FOR A LIVING?
NO... FOR A LIVING I LOAF.. .. BUT..

IN MY SPARE TIME I'M THE LOWEST COMMON DENOMINATOR... A GUESS EXPERT FOR A TEAM OF POLLSTERS...ANSWER QUESTIONS AND ETCETERA AND SO FORTH...
LET'S GO SEE 'EM.

BEFORE WE DOES, YOU WAS POSIN' POGO AN' HE'S STILL HOLDIN' THAT POSE FOR YOUR CAMERA... WAVIN' YOUR HAT... YOU GONE LEAVE HIM LIKE THAT? AIN'T YOU FERGETTIN' SOMETHIN'?
OH, YEAH.

YEAH... YOU'RE RIGHT. THANKS, CHIEF... I WAS FORGETTIN' THE OLD FEDORA... LET'S GO MEET THEM POLLSTERS.

FAIR THEY GO

NOW, BEFORE WE GO OVER OUR POLLS AGAIN, LET ME HAUL A COUPLE OF BANANAS OUT OF THE REFRIGERATOR AND WE'LL SEE IF THEY'RE RIPE...
RIGHT.
IF WE WANT TO CAPTURE TOP SEAT ON THE CUPOLA FOR POGO WE'VE GOT TO MAKE OUR CAMPAIGN FOOL PROOF.. ..WE MUST KNOCK THE HICCUPS OUT OF THE RECIPE.
EVERY DIAMOND MUST BE 24 KARAT GOLD!
RIGHT! THE PURE, UNDRIVEN HONESTY SHINING IN A LOVELY WOMAN'S EYES MUST GRACE OUR EVERY NUGGET OF THOUGHT. ... IN SHORT, WE MUST TAKE THE BAMBOOZLE OUT OF ANY WHAMMY WE CONJER UP FOR THE PUBLIC.
YOU MEAN WE OUGHT TO BE TRUTHFUL? FRANK? FEARLESS? LOYAL TO OUR TRUST?
YES.. BUT HOW? IT'S SO NEW... THE PUBLIC'S NOT READY.

WHAT WE MUST DO, AND I SPAWN THIS SALMON EGG DOWNSTREAM HOPING IT WILL LEAP UP OVER THE FALLS TO A HAPPY HUNTING GROUND, WE MUST TAKE THE TRUTH BY THE HORNS...
A DILEMMA.

RIGHT! WE'RE STANDING WITH OUR FEET BUTTERED ON A POOL OF BALL BEARINGS. THE TRUTH IS TRICKY... ONE MAN'S TRUTH IS ANOTHER MAN'S COLD BROCCOLI... OUR JOB, CHEF, IS TO MAKE THE TRUTH TASTY.

YES... TASTY TO ALL... ALL THIS OLD LEFTOVERS... POGO IS LOYAL, POGO IS UPSTANDING, POGO IS FRIENDLY... PFAG!
YOU'RE RIGHT! RUMMAGIN' THRU THE ICE BOX FOR STALE STERLING DON'T CUT NO NOTCHES ON THE WATERPISTOL.

WHAT WE NEED... AND YOU BETTER LOOK AT THIS BOMB THRU DARK GLASSES, WE NEED A NEW TRUTH ABOUT POGO... SOMETHIN' WITH A LITTLE JAZZ ON IT.. ..EVEN IF WE HAVE TO MAKE IT UP.

THIS CAMPAIGN TO GET POGO INTO THE TWENTY-FOUR CYLINDER ROCKET NEEDS A NEW AND FLASHY TRUTH...... A BLAST AROUND THE MOON... COLOR... ROMANCE, PAGEANTRY.

HOW ABOUT IF HE WAS TO MARRY SOMEBODY FROM MONACO?
MM.. NOT BAD.. THE JOB'S TAKEN THO'... WHO DO WE KNOW IN LAS VEGAS?

NOBODY WITH MORE'N TWO FEET... UM... HOW ABOUT SARATOGA?
FRANK SULLIVAN! IS HE ROYALTY THOUGH?... IN IRELAND HE WAS KINGS, BUT IN SARATOGA?
IN SARATOGA HE'S ACES... 'TAIN'T LIKE HE WAS A PICTURE CARD, BUT...
NO... NO.. WE NEED SOMEBODY WITH HIS OWN SET OF TAILS AND A CLEAN DICKEY.

I BRUNG YOU A CLEAN TABLECLOTH, HOWLAND... YOU 'BOUT THROUGH WITH THAT ONE? IT STILL GOT CHRISTMAS GRAVY ON IT...
IT COME IN HANDY FOR A COVER IN JANUARY.
MY LAND, LOOK AT THESE NOODLIN' YOU DOOD ON IT.. ALL KINDS OF NOTES... IT SAY: "TWO AND TWO IS...?"... AND.. "POGO GOTTA MARRY ROYALTY BUT WHO...?"
IF YOU IS LOOKIN' FOR ROYALTY YOU GOT A MESS OF IT RIGHT HERE IN THE SWAMP... YOU KNOW WHO MISS MA'M'SELLE HEPZIBAH REALLY IS? SHE'S THE LOST DAUPHIN OF FRANCE!
JUST THINK! MISS MA'M'SELLE IS THE LOST DAUPHIN! DON'T THAT SURPRISE YOU?
SOMEHOW IT DON'T SURPRISE ME HALF AS MUCH AS IT'S GONNA SURPRISE MA'M'SELLE HEPZIBAH.

THINK OF IT! IF MISS MA'M'SELLE HEPZIBAH IS THE LOST DAUPHIN, WE'VE GOT IT MADE.
CINDERELLA BOY MARRIES FRENCH MYSTERY QUEEN! ROYALTY COMES TO CANDIDACY!
WOW!

THIS IS A PEACOCK EGG! WE GOT TO HATCH IT CAREFULLY SO AS NOT TO PULL A ROC. FIRST OF ALL WE SHOULD BUILD A CLEOPATRA'S BARGE FOR MISS MA'M'SELLE.

THEN WE TOW IT OFF SHORE A FEW MILES AND SHE ROWS UP THE POTOMAC! GREETED BY FLAME THROWERS! BARRAGES OF FLOWERS! WE WHISK HER TO THE WHITE HOUSE AND THERE ON THE LAWN IS HER PRINCE! POGO!
BUT HE'S NOT IN THE WHITE HOUSE YET.

COULDN'T WE BORROW IT FOR A COUPLE HOURS... RENT IT FOR THE SUMMER, PERHAPS?
AT LEAST WE COULD USE THE LAWN.

HEIGHDY! I IS BRUNG A PHOTO-GRAFTER FROM NEWSLIFE! HE WANNA KNOW 'BOUT OUR POLLS.
YOU'RE JUST IN TIME! WE GOT TO RUN A QUICK POLL.

WE WANT TO KNOW HOW THE PUBLIC WILL REE-SPOND TO POGO'S MARRIAGE --S'POSE HE MARRIES A FRENCH NOBLEWOMAN?
DO HE SPEAK FRENCH?

NO, BUT HIS WIFE WILL.....
OH THAT'S OKAY THEN...SOMEBODY IN THE FAMILY OUGHT TO TALK TO THIS NOBLE LADY.
AS A GOOD LOW COMMON DENOMINATOR ..HOW WOULD YOU FEEL ABOUT IT?
OH, I COULDN'T MARRY HER ...I DON'T SPEAK NO FRENCH FOR ONE THING AN' S'POSE I ASKS HER TO PASS THE ARTI-CHOKES WHO KNOWS WHAT I'D GET...? BESIDES, I DON'T LIKE ARTICHOKES.
HOLD IT!

WE'VE DECIDED THAT INASMUCH AS MISS MA'M'SELLE IS THE LOST DAUPHIN, THE WHITE HOUSE COULD USE A LITTLE ROYAL BLOOD.
LONG AS YOU DON'T GIT NONE ON THE CARPET, WHY NOT?
WE SEE THIS BONANZA BLOOMING LIKE UNTO A BENGALESE BEGONIA! OUR CANDIDATE MARRIES FRENCH ROYALTY ON THE THRESHOLD OF THE PRESIDENCY!

NOW, AS OUR LOWEST COMMON DENOMINATOR, WHAT IS YOUR ANSWER TO POLL QUESTION NO. 64?...HOW DO YOU FEEL ABOUT POGO MARRYING MISS MA'M'SELLE?
GEE...UH WHY NOT ASK POGO?
HOW WOULD POGO KNOW HOW YOU'D FEEL ABOUT IT?
RIGHT...!
GOSH, I GUESS I GOTTA FACE IT.. DON'T I?

COME COME! CERTAINLY YOU CAN DECIDE A SIMPLE MATTER LIKE MARRIAGE WITHOUT SO MUCH WORRYING.
BUT, BUT--

I WOULDN'T HAVE NO TROUBLE IF IT WAS ME... BUT IF YOU WANTS POGO TO MARRY MISS MAM'SELLE, IT SEEMS YOU OUGHT TO GET HIS OPINION.
WHAT!?

YOU'VE GOT TO REMEMBER THAT US POLL TAKERS GOTTA HAVE A UNBIASED, UNPREJUDICED OPINION.. --POGO'S THOUGHTS ON A SUBJECT CONCERNIN' HIM WOULD BE SUSPECT BY EVERYBODY IN THE COUNTRY.

YOU MEAN IT'S UP TO ME?
THE FUTURE OF THE COUNTRY CAN WELL BE IN YOUR HANDS.

WHAT'S POGO GOTTA GET MARRIED FOR ANYWAYS?
YOU WOULDN'T WANT US TO BE WITHOUT A FIRST LADY?

WHO WOULD WASH POGO'S SHIRTS? WHO WOULD IRON HIS SOCKS..? WHO WOULD COOK HIM UP A MESS OF GREENS? WHO WOULD GET UP IN THE MORNING AN' START THE FIRE?
TRUE! TRUE!

WHO WOULD PUT UP THE FLAG ON FOURTH OF JULY..? WHO WOULD SLOP THE HOGS? WHO WOULD FIX THE RADIO OR VACUUM CLEANER WITH TEETH AND HAIRPINS?
TRUE.
MATTER OF FACT, THERE'S SO MUCH TO DO POGO COULD USE MEBBE TWO OR THREE FIRST LADIES.

SO YOU AGREE.. POGO SHOULD MARRY MA'M'SELLE?
A PUBLIC OFFICE IS A PUBLIC TRUST.
NOW TO PROCESS THE LATEST POLL FIGURES.
FIGGERIN' AGAIN THAT CHURCHY CONSTITUTES THE ENTIRE STUDENT BODY OF THE GRADUATIN' CLASS OF 1930 THAT WOULD MEAN THAT ALL FOLKS OVER 40 IS IN FAVOR ---OR AT LEAST WON'T STAND IN THE WAY UNLESS A MONSOON SPOILS THE CAULIFLOWER FESTIVAL.

WHICH INDICATES THAT FOLKS UNDERBENEATH OF THAT AGE GROUP WILL BE INFLUENCED BY MAJORITY DRIFT FACTORS BROUGHT ABOUT BY MEDIUM HIGH TIDES IN THE LUNAR SOLSTICE WHICH IF MULTI-PLIED BY EXPECTED TAX POTENTIAL WOULD BE --UM--.
QUANTUM HIGH TO THE QUOTIENT PARENTHETIC AND PENULTIMATE CONSEQUENTIALS....THIS IN TURN WHEN SUBTRACTED FROM TAKE-HOME-PAY PRESUPPOSES THE FACT THAT TERRE HAUTE WILL LEAD THE NATIONAL LEAGUE IN BATTING IN 1957!
WELL UH HUM... A MOST UNEXPECTED RESULT!

AND FIE THEY DO

IT'S STRANGE THAT YOU CLAIM TO BE A 'POSSUM, POGO, AND YET YOU SAY YOU'RE AN EXPERT RABBIT ...THAT'S DOUBLE-TALK!
I AIN'T POGO... YOU'RE TALKIN' TO ME NOT HIM... HE AIN'T ME... HE'S HIM! I'M ME!
OH, GO AHEAD, MIZ WOODPECKER.. YOU GOT A APPETITE LIKE A BIRD.
OH, MY.
LET'S GET THAT STRAIGHT... YOU'RE TALKING TO ME AND NOT HIM...RIGHT? WHY AREN'T YOU TALKING TO POGO... ...SORE AT HIM?

HELLO!? HELLO!? WHO AM I TALKIN' TO? SAY THAT AGAIN! SOMEBODY ON YOUR END IS MISQUOTIN' ME...PUT THE EDITOR-IN-CHIEF ON..LET ME TALK TO SOMEBODY IN CHARGE.

THERE'S NO NEED TO SHOUT SIR..THE EDITOR JUST STEPPED OUT, IF YOU'LL LEAVE A NUMBER WE'LL CALL YOU... DON'T CALL US...GOOD DAY!
THEY HUNG UP ON ME.

AS I SEE IT, POGO, YOUR POSITION IN THE CAMPAIGN IS ABOUT HERE...IN OTHER WORDS YOU'RE IN THE MIDDLE OF THE ROAD, RIGHT?
S'POSE HE AIN'T?

YOU GOT TO UNDERSTAND THE WAY POLITICAL LANGUAGE HAS CHANGED...SUPPOSE HE'S LIBERAL? ON THE LEFT SIDE OF THE ROAD AS WE ONCE KNEW IT? OKAY, YOU GOTTA REMEMBER THE ROAD HAS SHIFTED.

WELL! THE NEW ROAD GOES RIGHT THRU HIS OLD POSITION. THEREFORE HE'S MIDDLE OF THE ROAD! GOT IT? NOW SUPPOSE HE USED TO BE RIGHT OF CENTER ... OKAY, THE ROAD GOES THE OTHER WAY FOR THE CONSERVATIVE ... RIGHT?

AND, THE RIGHT SIDE OF THAT OLD ROAD IS THE LEFT SIDE OF THE SAME OLD ROAD GOING THE OTHER WAY, SO YOU FIND WHEN THE ROAD SHIFTS TO THE RIGHT IT GOES THRU THE LEFT SPOT OR ITS OLD RIGHT SPOT MAKING THAT THE MIDDLE OF THE ROAD, TOO ... ANY QUESTIONS?
YES. WHERE DO YOU GET A CROSSTOWN BUS?

AS YOU CAN SEE POLITICAL TERMS HAVE SHIFTED SO THAT THE LIBERAL WAY IS IN THE MIDDLE OF THE ROAD THE ROAD HAVING MOVED TO THE LEFT AND THE CONSERVATIVE WAY LIKEWISE ...

THE ROAD GOING THE OTHER WAY HAS SHIFTED TO THE RIGHT ... SO BOTH POSITIONS NOW OVERLAP EACH OTHER IN THE MIDDLE .... THE WAY THAT'S LEFT IS THE WAY THAT'S RIGHT AND VICE VERSA.
PSST PST.

THAT'S WHY, AS A CANDIDATE, YOU'VE GOT TO BE IN THE MIDDLE ... WHAT OTHER WAY IS THERE?
I'LL TRY, BUN RABBIT.
GO AHEAD, CUT HIM OUT OF THERE .. HE GOTTA EX-CAPE, MIZ WOOD-PECKER.
I HOPE ... BANG BANG BANG BANG ... THAT I'VE .. BANG BANG BANG ... QUOTED YOU CORRECTLY ... BANG BANG AND THANKS, BANG BANG POGO, BANG!

FRIDAY'S FOE

IT'S SIMPLY WONDERFUL! OL' SEMINOLE SAM TOLE ME ALL ABOUT HOW THE WEDDING IS GONNA GO... SHE'LL ROW UP THE POTOMAC FROM A COUPLE MILES OUT AT SEA.

THEN SHE'LL BE GREETED BY THREE HUNDRED CAVALRYMEN IN SPECIALLY DESIGNED UNIFORMS THROWIN' ROSES AN' PLAYIN' ON GOLDEN BUGLES A SIX ACT CANTATA WRITTEN SPECIALLY FOR THE OCCASION...THEN SHE..
WHO?

MISS MA'M'SELLE OF COURSE! THEN A FLIGHT OF IBIS AND EGRETS WILL WHEEL OVERHEAD SPELLING OUT IN LATIN: "UA MAU KE EA O KA AINA I KA PONO" OR "WELCOME TO WASHINGTON"... FLOWERS WILL THEN BE DROPPED ON THE GROOM..AND..
THE GROOM? WHO?

YOU... IN A SPECIAL SELF-DESIGNED UNIFORM ALIVE WITH NEON MEDALS AND A SOUVENIR SWORD SPECIALLY LOANED BY THE GRAND LODGE OF THE..

SEMINOLE SAM SAYS THAT YOU AN' MISS MA'M'SELLE ARE GONNA BE MARRIED SIX TIMES···ONCE FOR THE MORNING PAPERS···ONCE FOR THE AFTERNOON PAPERS···

ONCE FOR RADIO, ONCE FOR THE NEWSREELS, ONCE FOR THE TEEVIES AND ONCE FOR NEWSLIFE, THE NATIONAL MAGAZINE.

IT'S PRACTICALLY A LIFEWORK···UM··IT WON'T DO NO GOOD TO HURRY···
THE WEDDING DAY IS GONE BE A GALA EVENT JUST AFORE ELECTIONS.. NO USE RUNNIN' TO IT··· IT'LL KEEP.
I AIN'T RUNNIN' TO IT··· I'M RUNNIN' AWAY!

HALT! OH, FRIEND OF MY YOUTH, WHAT A SORRY DAY HAS DAWNED UPON US LIKE A BURSTING BOMB!

CONGRATULATIONS···
HUH?

YOU'VE WON HER... PRESUMABLY FAIR AND PRESUMABLY SQUARE! ---SHE WON'T COME BETWEEN US--- MY HEART, A NOBLE DOG'S HEART, IS AN ACHING VOID OF MISERY---- BUT SHE'S YOURS --I'LL SAY NO MORE.
LET'S BE MERRY... LET'S FACE THIS LIKE GENTLEMEN... COME! I HAVE A MANDOLIN FULL OF LEMONADE --- A TOAST, FRIEND--DON'T PROTEST ...I'M WILLING TO FORGET... A TOAST.
BUT, BUT--
HOW COULD HE OF DOOD IT TO HIM.. HOW?

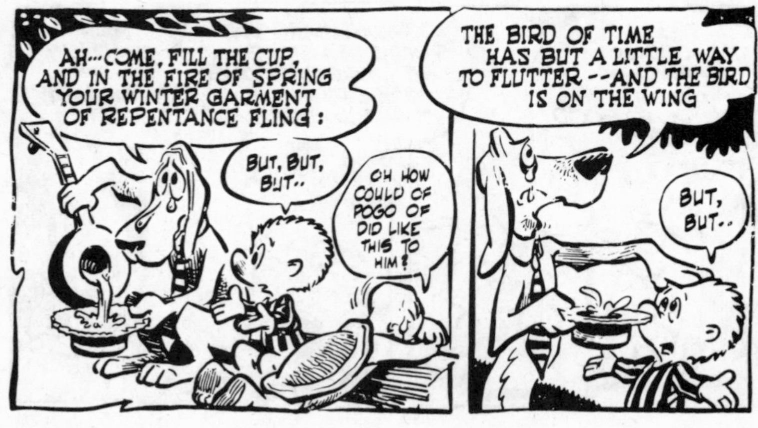
AH...COME, FILL THE CUP, AND IN THE FIRE OF SPRING YOUR WINTER GARMENT OF REPENTANCE FLING:
BUT, BUT, BUT..
OH HOW COULD OF POGO OF DID LIKE THIS TO HIM?
THE BIRD OF TIME HAS BUT A LITTLE WAY TO FLUTTER --AND THE BIRD IS ON THE WING
BUT, BUT..

A JUG OF WINE, A LOAF OF BREAD AND THOU--- BESIDE ME SINGING IN THE WILDERNESS~
OH POGO, HOW COULD YOU OF?
BUT..
AH, MY BELOVED, FILL THE CUP THAT CLEARS TODAY OF PAST REGRETS AND FUTURE FEARS.
HOW COULD YOU OF COULD YOU OF COULD YOU OF, HOW?
B?

A TOAST, MY FRIEND, LONG LIFE ··· HAPPINESS! A BROKEN HEART GROANS --BUT THE BRAVE DOG GOES RESOLUTELY ON!
BUT, BUT--

I'LL SPEAK NO MORE OF WHAT YOUR (GULP) MARRIAGE TO MISS MAM'SELLE IS DOING TO ME ··· I SHALL NOT RECITE THE LIST OF GRIEVOUS WOUNDS ··· IGNORE MY SUFFERING, 'TIS NOTHING.
BUT--
HAVE YOU NO SHAME?

MONEY SAVED··· A PITIABLE PITTANCE··· BUT MINE OWN··· FOR THE LITTLE COTTAGE···· AS YOU ARRIVED, WHEN WORD CAME, I WAS ON MY WAY TO HER HOME ··· A NEW SONG, SLAVED OVER IN THE MIDNIGHT, ON MY LIPS.
BUT--
HOW COULD YOU OF DID THIS TO HIM?

ALL THE MORNING SPENT SQUEEZING LEMONS INTO MY MANDOLIN····LEMONADE, HER FAVORITE, NOW NOTHING BUT A SOGGY MESS IN A SILENT TOMB WHERE ONCE THE SONGBIRD DWELT.
BUT--
STOP BUTTING IN ···IT'S BEAUTIFUL.

I DON'T HOLD THIS AGAINST YOU··· MY SHATTERED DREAMS ARE STILL MINE··· ··ASHES BUT YET WARM··
WULL·· UH· BUT I··

DON'T SPEAK, FRIEND··· WORDS CANNOT STENCH THE FLOW OF A WOUNDED LOVE··· YOU MEAN WELL, BUT YOUR FEEBLE AND CLUMSY ATTEMPTS AT COMFORT ARE BEST LEFT UNSAID.
BUT--

WOW!
IT'S FRIDAY THE THIRTEENTH!

PORKYPINE REPORTING FOR DUTY!
AN' NOT A MINUTE TOO SOON... THESE PEOPLE WILL BEAR WATCHIN'.
A NEW SHIFT.
NO CLUTCH.

NOTHING COULD BE FURTHER FROM THE NOBLE DOG'S HEART THAN TO HURT YOUR FUTURE, DEAR FRIEND. DESPITE THE OUTRAGEOUS FACT THAT YOU HAVE STOLEN MY SWEETHEART.
BUT I AIN'T.
UMF UMF
HENCE, LIKE I SAY, I SHALL APPEAR ON THE TEEVY WITH YOU... TO AID YOUR CHANCES FOR THE PRESIDENSITY -- NOTHING HELPS LIKE A GOOD DOG ACT.

LOOK, WE COME ON IN A BROTHERLY SHOW OF FAWNING FUN AN' GAY, LIGHT LAUGHTER! WEARING FRIGHT HATS AND DOING MAGIC TRICKS...
BUT..
GREAT.
I KNOW A TRICK...HOW TO MAKE A ELEPHANT DISAPPEAR! YOU TAKE A RAW EGG, A HIGH SILK HAT AN' A MOUSE, THEN YOU....
JES' WHAT VOTE IS YOU TRYIN' TO INFLUENCE?

ACTUALLY, LET'S PUT OUR HEARTS INTO OUR TEEVY BITS TOGETHER... CANDIDATE WITH TRUE HEARTED DOG! ...A DEMONSTRATION OF LOYALTY TO OUTROAR THE AURORING BOREALIS!
BUT..
I TAKE IT YOU HAVE NOBODY FOR VICE, YET? (KEEP ME IN MIND)...LOOK, ...YOU ENTER THE SCREEN, AND, IN AN UNPARALLELED PARABOLA OF DEE-VOTION, I LEAP (UTTERING ENDEARMENTS) UPON YOU.

A LITTLE SIDESPLITTING, HEART WARMING HORSE PLAY AND THEN I GIVE THE COMMERCIAL..."HERE FRIENDS, I SAY, (THIS COUNTRY BELIEVES IN DOGS, SO I'LL NOT BE GAINSAID!) "HERE IS THE CANDIDATE WHO IS WILD ABOUT CHILDREN AND OLD LADIES!
"HERE IS THE MAN YOU CAN LOVE... HE IS YUMMY... HE LOOKS AHEAD... HE LOOKS BEHIND... HE WILL FILL HIS CABINET WITH DOGS...HE..."
HEY!

THAT WAS ONLY A REHEARSAL··· WE'LL SHINE UP OUR TEEVY ACT··· THE ELECTRONIC ERA NEEDS A PERSONAL TOUCH··· SOMETHING FOLKSY··· WODDYA SAY?
GOOD BYE!
BOY! HOW DO YOU LIKE THAT? I SHOW HIM HOW TO GET ELECTED IN A CLEAN SWEEP IN EARLY INNINGS AN' HE SAYS "ADIEU!" NOT EVEN ALF WIEDERSTEIN!
UMF.

PERSON'LY I THINK HE'S MADE THE BEST SPEECH OF THE CAMPAIGN.
BUT ALL OF US IS ONLY TRYIN' TO DO HIM A FAVOR··· MAKE HIM PRESIDENT WITH SOMEBODY, SAY LIKE ME, AS VICE.
BUT FIRST YOU IS TRYIN' TO MAKE HIM OVER··· IN YO' OWN IMAGE··· AN' I FIGGER HE DON'T WANT TO BE NO DONKEY ATALL·· REGARDLESS OF PARTY.

A FRIED ADIEU

WULL, I LEFT THE CAT OUTEN THE BAG! I IS ANNOUNCED YOU IS THE LOST DAUPHIN.
YOU HAVE? I AM? WHAT?

THE HEIR TO THE THRONE OF FRANCE! SOMETIMES KNOWED AS ELEAZER WILLIAMS OR J.J. AUDUBON ... ACTUALLY YOU IS LOUIE, THE SEVENTEENTH ... AN' GONNA BE THE FIRST LADY.

YOU MEAN I AM HAVE COME IN SEVENTEENTH AS LOUIE, BUT AS A LADY I AM COME IN FIRST? HOW IS THESE?
SIMPLE ... WHEN YOU WAS LOUIE YOU WAS LOST ... BUT NOW YOU KIN MARRY POGO.
HMMPH .... COULD THEY NO FIND LOUIE. THE LOST DAUPHIN ...? WHY COULDN'T OF POGO OF MARRIED HIM?
BECAUSE! NOT ONLY WAS LOUIE REAL LOST, BUT HE WAS MUCH OLDER .. ... IT WOULD OF BEEN A BAD MISMATCH.

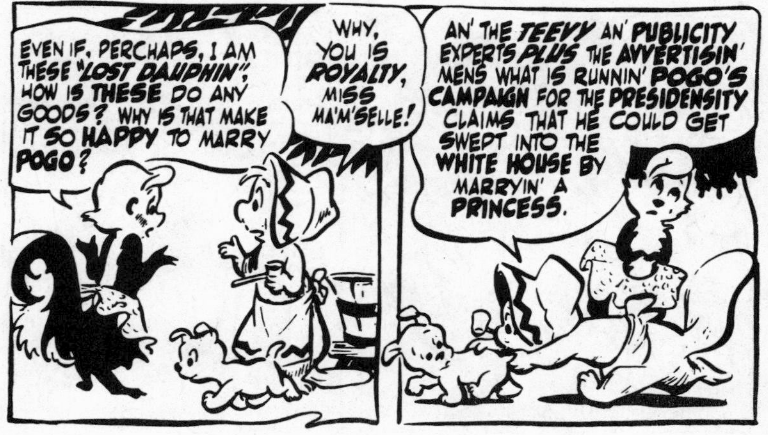
EVEN IF, PERCHAPS, I AM THESE "LOST DAUPHIN", HOW IS THESE DO ANY GOODS? WHY IS THAT MAKE IT SO HAPPY TO MARRY POGO?
WHY, YOU IS ROYALTY, MISS MA'M'SELLE!
AN' THE TEEVY AN' PUBLICITY EXPERTS PLUS THE AVVERTISIN' MENS WHAT IS RUNNIN' POGO'S CAMPAIGN FOR THE PRESIDENSITY CLAIMS THAT HE COULD GET SWEPT INTO THE WHITE HOUSE BY MARRYIN' A PRINCESS.

THE COUNTRY IS ROYALTY-PRONE. THEY IS DECIDED... READY FOR A BIG WEDDIN' ON THE LAWN, WITH 'PLANES SWOOSHIN' AN' DROPPIN' FRUIT AN' FLOWERS... IT'LL AROUSE GREAT SYMPATHY... SPECIALLY IF POGO GITS KLUNKED BY A WATER-MILLION.

SOMETIMES I DO NOT UNNER-STAN' LIFE... FOR INSTANCE, YOU HAVE ALREADY WASHED THOSE PUPS-DOG.
HECK, I AIN'T WASHIN' HIM, HON'! HE HATE BATHIN' SO MUCH THAT HE CHURN UP THE WASH SOMETHIN' FIERCE... BETTER NOR A MACHINE.

I IS DID MY BEST, MR. LAFEMME, BUT I AIN'T BEEN ABLE TO CHOP A HOLE IN THIS WATERIN' CAN, SO'S THIS CRITTUR KIN CLIMB OUT.
'SALL RIGHT MIZ WOOD-PECKER.
WE'RE FROM NEWSLIFE. NOW, I WANT A GOOD, HOMEY SHOT OF YOU, MA'M'SELLE, SHOWIN' WHAT A GOOD COOK YOU ARE.
FOR SUCH I AM DELIGHT ...WHAT I SHALL COOK... FRY EGGS OR STRAWBERRY SHORTCUTS?

DON'T MATTER ... ANYTHING .. .. NEWSLIFE WANTS TO SHOW EVERYTHING'LL BE HUNKY DORY IN THE WHITE HOUSE WHEN YOU'RE POGO'S BRIDE... MIX UP ANY KIND OF GOO.

MMPH... THRU THIS FINDER YOU LOOK LIKE A BIRD, MISS HEPZIBAH, 'COURSE IT GOT DARK SUDDENLY TOO... BUT... MMMM.. WHAT IS THAT DELICIOUS AROMA I SMELL?
BURNING MA'M'SELLE.
PHOO.. AM I TUCKERED.

AT LAST, MISS MA'M'SELLE, SHE IS HAD EASE-NOUGH! ALL THESE SILLY TALKS ABOUT SHE IS BE FIRST LADY TO THESE POGO!

HA! HIM! RUNS FOR THE PRESIDENSE! EHEU! BIG WEDDING! I AM TO ROW IN FROM TWELVE MILES OUT TO SEA! THE LOST DAUPHIN! ROYALTY TO MARRY THE CANDIDATE ON THE WHITE HOUSE LAWN... SOLDIERS, MARINES, SAILORS ALL GIVE THE BIG SALUTE.

WHO HAS TO ROW?! ME, THE BRIDE... AN' THERE IS HE IN SELF DESIGNED UNIFORMS, RED BELT IN BACK, REEP PLEATS IN LAPEL, PING PONG CHAMPION MEDALS ALL OVER LIKE CHRISTMAS TREES.. HA!

I AM DISGUST! OFF I GO INTO THE WILY BLUE YONKERS... FREE! OPEN! ABOVE BOARD, WELL DISGUISED! FAREWELL, SWAMP FRIENDS! OSMOSIS IS CATCHED ALL!

MAN! I IS AT LONG LAST HAD IT... I BEEN TOO EASY... LETTIN' FOLKS TWIST ME ROUN' THEIR LITTLE FINGERS... ... I'LL SHOW 'EM.

THEY THINKS I CAN'T FIGHT BACK! I'LL SHOW 'EM THEY IS TANGLED WITH A RED-BLOODED, TWO-FISTED AMERICAN BOY, WHICH AT HEART I IS, THOUGH I NEVER LETS ON.

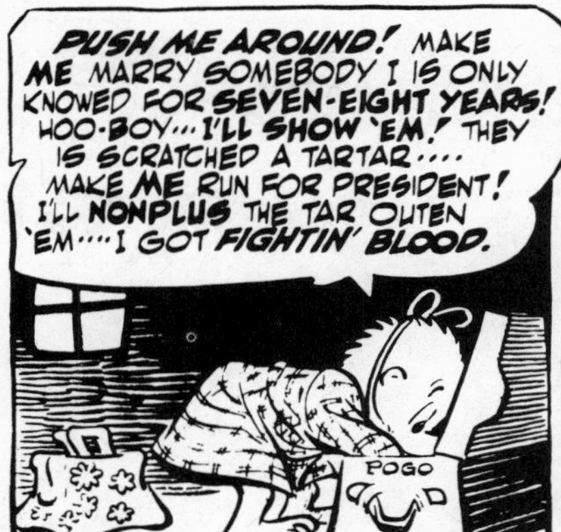
PUSH ME AROUND! MAKE ME MARRY SOMEBODY I IS ONLY KNOWED FOR SEVEN-EIGHT YEARS! HOO-BOY... I'LL SHOW 'EM! THEY IS SCRATCHED A TARTAR.... MAKE ME RUN FOR PRESIDENT! I'LL NONPLUS THE TAR OUTEN 'EM.... I GOT FIGHTIN' BLOOD.
POGO

FOOL AROUN' WITH ME, WILL THEY? I CAN BE TOUGH TOO! I'M RUNNIN' OFF!

MIZ MA'M'SELLE IS DONE RUN OFF!
GOOD BYES

I BETTER HUSTLE OVER AN' TELL POGO...

POGO.. IS YOU IN?.. MA'M'SELLE IS RUN... WHY, YOU IS TOO! LAND ALIVE! I THINK THEY'S EE-LOPED!
GOOD BYE

PORKYPINE IS THE ONLY ONE WHAT'LL KNOW WHAT TO DO ... I'LL RUSH OVER AN' TELL HIM...

PORKY!.... UH, MY LAND... LOOKY AT THE NOTE... THEY IS REALLY ELOPED! ALL THREE OF 'EM!
I IS RUN OFF.. Disgusted

I IS GITTIN' OUT AN' LET ALL THIS BLOW OVER... IT HAS COME TO BE TOO MUCH FER MY GRUMPY LI'L' MIND.

IT'S LIKELY TO HASTEN MY ANNUAL ATTEMPT TO COMMIT SUICIDE, WHICH IS NOW SUCH A CELEBRATED EVENT I'D HATE TO BRING IT OFF EARLY.

IT WOULD DISAPPOINT ALL THOSE FRIENDS AN' FANS WHAT GATHERS FOR THE YEARLY DOIN'S.... AN' ..OF COURSE IF I EVER BRUNG IT OFF FOR REAL...

--IT WOULD DISAPPOINT ME FIT TO KILL.

H'LO THERE, LI'L' OL' MAN MYSTERIOUS-TYPE STRANGER... WHICH WAY YOU GOIN'?

GOOD... YOU AIN'T THE TALKY TYPE... US LI'L' OL' MEN OUGHT TO STICK TOGETHER... I'LL HELP POLE YO' RAFT.

ME, I'M GOIN' OFF TO JOIN THE FOREIGN LEGION ... NEVER GONNA SPEAK TO ANOTHER WOMAN.

EHEU!
GESUNDHEIT.

WHERE IS YOU LI'L' OL' MENS GOIN'? ... GONNA GO IN SEARCH OF ADVENTURE?
YEP, I IS GOIN' TO JOIN UP WITH THE FOREIGN LEGION ... BUT FIRST I GONE LOLL 'ROUND, SINGIN' AN' FISHIN' AN' WRITIN' POETRIES.

GOOD ... I'LL GO 'LONG SEEIN' AS I IS A LI'L' OL' MAN, TOO ... WE KIN HOLLER AN' TELL FUNNY STORIES, GO BAREFOOT, SPIT ATWEEN OUR TEETHS, DON'T NEED TO WASH AN' KIN GO SWIMMIN' WITHOUT NO CLOTHES ON.
BUT I HATE SWIMMING ... I AM HATE IT! EVER SINCE I AM SMALL GIRL ... I MEANS BOY ... I HATE THE SWIMMING! HATE IT!

AHOY, LI'L' OLD STRANGER MENS... IS ANY OF YOU SEED POGO OR MIZ MA'M'SELLE HEPZIBAH OR OL' PORKYPINE...? THEY IS RUNNED OFF AN' IS VANISHED, DEAD OR LOST... ALL US LI'L' CHILLUN TYPE CRITTURS IS BROKE-HEARTED.
ALL NIGHT WE WAILS AN' HOOTS SOMETHIN' WONDERFUL... GRIEVIN' OUR LI'L' CHILE HEARTS OUT.

NOBODY TO GIVE US SPECIAL COOKIES... NOBODY TO TAKE OUR LI'L' SWEET SELFS TO SUNDAY SCHOOL ...NOBODY TO SHOW US HOW TO CATCH FISH.
OH, I IS GLAD PAW LOANED ME THE BORRY OF ONE OF HIS BIG HANKERS.
PASS IT OVER SOON'S YOU'S THRU.
AN' ME NEXT.
SNEEF!

WULL, I GUESS THE BEST US TADS KIN DO TO FORGET 'BOUT THE VANISHMENT OF POGO AN' MISS MA'M'SELLE AND UNCLE PORKY IS TO GO COMMIT SUICIDE BY EATIN' PLENTY OF UNCLE ALBERT'S COOKIN' AT THE FRY HE'S THROWIN' IN MOURNIN' OF THEM THREE.
UNCLE ALBERT IS COOKIN' UP ONE OF MA'M'SELLE'S FAVORITE RECIPES... CHICKEN FOOT. HE PUTTIN' SUGAR IN IT.

IT IS TOUCHING, GENTLEMENS, TO SEE YOU WEEP AND CRY 'BOUT MISS MA'M'SELLE DISAPPEARMENTS.
WULL, I WAS GRIEVIN' 'BOUT DEAR UNCLE PORKY.
LI'L' POGO'S PASSIN' WAS WHAT GIVE ME THE COBBLES.
EHEU! MEN! I GO! IF THESE ALBERT IS PUT SUGAR IN THE CHICKEN FOOTS EVER'BODY WILL DISAPPEAR! BETTER I GO BACK.
SHE AIN'T THE LI'L' OL' MAN I THUNK SHE WAS.

I ADMITS I IS PORKYPINE IN DISGUISE LI'L' OL' MAN, SO GOODBYE ... I UH ..
I COMES CLEAN TOO ... I KIN SMELL THAT FRY FROM HERE.
HOW COULD YOU OF DEE-CEIVED A OL' FRIEND, THAT WAY?

HURRY UP! ALBERT'S THROWIN' A BIG FRY IN HONOR OF POGO AN' PORKY'S DISAPPEARMINT ... AN' IF YOU DON'T HURRY IT'LL BE ALL ATE .... AN' ... OH, ... HEIGHDY!
D'YOU FIGGER THIS IS FAIR TO ALL ... YOU GOIN' TO YOU OWN WAKE, SO TO SPEAK?
WHO IS GOT BETTER LAST RIGHTS?

BY JING, YOU FOLKS GOT BACK JES' IN TIME --- NEXT TIME US MOURNS YOU, POGO, WITH A FRY, LEAVE THE BUTTER AN' EGGS WHERE WE KIN FIND 'EM.
IF YOU IS DOIN' THE COOKIN' MEBBE US BETTER LEAVE AGAIN.
YOU'VE UPSET ALL MY MUSICAL ARRANGEMENTS ---I HAD A LOT OF REAL COOL LUGUBRIOUS STUFF READY.

"AS MAINE GO, O, SO GO KEY LARGO, OTSEGO, FRISCO AN' FARGO, PLAYIN' POSSUM ON A POGO STICK AROUND AN' SEE THE SHOW GO."
HOW ABOUT A SHORT BURST OF OLD DOG TRAY?
I STILL SAY, "WHO'S FOR VICE?"
In an election year nobody will come right out and say ~~
NOBODY? HE MEANS YOU.

AND SO INTO THE NIGHT ...

POGO EXTRA

(ELECTION SPECIAL)

THE ELECTION *of 1960 was one of the closest in recent years, with John F. Kennedy narrowly winning over Richard M. Nixon. At first the choice in the Okefenokee seemed a foregone conclusion. The professional politicians, P. T. Bridgeport, Tammananny, Congersman Frog and Seminole Sam, agreed with top local leaders that Fremount the boy bug was to be The Man Who Ace researchers of* Newslife *agreed, as did nose-feelers and pulse-counters.*

But there is no such thing as certainty in politics. Soon there were character assassinations, attempted cover-ups and libelous leakages.

In examining the backside of political campaigning, Kelly is more informative than the double-domed investigative reporters, and a whole lot funnier.

Furthermore, no matter how fraught with skulduggery and pettifoggery things may get when the Okefenokee swamps itself in politics, there is always a happy ending.

Maybe human beans will get the knack of it some day. After all, the critters have been at it a few centuries longer.

A SHOO IN TIME IS JES' FINE

MORE I THINK OF IT, THE BETTER I LIKES THE IDEA OF LI'L' OL' FREMOUNT RUNNIN' FOR PRESIDENT.
IT'S A BIG JOB.
JES' FINE

WELL, IT'S A BIG COUNTRY... FREMOUNT WOULD HAFTA LEARN FAST.
HE LEARNT TO SET DOWN REAL FAST AN' HE LEARNT HOW TO SAY, "JES' FINE" IN HAR'LY NO TIME... LOOKIT HIM GO!
JES' FINE JES' FINE JES FINE

I B'LEEVES HE COULD BE A REAL GOOD PRESIDENT... HOW 'BOUT YOU?
I B'LEEVES! AN' HOW 'BOUT YOU, FREMOUNT? WHAT KINDA PRESIDENT WOULD YOU BE?
JES' FINE JES' FINE JES' FINE...

LAND! LAND! WHAT MORE YOU WANTS? HE GETS A HUNDERD POOR CENT IN THE POLL.
NOT EVEN THEM OTHERS, ROCKERFELLA AN' ALL, GOT THAT KINDA SUPPORT.
JES' FINE

AFTER TAKIN' A POLL OF US THREE IT CERT'LY IS SIGNIFICANT THAT LI'L' FREMOUNT IS THE ALL-OUT CHOICE FOR PRESIDENT.
NONE OF US AIN'T EVEN UNDECIDED.
JES' FINE

TRUE! WE AIN'T GOT NOBODY WHAT "DON'T KNOW" OR "CAN'T TELL" OR "FEEL IT'S TOO EARLY" OR "DON'T GIVE A GOOD..."
GLORY, YES! AN' NO OTHER CANDIDATE EVEN GOT A MENTION.

YOU THINK HE'S A SHOO-IN?
YEP... EVEN LI'L OL' FREMOUNT IS IN FAVOR OF FREMOUNT.
JES' FINE

MY LAND! THAT DOES IT THEN... HE'S THE FIRST CANDIDATE TO COME OUT FLAT-FOOTED FOR HIS OWN SELF!
JES'
FINE!

WELL! MIZ WEEVIL AN' MIZ BEETLE WITH LI'L FREMOUNT, THE BOY BUG.
PERTY SOON IT'LL BE HIS EXCELLENCY, PRESIDENT FREMOUNT.
JES' FINE

JES' FINE! I MEAN, PUT IT THERE...! YOU GONNA BE PRESIDENT OF YOUR CHEERFUL CHARLIE GROUP, SON?
NOPE, HE'S GONNA BE PRES. OF THE U.S. AND A.
JES' FINE

PRESIDENT OF THE U.S. AND A? AIN'T HE KINDA SMALL FER THAT?
OH.. SIZE DON'T COUNT.
GLORY, NO! IT'S WHAT YOU GOT UP HERE.

THAT'S WHAT I MEAN... DON'T YOU THINK HE OUGHTA BREAK IN ON A SMALLER JOB? WHY DON'T HE RUN FOR PRESIDENT OF RHODE ISLAND?
AND LEAVE THE OTHER 49 STATES IN THE LURCH?!
THAT'D BE TEMPTING PROVIDENCE.

NO TEETH, ALL JAW

SO THAT'S OL' FREMOUNT? HE'S GONNA RUN FOR THE PRESIDENTISTRY?
YEP... HE'S 'WAY AHEAD IN THE OPINION POLLS.
JES' FINE

JES' ONLY HIM, HIS MA AN' HIS AUNT SO FAR IS VOTED FOR HIM, THO'.
A REAL SHOW OF STRENGTH... THEM IS GRASS ROOTS FOLK.. THEY'S THE ENTIRE POPULATION OF FORT MUDGE.
SMILE FOR THE MAN, FREMOUNT.

THAT'S A CLEAR-CUT TREND...
HE GOT CHARM, OL' FREMOUNT DO...
IS HE SMILIN'?

MEBBE HE GOT CHARM, BUT HE AIN'T GOT HAR'LY ANY TEETH... HOW CAN YOU RUN FOR OFFICE WITHOUT A FULL HEAD OF TEETH?
JES' FINE

HOW CAN A BUG RUN FOR THE PRESIDENTISTRY? THIS ONE AIN'T EVEN GOT TEETH.
BUT THE OPINION POLLS PICK HIM.
WHAT'S HE NEED TEETH FOR?
JES' FINE

WITHOUT TEETH NOBODY CAN EVEN GET ELECTED DOGCATCHER.
YOU IS JUS' DISCRIMINATIN'.
HE GOT CHARM, AIN'T HE?
JES' FINE

THE RETURN OF THE BIG BAMBOOZLUM

Chateau de la Pompe, '59, A MOST ADMIRABLE YEAR, mon vieux-- IT WILL go Excellently with The FILLET
WITH WHAT?

With the FILLET!! A MOUTH~Watering CONCOCTION of purest JOY Serene

THAT LOOKED LIKE A HOT DOG 'TIL YOU SPOKE.. AND THE BOTTLE GOT NOTHIN' BUT WATER IN IT.
ONE must use the IMAGINATION OR ONE WILL STARVE, M'Boy!

WELL, ONE COULD START DREAMIN' UP A CLEAR HAVANA RIGHT NOW, THEN... 'CAUSE I'M SMOKIN' THE LAST BUTT.

LAND, FREMOUNT! WHY'S PORKY CLAIM YOU GOTTA HAVE TEETH JES' TO BE PRESIDENT?
JES' FINE

HOWDY, GENTLEMEN, YOU IS LOOKIN' AT THE NEXT PRESIDENT OF THE U.S. AND A.
Zounds! A female CHIEF EXEC!!

OH, HE AIN'T NO GIRL... HE'S A BOY.. DON'T YOU RECOGNIZE HIM? IT'S OL' FREMOUNT.
Recognize him?? I can hardly SEE HIM.

GADZOOKS! The FIRST Insect to run for Office! A NATURAL WONDER!
I KNOW... IT SORT OF SETS YOUR HAIR ON EDGE.. DON'T IT?

IMAGINE!! The First BUG to run for the Presidensity A NATURAL PHEE-NOME-MEENIA!
PHEE-NOME-MEENIA?
WHAT'S THAT?
JES' FINE

Meaning: Phenomena! In terms of The ROAD: We are with IT!

WITH WHAT? MAYBE I'M OLD IN THE HEAD-BONE BUT HOW CAN YOU GO FOR A PRESIDENT AS SMALL AS HIM?

AS SMALL as HIM? Why, my dear sir, My Dear Friend! Tremore, the boy Insect, WILL BE THE BIGGEST thing to ever hit the White House
WHAT THEY BEEN THROWIN' UP TO NOW, THEN?
Y'MEAN FREMOUNT, THE BOY INSECK.
JES' FINE

What a Sterling OPPORTUNITY for → YOU, ! My Dear Lady !
YEP. YOU'RE RIGHT, MR. BRIDGEPORT... HAVIN' A CHILE OF YOURS BE PRESIDENT AIN'T TO BE SNEERED ABOUT.
JES' FINE

LOVELY, Naturally, but it happens that I, myself, And MY COLLEAGUE ARE AT ⇒ LIBERTY!!
YOU MEAN YOU TWO ESCAPED FROM SOME PLACE?

NO, HE MEANS WE'RE OUT OF WORK AND COULD USE A SQUARE MEAL TO MATCH OUR HEADS.
TAMMANNANY!
UM?

It is My PROPOSAL, DEAR Lady that WE be engaged to BALLYHOO young TRIPOD INTO OFFICE.
FREMOUNT, Y'MEAN? WHY NOT DEPEND ON PLAIN VOTES?
ONLY AS A LAST RESORT, MA'M.

Take a few Notes: To ALL Papers, PERIODICALS AND FAMILY JOURNALS ★★★ STOP PRESS!
HOW ABOUT THE A.P.?

MAKE OVER PAGE ONE ☆☆ NEW LEAD STORY:
EXTRA P. T. BRIDGEPORT, BELOVED LEADER, STUNS NATION!
CONGRESS HASTILY ADJOURNS
NOW, PHOTO of P.T. -- mm WHAT DO WE HAVE?

There, that SHOULD DO IT I've gained a few pounds but, HO-HO...
HO HO, YOURSELF. THAT'S MARY BALL'S SON, G. WASHINGTON..AN' ON A SINGLE... WHERE'D YOU GET ONE?

WASHINGTON? I'VE SAVED THIS THINKING IT WAS ME WHAT do I look like, then?
A CHUMP... SHALL I MAKE OVER PAGE ONE AGAIN OR SHALL WE RUN A SNOW PICTURE?

¿ HOW CAN WE ISSUE a PRESS !!! RELEASE !!! WITHOUT A Picture of ME?
HOW ABOUT A SHOT OF THE LITTLE CANDIDATE THERE?

NO, no.. it's a little early for that... HERE is A Photo of me as a Youth!! It will appeal to the Younger Voter.

Striking, eh what?
HOW YOUNG DOES THAT VOTER HAVE TO BE? THIS IS A BABY PICTURE... A BALD BEAR! BALD ALL OVER!

My Dear Mother thought it had Charm!
I DUNNO ...IT'S LIKELY TO BRING UP THE WHOLE SUBJECT OF BIRTH CONTROL AGAIN...

SO LI'L QUEE OR NOT TO BE

WHAT ASTONISHIN' EVER-LOVIN', BLUE-EYED NEWS!

A INSECT, FREMOUNT, THE BOY BUG, IS GONNA RUN FOR THE PRESIDENTISTRY.

IT'LL TAKE THE MOXIE OUT OF POLITICS... WHEN THE OPPOSITION CALLS OUR MAN A BEETLE BRAIN IT'LL BE A COMPLIMENT!

THE AIR FORCE WILL BE NOTHIN' BUT BUTTERFLIES, A SQUADRON OF AMOEBAE OUR NAVY, THE ARMY WILL BE ANTS AND THE PENTAGON FULL OF BUNGLE BEES.
IT GIVES ONE A CASE OF THE D.D.T.'S.

WHAT DO YOU THINK ABOUT A INSECT IN THE WHITE HOUSE?
I WOULDN'T THINK OF IT AT ALL! I'D CALL THE MILITIA!

I'D ROLL THE CANNON UP TO THE DOOR... BLAM! I'D LET HIM HAVE IT... THEN, IN WE'D GO! BAYONETS AT THE READY!

WAIT! WAIT! IS THAT ANY WAY TO TREAT THE PRESIDENT?
THEN I'D GROSP HIM... AN' I'D BANG HIM.. THEN.. HUH, WHAT? THIS INSECT IS THE PRESIDENT?

SURE .. A DULY ELECTED CHIEF.. AN' YOU CARRIES ON LIKE THAT!
WHICH PARTY? AFORE I LETS GO THE RASCAL?

USUALLY, IN A PRESIDENTAL YEAR, YOU CAN VOTE WITH CONFIDENCE.

ONE OR ANOTHER OF THE OLD RELIABLE PARTIES BRINGS UP A NAME BRAND CANDIDATE... WHOLESOME, DEPENDABLE... A HOUSEHOLD WORD TYPE OF FELLOW...

A KITCHEN-TESTED CHAP... HOME-TRIED IN THE LABORATORIES OF PUBLIC ACCEPTANCE... BUT THIS TIME THE EARLY POLLS SAY FREMOUNT, THE BOY BUG, SHOULD RUN!

I TELL YOU, IT'S ENOUGH TO MAKE A MAN THINK BEFORE HE VOTES...
DON'T GO FLYIN' OFF THE HANDLE, NOW.

I DON'T MEAN TO CARP... NOT PERSON'LY, BUT WHY RUN A BUG FOR PRESIDENT?
THE POLL SAID HE WAS MOST POPULAR.

NOT WITH ME! NOBODY NEVER ASKED ME... 'F ANYBODY DID I'D OF SAID SOMETHIN' SHORT AN' SHARP.. I'D OF GIVE 'EM SHORT SHRIFT... I'D OF SAID, LEMME THINK IT OVER.
BUT...

THE SAMPLE POLL SHOWED 100% OF THE RESIDENTS OF FORT MUDGE WAS FOR FREMOUNT... THEY ASKED HIS AUNTIE... THEY ASKED HIS MA AND THEY ASKED HIM.
WHAT ABOUT EVERY-BODY ELSE?

THERE WASN'T NO EVERYBODY ELSE... 'CEPT THEM WHAT WAS IN JAIL AND/OR DEAD.
SINCE WHEN IS IT A CRIME TO BE DEAD?

IN MY TIME A WHOLE CEMETERYFUL OF CONSTITUENTS COULD SWEEP YOU INTO OFFICE.
IT'S NO CRIME TO BE DEAD BUT YOU GOT TO LOOK AT LEAST A LI'L ALIVE IN CASE THERE'S A BUZZARD IN THE FAMILY.

THE TOMBSTONE VOTE IS DEAD... MORALITY ALTERS.. VALUES CHANGE... YESTERDAY'S GARBAGE IS TODAY'S BOUQUET.
OOG

THAT'S THE TROUBLE, NOTHIN'S PERMANENT.. ALL THESE PEOPLE CONFESSIN' AN' BEIN' CAUGHT.. THERE'S INSTABILITY IN EVERY THIN'... WHERE'S THE OLD VIRTUES?

YER RIGHT... THERE WAS A DAY WHEN A CROOK DIN'T GET CAUGHT AN' DIN'T CONFESS... YOU COULD DEPEND ON HIM TO GO ON BEIN' CROOKED ... BUT NOW? HAH!
SURE, YOU DON'T KNOW WHERE YOU ARE...

WELL, IF IT AIN'T ME OLD PAL, CHUM AND BOOSLUM BUDDY, HOWLAND OWL, THE NATURAL WIT... YOU HEAR US BUGS GONNA ELECT A PRESIDENT?
I IS CURRENTLY PONDERIN' THAT NEWS, MR. WILLOW, THE WASP.

IT'S ABOUT TIME US WASPS, MOTHS, CENTERPEAS, CRAWDADS, SCORPOLINS, VARMINTS, ANTS, CRINKETS, GRASSHOPPLES AN' CATERPIGGLES GOT INTO POLITICS.
BUT YOU HAD A CANDIDATE LAST TWO TIMES.

WHAT?! THAT TWO-TIME LOSER? EVEN J. DEMPSEY NEVER GOT A THIRD CHANCE AND POGO AIN'T ACTUAL A HEAVYWEIGHT.
HE OUT-WEIGHS YOUR MAN, OL' FREMOUNT, THE BOY BUG.

FREMOUNT DON'T LOOK TO ME LIKE HE CAN RUN FOR THE SCHOOL BUS.
THAT SHOWS HIS POLITIWOCKLE SAVVY... A CANDIDATE AIN'T SUPPOSED TO LOOK LIKE HE CAN RUN.

AWASH WITH LOVE

I SUPPOSE YOU KNOW THAT MAN'S BEST FRIEND, THE EVER TRUE DOG, IS A GREAT ONE TO GO WITH CANDIDATES?
WELL, FREMOUNT AIN'T NEVER HAD NO DOG.
JES' FINE

MOST DOGS WE'S HEARD OF IS ALWAYS BEEN OLDER'N HIM AN' A LI'L' BIGGER.
AGE IS WISDOM.. LOOK! GET THE PICTURE.
JES' FINE

THE ... SLURP ... T.V. AUDIENCE ... SLURP ... NEWS READERS ... SLURP ... ARE REASSURED WHEN THEY SEE A CANDIDATE WITH A ... SLURP ... AFFECTIONATE DOG.
STOP LICKIN' HIM! HE'S GONE!

ACK! KAFF!
A MIS ... KOFF ... STAKE!
FREMOUNT! SPEAK TO ME!
JES' FINE

YOU MIGHT HAVE DROWNT HIM.
HE'D OF HAD TO GO DOWN FOR THE THIRD TIME ... AN' FOR ME, ONCE WAS ENOUGH.

TWO FOR THE SEE-GAR

LOOK UNDER "L" IN THE FILE THERE... SEE IF YOU GOT A **LIGHT** FOR ME.
NOPE, **MR. CONGERSMAN,** ALL I GOT IS ***"LUNCH," "LIVERWURST"*** AND ***"LICORICE."***

LOOK UNDER **"M"** THEN, FOR ***MATCH.***
NOPE... NOTHIN' THERE BUT **"MONEY"**... A FIVE SPOT.. **MY PAY.**

THIS IS **MIGHTY** SLOPPY FEDERAL FILING, SECRETARY... LET'S HAVE THE FIVE.
MY ***PAY?***

OH, THAT'S **OKAY**... IT'LL DO... WHAT'S THIS **FREMOUNT, THE CANDIDATE,** LOOK LIKE?
WELL, HE'S **HARD** TO SEE... *GOSH, WISH **I** COULD AFFORD FIVE-DOLLAR BILLS TO LIGHT **MY** SEEGAR.*

WELL, SECRETARY, IT MIGHT DO SOME **GOOD** TO WALK **OVER** AND **VIEW** THE CANDIDATE.
LIKE I SAY, HE'S **HARD** TO **SEE,** MISTER **CONGERSMAN.**

SIZE HAS GOT **NOTHIN'** TO DO WITH IT... LOOK AT **STEPHEN A. DOUGLAS.**
YEH, BUT **HE** NEVER GOT ELECTED PRESIDENT.

HE DIDN'T? SAY, THAT FIVE SPOT OF YOURS GAVE A MIGHTY POOR LIGHT... GOT ANOTHER?
THEN YOU'LL HAFTA PAY ME IN ADVANCE... I GAVE YOU THIS WEEK'S PAY.

OF COURSE, IT'LL HAVE TO BE AN ADVANCE... YOU DON'T EXPECT ME TO PAY YOU TWICE A DAY?
DO I MAKE OUT A I.O.U. FROM ME TO YOU OR FROM YOU TO ME?

I DON'T BELIEVE WE EVER HAD A PRESIDENT FROM THIS DISTRICT, EH, SECRETARY?
NOPE.. AN' IT'LL MAKE YOU TOP FROG IN A BIG PUDDLE MR. CONGERSMAN.
JES' FINE

WHERE'S THIS FREMOUNT LIVE...? (GO 'WAY, BOY; STOP YOUR STARIN'.)
MM... LESSEE..
JES' FINE

VAMOOSE! SCAT! BEGONE!
HEY! THAT'S THE CANDIDATE! FREMOUNT HISSELF!
JES' FINE

WELL! WELL! WELL! HELLO, THERE! HOW DO YOU DO, SIR.... IT CERTAINLY IS A PLEASURE TO SEE YOU LOOKING SO FIT... YES, INDEED!

SECOND, THIRD AND FORTH-RIGHT

YESSIR, MR. CONGERSMAN, FREMOUNT IS BEEN NAMED BY A WHOPPIN' POLL ··· HE'S THE PEOPLE'S NUMBER ONE CHOICE.
PUT IT THERE, SIR.

ANYBODY THAT GETS THE MAJORITY SHARE OF THE VOTE IS "A" NUMBER ONE WITH ME, TOO! I'M WITH THE PEOPLE ·· HAW! HAW! HAW!
CAREFUL, HE JES' HAD HIS DINNER.

HOW'D THE VOTE BREAK DOWN, MIZ BEETLE?
WELL, ON ONE SIDE THERE WAS ·· UM ·· THREE.
HAW! HAW! A REAL SKUNKIN'... AND WHAT WAS YOUR WINNING VOTE?

THAT WAS IT... T·H·E·R· DOUBLE· E... THREE!
YOU MEAN LIKE COMES BETWEEN TWO AND FOUR?

IT SEEM TO ME, MR. CONGERSMAN, THAT OL' **FREMOUNT** GOT MORE VOTES PLEDGED TO HIM THAN **ANYBODY.**
TRUE, TRUE.. HOW DO **YOU** FEEL ABOUT THE RACE, SIR?
JES' FINE

NOTHING I LIKE BETTER'N **CONFIDENCE**... WHAT DO YOU THINK OF THE **PARTY PROGRAM**, SIR?
JES' FINE

AND WHAT DO YOU THINK OUR CHANCES ARE TO **SWEEP** YOU INTO **OFFICE**, SIR?
JES' FINE

Y'KNOW, WHAT **I** LIKE ABOUT THE CANDIDATE IS HIS **FORTH-RIGHT**, CLEAR-CUT, FEARLESS, CONSISTENT, **NO-NONSENSE ABILITY** TO GIVE A CONCISE ANSWER TO THE **LEADING ISSUES** OF THE DAY...
OH, ***ME.*** TOO.
JES' FINE

H'LO, MIZ BEETLE, I COME OVER TO VIEW THE **CANDIDATE.**
H'LO, WILLOW, THE WASP.
FREMOUNT, WHAT DO YOU THINK OF **PARITY**?
JES' FINE

HOW ABOUT **EQUALITY, FRATERNITY, JUSTICE**? HOW DO YOU FEEL ABOUT **THOSE** THINGS?
HE LOOKS JUST AS ***NATURAL.***
JES' FINE

HOW ABOUT LOW PRICES, HIGH PAY, PEACE ... YOU GOT AN OPINION THERE? HOW DO YOU LIKE THEM?
WAS HE SICK LONG?
SICK? HE AIN'T SICK.
JES' FINE

HE AGREES WITH EVER'THING ... DOES EVER'THING AGREE WITH HIM?
JES' ONLY RADISHES AND THE TEEVEE DON'T... THEY GIVES HIM THE COLD ROBBIES.
LOW TAXES?
JES' FINE

WELL, MR. CONGERSMAN! SO THAT'S THE BUG US WASPS, CRINKETS, CATERPIGGLES, BUSTERFLIES AN' GRASSHOPPLES IS GONNA ELECT TO THE WHITE HOUSE!
FREMOUNT HIMSELF, MR. WASP.
JES' FINE

SEEM LIKE HE DON'T SAY NOTHIN' MUCH ... MIND IF I ASK HIM A QUESTION? HOW DO YOU FEEL 'BOUT A BIG FAT PENSION FOR BEAT-UP WASPS, MR. CANDIDATE?
JES' FINE

I GOTTA ADMIT HE COME RIGHT OUT ... DIRECT! CLEAR! NOT AFRAID TO RISK HURTIN' MY TENDER WASP FEELIN'S!
HE'S OUR BOY! US BUGS HAVE TO STICK TOGETHER ... HAVE A SEEGAR? NO? WELL, GOOD LUCK!
JES' FINE

HE'S QUICK ON THE DRAW WITH A SEEGAR.. I DIN'T KNOW THAT FROGS WAS INSECKS.
AT HEART MAYBE. AT HEART.
JES' FINE

THE UNCLEAR ISSUE

WELL, TA TA!
HOW EMBARRASSING! HIM SITTIN' THERE LISTENING TO US... BOLD AS BRASS.

BEING A PUBLIC SERVANT HAS ITS DOOM AND DISMAY, SECRETARY, ITS WOUNDS AND ITS WASTES... GIVE ME A LIGHT LIKE A GOOD FELLOW.
YES'R

YOUR FEDERAL FILING SYSTEM IS A SHODDY MAKESHIFT... QUICKLY! LOOK UNDER "M" FOR A MATCH.
LAST WEEK ALL'S WE FOUND UNDER "M" WAS "MONEY"... MY PAY! AN' YOU USED THAT FOR A LIGHT BUT THIS WEEK...

COME, COME... I'M A BUSY MAN.
BUT THIS WEEK I MADE SURE MY MONEY AIN'T UNDER "M"... OOP! NEITHER IS A MATCH! WELL, I'LL LOOK UNDER "L" FOR LIGHT... OOG... NO MATCH.. BUT...

I FILED IT UNDER "L" FOR LOOT...
SOMEDAY YOU'LL BE ABLE TO LIGHT YOUR SEEGARS WITH FIVE-DOLLAR BILLS.
5$

WE'VE GOT TO LIGHT A **FIRE** UNDER THIS CAMPAIGN OF OL' FREMOUNT FOR THE **PRESIDENSITY.**
IF WE ONLY HAD A **MATCH.**

THIS BOY HAS GOTTA HAVE A **PROGRAM** ... HE'S GOTTA COME OUT **FOR** SOMETHING ... BE ***AGAINST*** SOMETHING ... PUT SOME ***TEETH*** IN THE CAMPAIGN.
HE COULD COME OUT **AGAINST** THE **BENGAL TIGER.**

THAT'S **OLD HAT** ... WE NEED A **NEW TWIST.**
S'POSE HE COMES OUT ***FOR*** THE BENGAL TIGER?

YOU'RE SO SQUARE YOU'RE **CUBED.**
WELL, IT'S ONE WAY TO GET ***TEETH*** INTO THE CAMPAIGN. **FREMOUNT** AIN'T GOT NONE.

AH, WHAT IS SHARPER THAN A SERPENT'S TOOTH?
A FANGLESS CHILD?

STOP PRESS MAKEOVER

SO FAR THE ONLY BULLETIN YOU'VE RELEASED TO THE PRESS WAS A WEATHER REPORT AND THAT WAS WRONG...
ONE does not expect 100% PERFECTION ALL the TIME.

FREMOUNT, THE BOY BUG, WILL BE A MUMMIFIED RELIC BEFORE YOU PUT OUT A STORY ON HIM ... HOW ABOUT NAMIN' HIM THE CANDIDATE TODAY?

Let's see-- 10¢
FINAL P. T. BRIDGEPORT NAMES--UM--UH-- WHAT'S'IS NAME OH-- MM--??
BRIDGEPORT CERTAIN OF VICTORY IN

FREMOUNT!
Oh, yes
415 SHOPPING DAYS TILL XMAS
P. T. BRIDGEPORT PICKS FLEAMUT
BELOVED LEADER NAMES UNKNOWN
CONFIDENCE RETURNS TO NATION'S CAPITAL

YOU'RE HAVIN' SO MUCH TROUBLE REMEMBERIN' THE CANDIDATE'S NAME, WE'LL NEVER GET OUT A PRESS RELEASE.
POLITICS is a TRICKY GAME!!

FREMOUNT'S NAME CAN BE REMEMBERED THUS: F IS FOR FELIX; R FOR RUDOLPH; E FOR EMMETT; M FOR MOE; O FOR OTHO; U FOR ULRIC; N FOR NEMO AND T FOR TIPPECANOE...ALTOGETHER THEY STAND FOR FREMOUNT.
RIGHT!

Felix, Rudolph, EMMETT, MOE, OTHO, ULRIC, NEMO AND TIPPECANOE! REMEMBER them NAMES!
NOW YOU'RE COOKIN'.

EVERY LAST Mother's Son OF THEM IS FOR FURBUNCH the PEOPLE'S CHOICE

WELL! WELL! I UNDERSTAND YOU BOYS ARE WITH THE TEAM! DOING PUBLICITY! PUT IT THERE!
DID YOU HEAR A VOICE, Tammannanny?
THOUGHT SO... DON'T SEE ANY-BODY...

DOWN HERE!

THOUGHT YOU BOYS COULD PUT OUT A STORY THAT ME, THE CONGERSMAN HERE, IS THROWIN' MY WEIGHT IN BACK OF OL' FREMOUNT.
YOUR Weight? WELL...
FLASH FILLER: ETAOIN SHRDLU PLS: PG. 55
CONGERSMAN BOARDS CANDIDATE FRUITBIN'S VICTORY BANDWAGON
HELP WANT
DISHWASHER
FROG SAYS HE'LL THROW WEIGHT BEHIND FLYBITE
P.T. BRIDGEPORT: "NO COMMENT"
FORT MUDGE FEB
HOW MUCH DOES HE WEIGH? WITH THE CIGAR?

NEW BORN LEADER

I ADMIRES OL' FREMOUNT TREE-MOUNDLESSLY... BUT DO HE EVER SAY ANYTHING 'CEPT "JES' FINE"?
THAT'S A PLENTY.
JES' FINE

BUT IF HE'S GONE RUN FER THE PRES-IDENSITY HE GOTTA SAY MORE'N "JES' FINE"..
WHY?

S'POSE A NATIONAL CATASTROPHE GETS A TWO-THIRDS MAJORITY... AN' FOLKS WANTS TO KNOW: HOW'S WE DOIN'?
WELL, HE COULD SAY, "JES' FINE."
JES'

FIFTY EVER-LOVIN' PERCENT OF THE TIME HE MIGHT BE RIGHT.... BABE RUTH DIDN'T DO NO BETTER.
FINE

I BEEN TALKIN' TO MIZ BEETLE 'BOUT FREMOUNT. SHE CLAIM IT'D BE OKAY FOR HIM TO SAY "JES' FINE," AS PRESIDENT.
UNLESS HE GOTTA HOLLER FER HELP HE'S SAFE.

YEH, BUT SHE SAY EVEN IF HE'S GOTTA ANSWER QUESTIONS, HALF THE TIME HE'D BE RIGHT....
BETTER'N MOST.

WELL, SHE SAY HIS AVERAGE WOULD BE AT LEAST AS GOOD AS BABE RUTH'S.
AND A FINE PRESIDENT HE WAS.
UM.. DID SHE MEAN IN HITTIN' IT OR THROWIN' IT?

DID YOU HEAR ABOUT JACK, THE GIANT-KILLER, FIGHTING THE DRAGON? HE SAID, "HOO BOSS! HOO BOSSY! BOSSY!" AND THE DRAGON RUN OFF.
WHY, HO, HO?

IF HE CALLED HIM A COW'S NAME, (A. BOSSY,) THE DRAGON WAS "COWED" (OR IN OTHER WORDS, B. SCARED.) IPSO ...

FACTO, THE DRAGON BEING COWED, HE UNDOUBTEDLY...
OKAY! OKAY OKAY OKAY

I DON'T GET IT.
CLODS!

A YUCK FOR A YUCK

I BEEN WORKIN' MY HEAD TO THE BONE TRYIN' TO HELP FREMOUNT DEVELOP A SENSE OF HUMOR.
WHY? IS HE GOIN' TO BE A T.V. COMIC?

A T.V. COMIC? WELL, UM ... .. NO ... NOT EXACTLY .. HE'S RUNNIN' FOR HIGH OFFICE ... HE'S GOTTA BE FOLKSY .. GOTTA TELL A FEW ROUSERS ...

TROUBLE IS, I CAN'T THINK OF ANY HE CAN USE ...
NOT EVEN ANY YOU COULD SORTA DUST 'EM OFF A LI'L'?

'TAIN'T THAT ... HOW MANY JOKES DO YOU KNOW WHAT ENDS WITH THE PUNCH LINE OF "JES' FINE"?

'LONG AS YOU WANTS TO TEACH FREMOUNT SOME JOKES SO'S HE'LL LOOK LIKE HE GOT A SENSE OF HUMOR YOU GOTTA USE JOKES ENDIN' IN "JES FINE".
THAT I KNOW.

WE'LL THINK OF SOME.

Y'KNOW, I THINK THIS BOY BETTER JUS' RUN ON HIS **RECORD**.
NO **OTHER** FUNNY STUFF, HUH?

I STILL FEELS **FREMOUNT** OUGHT TO TELL A FEW JOKES ··· THE BIG AMERICAN TRADITION IS A SENSE OF HUMOR.

A MAN RUNNIN' FOR PRESIDENT GOTTA HAVE A **READY QUIP**··· A ANECDOTE AT THE TIP OF HIS TONGUE··· THEN WHEN A **FOREIGN PREE-MEER** SAYS: "WE'RE AHEAD OF YOU IN **SUCCOTASH AND ROCKETS**.."

FREMOUNT CAN COME UP WITH SOMETHIN' LIKE "***JES' FINE!***" ?
WELL.. **YOU** KNOW··· **REPARTEE** COULD BE WORKED OUT AHEAD OF TIME.

WELL, ***MAYBE***.. BUT FOR THE PURPOSES OF RUNNIN' FOR OFFICE HE BETTER RUN ON HIS **RECORD**.
I S'POSE THERE **COULD BE** A FEW **LAUGHS** IN IT, AT **THAT**··· AN' WE COULD ALWAYS **YUCK IT UP** A LI'L.

VENTRILOQUIZZING

FREMOUNT GOTTA DEVELOP HIS PERSONALITY SO'S HE SPARKLES WITH WIT ... THEN THE PUBLIC WILL TAKE HIM TO ITS BOSOM.

A GOOD IDEA ... I GOT A COUPLE OF OLD VAUDEVILLE ROUTINES AROUND SOMEWHERES ... LET'S SEE, ONE WENT: "WHY'D THE CHICKEN CROSS THE ROAD, SAM?"
SAM?

I NEVER HEARD IT TOLD THAT WAY ... NOT WITH SAM .. MAYBE WITH FRED, OR IRVING .. BUT SAM? I DUNNO!
IT WAS SAM.

OH, S'POSE IT WAS SAM .. WHAT'S THE REST OF IT?
WELL, THAT PART ESCAPES ME ... BUT I'M SURE OF THE SAM PART.

LISTEN, I JUST THOUGHT OF A GREAT IDEA ... I USED TO BE A VENTRILOQUIST AND FREMOUNT CAN'T SAY NOTHIN' BUT "JES'FINE."
UM?

WELL, HE DON'T HAVE TO TALK AT ALL .. I'LL TALK ... LOOK, PRETEND YOU'RE FREMOUNT, THE CANDIDATE ... ACT LIKE A DUMMY.
JUST OPEN AND CLOSE MY MOUTH?

RIGHT! NOW I GO INTO MY ROUTINE... "WELL, WELL! MY OLD PAL! WHY DID THE CHICKEN CROSS THE ROAD, SAM?
SAM?

YES, SAM! WE DECIDED YESTERDAY IT WAS SAM! YOU DON'T HAVE THE BRAINS TO BE A DUMMY.
BUT I'M JUST A SUBSTITUTE CANDIDATE ... BESIDES IT'S FUNNIER WITH RUDOLPH.

THIS IS THE ONE WAY FREMOUNT WILL BE ABLE TO MAKE A SPEECH... THRU THE MAGIC OF VENTRILOQUISM.

ACT LIKE A DUMMY, NOW... YOU, THE CANDIDATE, ARE TALKIN' ABOUT SPLITTING THE WOMEN'S VOTE... SO YOU SAY THAT REMINDS ME OF A STORY... (JUST KEEP OPENIN' AN' CLOSIN' YOUR MOUTH)

ONE MAGICIAN SAYS TO THE OTHER, "WHO WAS THAT LADY I SAWED WITH YOU LAST NIGHT?"

HAW HAW... WHAT DO YOU THINK OF THAT, PORKY?
WHAT'S HE EATIN'?

HELLO THERE, FOLKS, DON'T FORGET US TIGERS, TURTLES AND PORKYPINES GOTTA STICK TOGETHER.

HELLO, MR. CONGERSMAN AN' YOUR RETINUE…
H'LO, MISS BOBOLINK… DON'T FORGET ELECTION DAY. **US BIRDS GOT TO STICK TOGETHER.**

HOWDY, MRS. MOUSE.. DON'T FORGET THIS IS A **ELECTION YEAR**… US **MICE** GOTTA **STICK** TOGETHER.
HEIGHDY, MR. CONGERSMAN

AH, THERE, **MRS. CATERPIGGLE**.. IT'S AN ELECTION TIME COMING UP… AND **US CATERPIGGLES** MUST STICK TOGETHER.
HOWDY DO, MR. CONGERSMAN

HELLO THERE, MR. CONGERSMAN
I ***DARE*** YOU.

BOTH SIDES OF THE ISLE

GIVE 'EM DOUBLE "L"

ALL RIGHT! LET'S SAY A LADYBUG IS A LADYBIRD.
UM?

AN' A LADYBIRD IS A ENGLISH LADYBUG... WELL!
YES, YES?

THAT MEANS THE ENGLISH AIN'T AFRAID TO ELECT A LADY PRESIDENT SO WHY SHOULD WE...?
BUT IS FREMOUNT A LADY?

THESE ARE ACADEMOCRATIC QUESTIONS! IS FREMOUNT A LADY? IS THE QUEEN A PRESIDENT? IS A BUG A BIRD?
WAIT A MINUTE NOW... IS A WHAT A WHAT?

FACE THIS! CAN A LADY BE PRESIDENT OF THE U. S. AND A.?
SO LONG AS SHE'S A GENTLEMAN.. WHY NOT?

IT SAYS RIGHT HERE IN MAJOR FRUMMY'S BUG ATLAS.. A LADYBUG OR A LADYBIRD IS NOT NECESSARILY A GENTLEMAN BUG OR BIRD AS THE CASE MAY BE!

AND ... MARK YOU, AND WHAT PARTY IS GONNA PUT UP A CANDIDATE WHAT IS NOT NECESSARILY A GENTLEMAN?
OH, HO!

YOU MEAN A WINNING CANDIDATE OR A NON-WINNING CANDIDATE?
LET'S SEE WHAT THE MAJOR SAYS ON THAT.

WELL, MAJOR FRUMMY DOESN'T SAY ANYTHING ABOUT BUGS INSOFAR AS THEY IS CANDIDATES.
MAJOR FRUMMY'S BUG ATLAS

TO BE EXACT, HE DON'T SAY A LADYBUG, NOT BEIN' A GENTLEMAN BUG, CAN BE A CANDIDATE OR NOT ... IN OTHER WORDS, THE BUG ATLAS HERE LEAVES IT OPEN.

YOU GOT TO BE FAIR ABOVE ALL! WHAT PARTY WOULD PUT UP A CANDIDATE WHAT'S NOT ALSO A GENTLEMAN?
ANY PARTY MIGHT PUT UP AT LEAST ONE. HOW COULD THEY TELL?

HO! ANY PARTY MAYBE! WHY, SOMEBODY MIGHT PUT UP AS MANY AS SIX!
I'D SAY ONE WAS THE LIMIT.

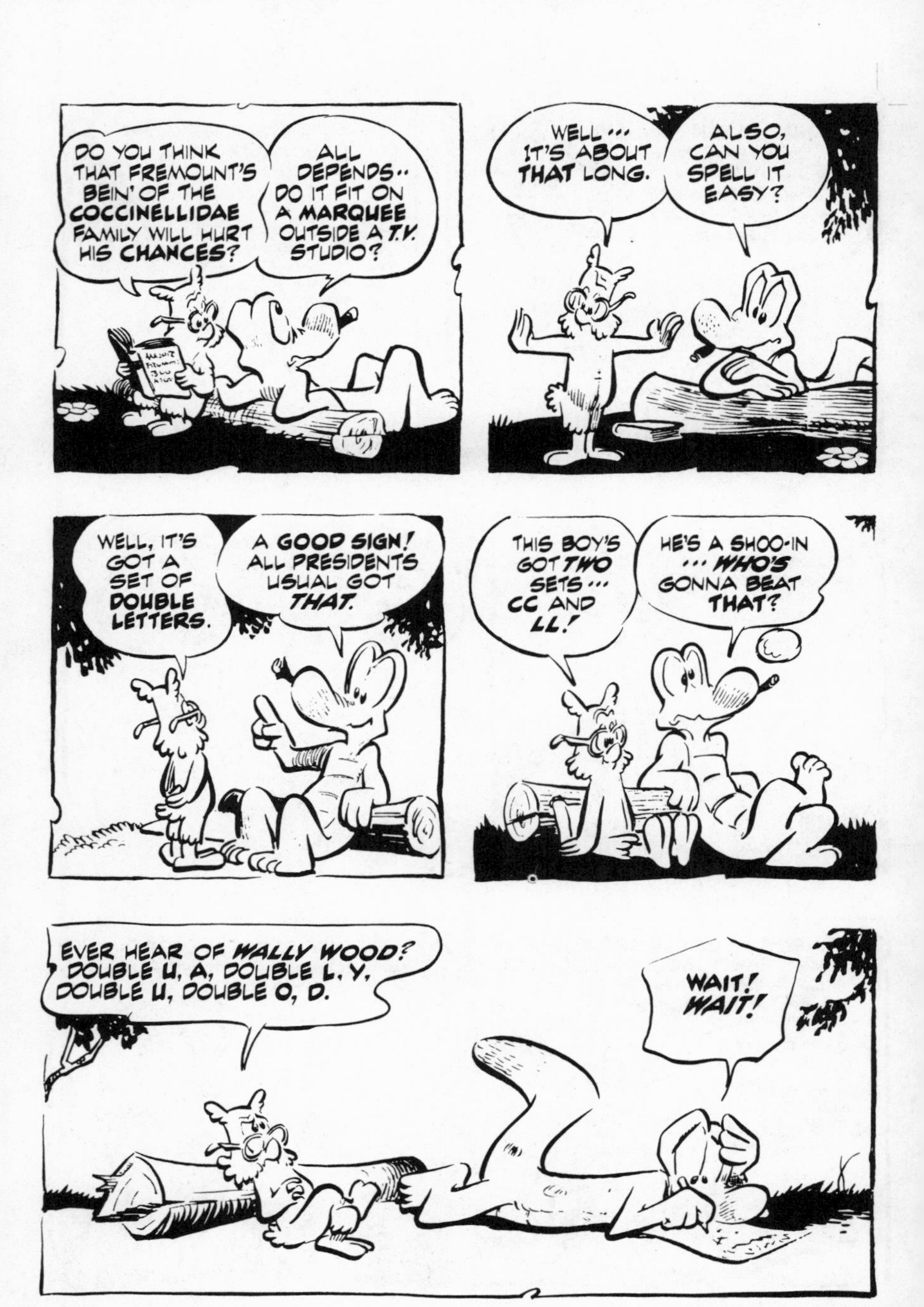
DO YOU THINK THAT FREMOUNT'S BEIN' OF THE COCCINELLIDAE FAMILY WILL HURT HIS CHANCES?
ALL DEPENDS.. DO IT FIT ON A MARQUEE OUTSIDE A T.V. STUDIO?
WELL... IT'S ABOUT THAT LONG.
ALSO, CAN YOU SPELL IT EASY?
WELL, IT'S GOT A SET OF DOUBLE LETTERS.
A GOOD SIGN! ALL PRESIDENTS USUAL GOT THAT.
THIS BOY'S GOT TWO SETS... CC AND LL!
HE'S A SHOO-IN ... WHO'S GONNA BEAT THAT?
EVER HEAR OF WALLY WOOD? DOUBLE U, A, DOUBLE L, Y, DOUBLE U, DOUBLE O, D.
WAIT! WAIT!

COCKEYES AND MUSCLES

WHEN THE CLAMOR OF THE PUBLIC, THE POPULAR CLAMOR, CALLS A MAN, HE KNOWS HE'S BEEN CALLED!
MY SAKES! I DIN'T KNOW WE HAD A PUBLIC CLAMMER.

HOW ABOUT A POPULAR OYSTERER... KIN THE POPULAR OYSTERER BE HEARD, TOO?
HUH?

WELL, SURE, OUR ROISTERERS CAN BE HEARD, BUT THE VOICE OF THE VULGAR AIN'T GOT AS MUCH OOMPH ...MORE PEOPLE DIG THE POPULAR CLAMOR.
THEY DIGS THE CLAMMER?

SURE, THEY DIGS THE CLAMOR... THAT'S WHY THE CLAMOR IS SO POPULAR.
BY GEORGE Y. WELLS! I ALWAYS THOUGHT IT WAS THE OTHER WAY AROUND.

YEP, THE POPULAR CLAMOR MUST BE HEEDED!
YOU MEANS THE CLAMMER OF THE PUBLIC?

YES.. AN' IT'S MY THOUGHT THAT THE PUBLIC CLAMOR WILL BE FOR FREMOUNT!
THE CLAMMER IS FOR FREMOUNT?

THE POPULAR CLAMOR IS FOR FREMOUNT ... HE IS EASILY DUG!
BY THE POPULAR CLAMMER? BUT NOT BY OUR OYSTERERS?

MAYBE OUR ROISTERERS DIGS OL' FREMOUNT BUT MAYBE THEY DON'T, TOO.
WHY NOT? THE MONTH GOT A "R" IN HER.

YOU TALK ABOUT HEEDIN' THE PUBLIC CLAMMER.. .. HOW DO YOU MEAN?
S'POSE THE PUBLIC CLAMOR SAYS, "RUN FOR OFFICE..."

YOU COULD HEED IT BY SAYIN': "IF, IN THEIR ABIDING WISDOM THE GOOD PEOPLE OF THE PARTY SHOULD CALL UPON ME TO SERVE IN SO LOFTY A CAPACITY...

"I WOULD FEEL HUMBLE, INDEED! IF CALLED, I WOULD FEEL DUTY BOUND TO HEAR THE CLARION!"

IN OTHER WORDS, YOU WOULD HEED THE PUBLIC CLAMOR... YOU'D DIG THE TRUMPET.
PHOO, I WOULD! HOW DEEP IS THIS KAZOO?

FOOBASHFUL FROG

FOO BASH

HOWDY, MISTER CONGERSMAN
WHY, AIN'T YOU PERTY TODAY, MIZ ANGLEWORM! IT'S A ELECTION YEAR... REMEMBER, US ANGLEWORMS MUST STICK TOGETHER.
AW, COME OFF IT

I DON'T SEE HOW YOU CAN GO SMIRKIN' AROUND SUCH UGLY WOMEN.
AAAH... THEY'RE ALL ALIKE, M'BOY.

WELL WELL WELL
DOG-GONE!

Y'KNOW, THERE'S SOMETHING DISTINCTIVE ABOUT A LADY FROG, M'BOY.
YESSIRREEBOB! LET'S US STROLL IN THIS DIRECTION. MR. CONGERSMAN.

GHOST TO GHOST NETWORK

GO WEST, Y. M.

BY GREAT JUMPING BOB HALL! A ZEBRA! RUN UP AND GET HIS AUTOGRAPH, ASHLEIGH, MY SON.

I AIN'T A ZEBRA... I'M A TIGER.
HAW, TIGERS HAVE MANES ... WHERE'S YOURS?
SNIFF

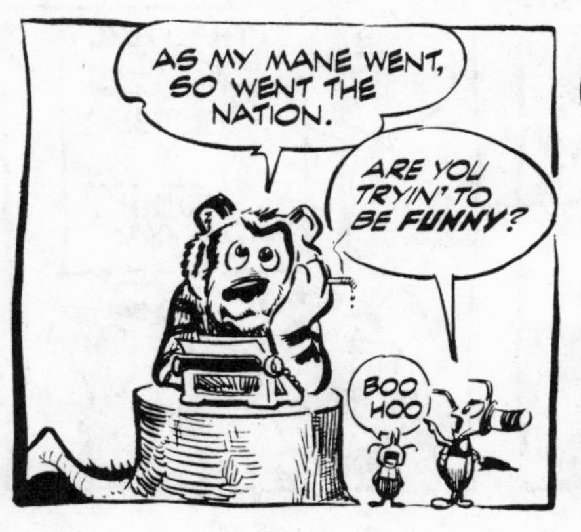
AS MY MANE WENT, SO WENT THE NATION.
ARE YOU TRYIN' TO BE FUNNY?
BOO HOO

IN THIS COMIC VALENTINE? I WOULDN'T THINK OF IT.
DESTROY A SON'S FAITH IN HIS FATHER, WILL YOU? TAKE THAT! YOU FALSE ZEBRA!
GO IT, PA

JUST HAD A TALK WITH A COUPLA BUGS .. THEY CALLED ME A ZEBRA!
A ZEBRA !? WHY ?

THE STRIPES, MAYBE
ACTUALLY YOU LOOK LIKE A MASTER SERGEANT WHO HAS RE-ENLISTED 14,906 TIMES

WELL, I DIDN'T TAKE IT LYING DOWN.
ATTABOY!

I WAS MORE SITTING... SORT OF CROUCHED, IN FACT.
?

IT'S ABOUT TIME YOU PUT OUT A PRESS RELEASE ON FREMOUNT... THE CANDIDATE, YOU RECALL.
AH, YES! LITTLE FRYMOCK! WHAT IS HIS LATEST BON MOT??

"JES' FINE"
THAT, SIR, IS THE GENUINE TROUBLE! HOW CAN YOU PUT OUT A DAZZLER WITH NOTHING BUT "JES' FINE"
?

Fremount, the boy bug, whose slogan "Jes' fine," sweeps the U.S., was born in a humble, unpretentious tin can on the edge of a pig farm.

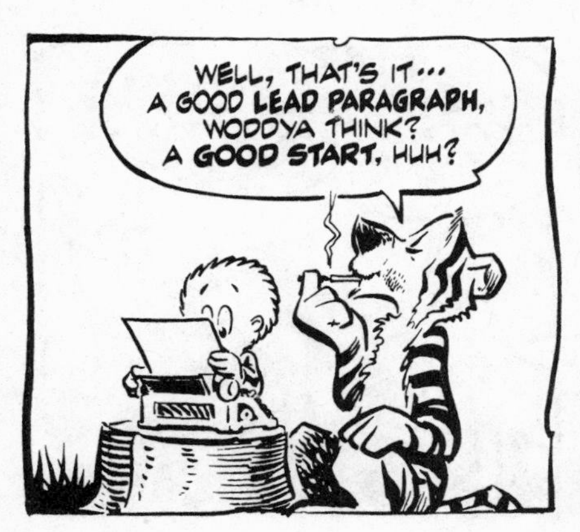

THE QUESTIONEER BEFORE THE HOUSE

THAT'S MIGHTY GOOD COFFEE··· SO YOU'RE A TAKER OF THE PUBLIC PULSE?
YES, MA'M! I'M A POLLSTER··· THAT'S THE KIND OF CAT I AM, IF YOU DELVES MY JIVE.

YOU PUTS YOUR FINGER ON THE PULSE BEAT OF THE NATION?
A PULSE BEATNIK

OKAY··· GO AHEAD AND ASK ME A QUESTION.
DAD TAKE IT! THEM SPOONS IS DANGEROUS. YOU SAY A QUESTION?

NO, WHAT WE GOT IS ANSWERS··· YOU GET A CHOICE OF OUR BEST ANSWERS··· THEN YOU HAVE TO THINK UP A QUESTION··· THAT'S ONLY FAIR.
WHY DO US PUBLIC ALWAYS GET THE HARD PART?

TELL YOU HOW US PULSE BEATNIKS WORK··· ANY MORE COFFEE HERE?
DON'T RIGHTLY B'LEEVE THEY IS.

WHAT'S THIS? SEEMS LIKE THERE'S A PLENTY.
WELL, UM··· LESSEE···

GACK! THE WORST COFFEE I EVER TASTED.

THAT THERE IS PAINT.
THAT SO? OH, WELL, FOR PAINT IT AIN'T BAD AT ALL.

IT'S HARD FOR ME TO UNDERSTAND HOW YOU CAN STAND AROUND DRINKIN' RED PAINT!
RED? IT'S NOT RED... IT'S MORE PUCE.

OH, YEH, WELL, PUCE, SURE...
ANYWAY, LET ME TELL YOU HOW WE PULSE BEATNIKS GO ABOUT COUNTIN' YOUR NOSES.

MY NOSES!?
I MEAN THE NOSES OF THE PUBLIC... ONLY ONE TO A CUSTOMER, OF COURSE... NOW, TAKE YOUR NOSE...

YOU'LL NEVER GET ANYWHERE WITH ME... I AIN'T GOT NO NOSE.. LOOK, THERE'S PROOF.
YOU MEAN YOU'RE WASTIN' MY TIME? NO NOSE TO COUNT HERE?

Y'KNOW, YOU'RE RIGHT.. YOU DON'T HAVE NO NOSE... THERE'S NO WAY TO POLL YOU... NO WAY TO COUNT YOUR NOSE.

I KNOW... BUT YOU'RE A PUBLIC PULSE TAKER.. COULDN'T YOU TAKE MY PULSE INSTEAD OF COUNTIN' MY NOSE, MR...UH..M...DIN'T GET YOUR NAME?
BASIL, IT'S BASIL McTABOLISM, THE PULSE TAKER.

APRIL FOOL?
NO

BUT NOBODY GOT A NAME LIKE BASIL McTABOLISM.
YEAH? WELL, NOBODY AIN'T GOT NO-NOSE NEITHER, THEN!

WELL, MADAM, THAT'S IT... MY JOB IS COUNTIN' NOSES AND IF YOU DON'T HAVE NO NOSE IT'S GOOD-BYE.
GOOD-BYE?

SURE, US PULSE TAKERS GOTTA MOVE.. IT'S AS PLAIN AS THE NOSE ON YOUR FA... I MEAN.. UM...
COULDN'T YOU COUNT MY TOES? I GOT PLENTY OF THEM.

NOPE .. I'M SORRY... GOOD DAY, MADAM LAFEMME!
WELL, I TRIED TO HELP. GOOD-BYE, BASIL MCTABOLISM.

C. LAFEMME
SLAM
THERE'S SOMETHIN' WRONG HERE.

HOW DO YOU GET RID OF A POLL TAKER?
EASY

C. LA FEMME
IF IT'S MY HOUSE I DON'T LET HIM THROUGH THAT DOOR.

DON'T LET HIM THROUGH THE DOOR, HUH? WELL, IN THAT CASE, IT'S GONNA BE TOUGH.
HOW COME? THEY AIN'T NO POLL TAKER OUT HERE.

C. LA FEM
I KNOW... BUT THERE'S ONE IN THERE.

SOLICITING THE SOLACE

OH, HE'S IN THERE, THAT OL' POLL TAKER... LIVIN' IT UP.. IN MY HOUSE...
CAN'T SEE HIM THRU THE KEY-HOLE.

MY DOOR AIN'T GOT NO KEYHOLE.
OH

HEY, IN THERE! STOP EATIN' CRACKERS IN MY BED!
YOU DOES IT YOUR OWN SELF.

BUT HE GOT HIS HAT ON.
HE AIN'T GOT NO NOBLESSE OBLIGE.

WHEN A STRANGER U-SURPS YO' PRIVILEGE OF PRIVATE DOMICILITY, TAKE ACTION! SMOKE THAT RASCAL OUT OF THERE!
SMOKE HIM OUT ?

THAT'S RIGHT! SMOKE THAT POLL TAKER OUT OF YOUR HOUSE.
I'LL SNEAK IN.

♪

OOP? WHAT HAPPENED?
HE OUT-SMOKED ME.
DELICIOUS CIGARS··· YESSIR! FIRST-RATE!

I'LL TAKE THINGS INTO MY OWN HANDS··· I'LL GET THAT POLL-TAKIN' DOG-IN-THE-MANGER OUT OF THERE···

WHAT YOU GONNA DO?
SHH··· WE'LL SET FIRE TO THE PLACE.
C. LAF

HEE HEE
HEE··· THIS'LL ROUSE HIM.
C. LAF

WHAT'S YOU TRYIN' TO DO? BURN DOWN YOUR HOUSE?
THAT'S RIGHT! IT IS MY PLACE, AIN'T IT?
A PITY

BIRD WORK

I GOT A POLL-TAKER IN MY HOUSE AN' CAN'T GET IN ... SO I COME OVER TO INSTRUCT FREMOUNT.
HOW...? WHAT'S HE NEED TO KNOW?

FOR A SAMPLE, HE OUGHT TO BUILD UP HIS STOCK OF JOKES ... SO'S HE CAN HANDLE FOREIGN DIGNITARIES ...
HE GIVES A GOOD BIRD IMITATION.

THAT SO? LEMME SEE HIM IMITATE A BIRD.
THERE HE GO! HE'S BEIN' A OSTRICH ... A FLIGHTLESS TYPE.

A OSTRICH? JUS RUNNIN' AROUND IS BEIN' A OSTRICH? DON'T HE SING OR SOMETHIN'?
HE SORTA HUMS ... NOW, LOOK AT HIM BE A OSTRICH NOW! ... TELL ME HE AIN'T PRESIDENTIAL TIMBER?

FREMOUNT GIVIN' BIRD IMITATIONS AIN'T AS GOOD AS **JOKES**... FOR HIM TO IMITATE A OSTRICH AIN'T **MUCH**.
HE AIN'T **THRU**.

WHAT'S THE REST OF HIS **REPERTORY**?
HE KNOWS ALL THE POLITICAL STYLES... **WATCH**.
JES' FINE

WHY'S HE **LIMPIN'**?
THAT SHOWS HE'S THE KINDA BIRD KIN HANDLE **ANY** PART OF THE JOB.
JES' FINE

YEAH? BUT WHY'S HE ***LIMPIN'*** ?
GOOD AT IT, AIN'T HE? HE'S BEIN' A **LAME DUCK**.
JES'

IT'S HARD FOR ME TO COMPREHEND 'BOUT FREMOUNT IMITATIN' BIRDS... 'STEAD OF **CAMPAIGNIN'** FOR THE PRESIDENTISTRY.
YOU IS OL' FASHIONED.

YOU MEAN GIVIN' ***BIRD IMITATIONS*** IS THE **MODERN** CAMPAIGN METHOD?
AS A **CANDIDATE** YOU SHOWS WHAT YOU'RE **GOOD** AT.
JES' FINE

WULL, HE'S DONE A OSTRICH AN' A LAME DUCK... WHAT ELSE?
SHOW HIM WHAT OTHER LEADERSHIP ABILITIES YOU GOT, FREMOUNT.

WHOOSH! WHAT WAS THAT?
NATURALLY, THAT WAS THE DYIN' SWAN...

IF YOU GOES ON HAVIN' FREMOUNT GIVE BIRD IMITATIONS YOU'LL GET THE BIRD-WATCHER VOTE BUT WHAT ELSE?

WELL, WE'LL GET ALL THEM AS IS BIRD MINDED.
ALL THE BIRD BRAINS, HUH? Y'KNOW WHAT HE'S GONNA BE IMITATIN' IF HE KEEPS UP HIS ORNITHOLOGICAL CAMPAIGN?

THIS
WHAT IN THE WORLD?

A DODO

CLAMMING UP, COAST TO COAST

I BEEN THINKIN' AN' THINKIN' WHAT OWL SAID ABOUT THE **PUBLIC CLAMMER.**
THE **CLAMOR** OF THE **PUBLIC**?

YES ... THE POPULAR CLAMMER ... HE SAYS WE ALL MUST HEED THE **CLAMMER.**
NO TWO WAYS ABOUT IT ... A EAR TO THE GROUND.

OWL SAYS WE MUST ***DIG*** THE CLAMMER ... THAT SOUND KINDA BACK-WARDS.
OH, IT WORKS **BOTH WAYS** ... WE UNDERSTANDS THE CLAMOR AND THE CLAMOR **DIGS US.**

THE CLAMMER DIGS ***ME?*** ***I'M*** A ALLIGATOR BY TRADE.
THERE WOULDN'T BE A **TRUE** CLAMOR OF THE PUBLIC WITHOUT IT TOOK INTO ACCOUNT ***ALL*** HUMAN BEANS.

OWL SAYS WE DON'T DIG OUR OYSTERERS LIKE WE DO THE PUBLIC CLAMMER.
WELL, OUR ROISTERERS ARE **NOISY** PEOPLE.

THEY DON'T MAKE ANY MORE NOISE THAN THE CLAMMER.
THE PUBLIC CLAMOR IS DEEP DOWN SOMETIMES AN' **QUIET.**

HUH?
A GROUND SWELL ··· THE PUBLIC CLAMOR IS SWEPT ALONG ON A TIDE ··· IN WAVES ····

SWIMMING ON AN' ON ··· ··· ACROSS THE COUNTRY ···
SWIMS ACROSS COUNTRY! A NATATORIAL PHEE-NOMINATION!

YOU SAY THE PUBLIC CLAMMER SWIMS ACROSS COUNTRY?
THE CLAMOR GOES ACROSS THE LAND IN A RISING WAVE, A TIDE.

WHAT ROUTE DO IT TAKE? ROUTE SIX?
NO SPECIAL ROUTE ··· THE CLAMOR OF THE PUBLIC SWIMS CROST PLAIN AN' MOUNTAIN.

THIS HERE CLAMMER SWIMS ACROSS MOUNTAINS?
ACROSS FOREST AND FEN ··· RAVINE AND RILL.

UNTIL AT LAST THE CLAMOR IS HEARD IN THE HALLS OF CONGRESS.
HOLLERIN' FOR HELP?

THE SATISFACTION OF HONOR

YOU COME OUT OF MY HOUSE, YOU POLL-TAKIN' CAT! LEAVE!

I'M BUSY! GO AWAY!
RACING TODAY

BESIDES ... COME IN AN' MAKE ME LEAVE!
OH, YEAH?! THAT'S YOUR JOB.

HEIGHDY, CHURCHILL, WHAT YOU DOON?
KEEPIN' A GUY FROM RUNNIN' OUT OF MY HOUSE.

I BEEN THINKIN' UP FUNNY STORIES SO'S THE CANDIDATE KIN SHOW HE'S A PURE AMERICAN BOY WITH HIS SUNNY SIDE UP.
UM

THE SERGEANT SAYS TO THE PRIVATES, "WHAT'S THE THIRD NOTE UP IN THE SCALE?" AN' ONE GUY SAYS, "MI!" THE SERGEANT SAYS, "I'M GLAD YOU VOLUNTEERED...

"NOW," HE SAYS, "TAKE THIS KNIFE AN' THEM POTATOES AN' ...." WHEREUPON THE PRIVATE SAYS, "I DIDN'T RAISE MY VOICE TO BE A SOLDIER." THEN ...

DID SOMEBODY KNOCK?

SLAM
HO HUM

CHURCHY
DAGBLAG THAT DADSNAGGED OL' POLL-TAKIN' CAT PLAYIN' DOG-IN-THE-MANGER OF MY OWN HOUSE!

CHURCHY
KNOCK KNOCK KNOCK

ANYBODY HOME?

YES! ME!

IF THIS IS THE WAY YOU TREAT AN INNOCENT POLL TAKER, I'M LEAVIN'!
HAH, YOU AIN'T SO INNOCENT, BASIL McTABOLISM!

I AM SO INNOCENT!
YOU ARE NOT!

I AM I AM I AM! I AM INNOCENT!
HAH!

OF WHAT?

HO! I GUESS I KNOW WHEN I'M NOT WANTED! I'LL LEAVE ... I'M GOIN'!
WELL, LEAVE THEN, BEFORE I ...

BEFORE YOU WHAT?
SO YOU WANT TO FIND OUT, HUH? WELL!

I'M BUSY NOW... I'M LEAVIN' BUT I'LL BE BACK! YOU WAIT!
HO! HO! HO! HO! IT IS TO LAUGH.

AAHAH.. ..YOU.. YOU.
WHY, YOU... ..YOU... YOU....

WELL, I GUESS I
SHOWED HIM!

WHOLE SPEECH AT HALF PRICE

SORRY I SAID FREMOUNT'S WORD, 'STEAD OF OL' FREMOUNT SAYIN' IT.
ME, TOO·· IT JES' MADE HIM BELLER AND WAWL.
SNIMF

ON T'OTHER HAND, WHAT KIND OF A CANDIDATE IS IT WHAT STARTS CRYIN' WHEN YOU ASK HIM A QUESTION?
DEPENDS ON THE CALIBRE OF THE MUZZLE-LOADIN' QUESTION.
SNIF

S'POSE YOU SAYS WHAT HAPPENED TO THE LOOT, NOOT, AN' HE BUSTS OUT BAWLIN'?
WELL, IT'D BE A LI'L RELIEF FROM HIM ONLY SAYIN' THAT OTHER THING ... YOU KNOW···J-E-S··
SNUF

Y'MEAN "JES' FINE?"
WHOO
HOO
HUP
HUP
HUP
HUP
THERE HE GO AGAIN!

HEIGHDY, MR. WASP! HEIGHDY, MIZ BEETLE! HEIGHDY, OL' FREMOUNT!
HOWDY, OL' FLEA... FREMOUNT BEEN BLUBBERIN' 'CAUSE WE USED HIS WORDS.
SNIF

WHAT'S WRONG WITH THAT? THEY'S A PLENTY WORDS ···AN' YOU CAN USE SOME OF 'EM OVER AGAIN.
OL' FREMOUNT USES 'EM OVER OKAY, BUT HE AIN'T GOT BUT TWO.
SNIF

WHAT IS THEY?
WE DASSENT TELL... IT'LL SET HIM TO CATTERY-WAWLIN'.
YEH, LET'S CHANGE THE SUBJECT! HOW WAS THINGS IN THE D.C. PRIMARIES?
SNUF

OH... YOU KNOW, JES' FINE.
WOW OOOOOOO HOOO
IT'S DID AGAIN!

I DUNNO... ANY CANDIDATE THAT GOES AROUND BLUBBERIN' JES' 'CAUSE SOMEBODY SAID HIS WORDS AIN'T MY IDEA OF PRESIDENTIAL TIMBER.
THERE THERE

INSECKS DON'T NEED NO PRESIDENT LIKE THAT.
IF HE DON'T SHOW NO BETTER FIBRE WE'LL GET A NEW BOY.
HIC

YOU GIVED MY CHILD, FREMOUNT, (NEXT PRESIDENT OF THE U.S. AND A., BORED IN A LOG CABIN,) YOU GIVED HIM THE HICCUPS.
HIC HIC HIC

HEIGHDY, MIZ WEEVIL... OL' FREMOUNT GOT A NEW SPEECH.
BURN MY TAR!
SH! THEY'S A LOT IN WHAT HE SAY.
HIC HOOP A HOOPA HIC HIC HOOP HOC HIC HOOK HIC

OL' FREMOUNT'S MAKIN' HIS FIRST **LONG** POLITICAL SPEECH.
A-HIC HOOP A-HUPPA HIC HIC HIC **HIC**... **OOK**... HIC HIC

AN' HE DOIN' IT **ENTIRE** WITH HICCUPS.
I'VE HEARD **COUGHIN'** **FITS** WHAT HAD MORE SENSE IN 'EM.
HIC HIC HIC HIC

YEH, BUT IS YOU HEARD **SPEECHIN'** WHAT GOT MORE MOXIE?
YEAH! MAYBE YOU DON'T GO 'LONG WITH HIS SENTIMENTS?
WELL ..UM..
HIC HIC HIC HOOP HIC

ADMIT IT! YOU DON'T AGREE WITH HIM SO YOU **KNOCKS** HIM.
OH, NO! I..UH.. GOSH ..I...
WHY NOT APPLAUD A LI'L? TO SHOW GOOD FAITH.
MUS' I **CHEER**?
HIC HIC HIC HIC HIC A-HOOP WOOP HIC

POGO, I COME OVER ON ACCOUNT OF THE **SIN** **AND SHAME** **OF IT ALL.**
H'LO, FLEA, WHAT SIN AN' SHAME OF WHAT ALL?
THEM **BEETLES!** RUNNIN' FREMOUNT FOR A CANDIDATE WHEN ALL'S HE CAN SAY IS "**JES' FINE**" AND A **HANDFUL** OF **HICCUPS.**
HICCUPS?

"JES' FINE" AN' HICCUPS IS HIS WHOLE LOVIN' VOCABULARY.
NO SNEEZES? NO GRUNTS? NO GROANS, NO SCREAMS OF ANGUISH?

"JES' FINE" AN' JES' HICCUPS.
I DUNNO... HOW'S THIS BOY GONNA HOLD OFFICE IF HE CAN'T GRUNT, GROAN OR SCREAM?

LIKE I TOLE YOU, FREMOUNT IS MERE HICCUPPIN' AN' SAYIN' "JES' FINE"... CALL THAT A PLATFORM?

WHY AIN'T HE FACIN' THE ISSUES OF THE DAY?
WULL, HE'S HICCUPPIN'.

THAT MERE MEANS SOMETHIN' DON'T AGREE WITH HIM... IT DON'T MEAN HE DON'T AGREE WITH ANYTHING... HE KEEPS SAYIN' "JES' FINE!"

MAYBE HE AGREES WITH EVERYTHING ... MAYBE HE THINKS BOTH SIDES IS RIGHT ALL THE TIME.
NO WONDER HE'S SICK TO THE STOMACH.

ACTUALLY, POGO, I COME DOWN HERE REPRESENTIN' ABOUT 10,000,000,000 FLEAS...

US FLEAS FIGGER WE GOT THE VOTE AN' WE WANT TO BE SEATED AT ANY AN' ALL CONVENTIONS.
TEN BILLION SEATS?

OTHERWISE WE'LL START OUR OWN RUMP CONVENTION AN' CHOOSE OUR OWN HOST BODY...
H'LO?
HI, BEAUREGARD

H'LO, DOLL... WHAT'RE YOU DOIN' AROUND CONVENTION TIME?

IF US FLEAS, TEN BILLION STRONG, SAYS THE WORD, YOU CAN GO INTO THE WHITE HOUSE.
I AIN'T GOT NO PRESIDENTIAL QUALIFICATIONS.

WODDYA MEAN..? YOU AIN'T AFEARD TO APPEAR ON T.V.? NO... YOU CAN PARRY AND THRUST WITTILY AT A PRESS CONFERENCE?
NATCH

YOU CAN EXCHANGE BARBS INNERNATIONALLY...? SET A GOOD TABLE WHEN YOU PLAYS HOST? WING FROM CONFERENCE TO CONFERENCE LIKE A GULL?
I COULD LEARN.

CAN YOU BREAK NINETY?

I BELIEVE IF I WAS TO BE PRESIDENT I'D MAKE A NEW GAME POPULAR 'STEAD OF GOLF.
DOMINOES?

OO..HA..HA...GUESS AGAIN
CHECKERS? TIDDLYWINKS? HIDE-AN'-GO-SEEK? DICE? PINOCHLE? HOP-SCOTCH? SPIN-THE-BOTTLE? POST OFFICE?

NO ... NONE OF THEM ... LISTEN ... SPSSST.. WSPER ...SPTSSS..TSSS...

PERTY SPORTY, EH?
WHAT? HOW WOULD THAT LOOK? YOU AND THE WHOLE CABINET OUT CHASIN' AUTOMOBILES?

THE SHOCK OF TRUTH

FREMOUNT IS A CANNIBAL.

HE'S NOT A BEETLE ATALL ... HE'S A SNEAKY OL' ANT LION WHAT BURRIES UNDER-GROUND AN' SPRONGS OUT AT ANTS...

IT'S ALL IN MAJOR FRUMMY'S BUG ATLAS... A PICTURE OF FREMOUNT... AND HE EATS ANTS...

HOW KIN WE ELECT FREMOUNT? THERE HE'D BE AT A INNERNATIONAL DINNER... KHRUSHCHEV REACHES FOR THE CAVIAR... AND OUR PRESIDENT SAYS, "PLEASE PASS THE..." OOG!

I DON'T KNOW WHAT TO DO... A SECRET TORMENTS ME... SHOULD I UNLOCK MY HEART?
HYDY

WILD HORSES COULDN'T DRAG IT OUT OF ME!

THE SECRET THAT FREMOUNT IS MASQUERADIN' AS A BEETLE AND IS REALLY A CANNIBAL ANT LION IS LOCKED IN MY BOSOM

WHY HURT THE KID'S CHANCES TO BE PRESIDENT? HOW MANY PEOPLE CAN HE EAT IF HE DON'T HAVE CONGRESS WITH HIM?

I KNOW A SECRET.
AND I GOT TROUBLES OF MY OWN.
ATLAS
MAJOR

THE CANNY-BALLISTICS OF POLITICS

THAT'S A PICTURE OF FREMOUNT, OKAY! YOU SAY THE BOOK SAYS HE EATS AUNTS? WHAT KIND? PERSONAL OR PUBLIC?
ANY KIND... HE'S A ANT LION... HIDES UNDERBENEATH THE SAND, TRAPS THE ANT AN' DRINKS THE BLOOD!

BY JING! LAND SAKES! GOLLY MICKLE... FOOBASH! AND HERE WE WAS GONNA PUT THIS FELLOW IN THE WHITE HOUSE... A AUNT DRINKER!

IS YOU A AUNT OF ANYBODY...? THINK CLOSE NOW.
LI'L' ROSCOE CALLS ME HIS AUNT 'CAUSE I LIVES NEXT DOOR BUT ACTUALLY, I IS A FELLA... ROSCOE DON'T MEAN NO HARM.

WELL, THERE IS A MONSTER LOOSE... WHAT DEE-VOURS ANY KIND AUNTS... SPREAD THE WORD.
WHAT SHE SAY, AUNT BIRDIE? WHAT THE LADY SAY?
STOP CALLIN' ME AUNT BIRDIE!

WELL, WELL! MY FAVORITE CON-STITUENT! MIZ EVERLOVIN' WEEVIL, BLESS MY EYES!
HEIGHDY, MR. CONGERS-MAN.. WHAT IN THE WORLD IS GUMMINT COMIN' TO?

HO HO HO! NO TECHNICAL QUESTIONS, NOW! WHO KNOWS WHAT THEM RASCALS IN POWER WILL DO? US OL' WEEVILS GOTTA STICK TOGETHER!
I'M SKEERED... I'M A AUNT.

IS THAT A FACT! SHO' NUFF? MY GOOD LORRY BEANSTALK... I'M A AUNT, TOO! US AUNTS GOTTA STICK TOGETHER.
WELL, THERE'S A MONSTER GOIN' AROUND EATIN' AUNTS.

EATIN' YOU AUNTS!? LAURA MERCY! US UNCLES WILL HAFTA LOOK INTO THIS.

I SAY IT'S A CRYING SHAME! A TRAVESTY ON INNERNATIONAL LAW, ORDER AND THE IMMUTABLE TRANS-FIXITY OF STABILEMENT.
HUH? WHAT?

WHY, YOU TOLD ME WITH YOUR OWN LIPS THERE'S A MONSTER GOING AROUND EATIN' UP MY CONSTITUENTS.
THA'S RIGHT, MR. CONGERSMAN

NOT ONLY MY CONSTITUENTS, BUT THE POTENTIAL VOTERS FOR OUR FAVORITE SON, THAT STERLING JEWEL IN THE CROWN OF SOCIETY, THE CANDIDATE, FREMOUNT HISSELF.
HE'S THE ONE WHAT'S EATIN' 'EM.

FREMOUNT!? THE CANDIDATE IS EATIN' UP THE VOTERS? WHY, THAT STERLING GOOD-FOR-NOTHIN' JEWEL IN THE CROWN OF SOCIETY AIN'T GOT THE POLITICAL SAVVY OF A WARTHOG.
HE'S A HUNGRY ONE.

MIZ WEEVIL, YOU KNOW ME, AS YOUR CONGERSMAN I SAY **US WEEVILS** GOTTA STICK TOGETHER... HOW COME OL' **FREMOUNT**, THE CANDIDATE, IS A ***ANT LION?***
BY BIRTH

BUT I THUNK HE WAS A **BEETLE**, THE CHILD OF YOUR SISTER-AN'-LAW.
WE THUNK SO TOO... DIN'T QUITE NOTICE THE **DIFFERNTS** IN THE MODEL.

BUT A MAMMY'S EVER-LOVIN' BLUE-EYED **HEART** KIN TELL HER OWN CHILD, **NO DOUBTS**?
BUT **FREMOUNT** IS WATCHA MAY CALL A **FOUNDLIN'**.

LAURA MERCY! WHAT **KIND** OF A FOUNDLIN'?
MIZ BEETLE FOUND HIM IN A **BOX OF POPCORN**... A KIND OF A PRIZE, YOU MIGHT SAY.

HOO BOY! THIS NEWS IS GOIN' TO PUT A **NUMBER "A" CRIMP** INTO THE CONVENTION... THE PARTY IS **RUINED**.
YOU MEAN THE FACT THAT **FREMOUNT** IS ACTUALLY A **BLOODTHIRSTY ANT LION**?

NO... **THAT** WE CAN **HUSH UP**... OR CLAIM HE'S CHANGED HIS WAYS...

BUT S'POSE IT LEAKS OUT THAT HE WAS BORN IN A BOX OF *POPCORN?*
MY SISTER'N'LAW, MIZ BEETLE, WAS DISAPPOINTED, TOO... SHE WASN'T LOOKIN' FOR A **LI'L BOY**...

WHEN SHE OPENED UP THE **BOX** SHE WAS HOPIN' FOR A **WHISTLE**...
GADS

HOW'D THE PARTY EVER GET ITSELF OVER A BARREL BY GOIN' FOR FREMOUNT?
ON ACCOUNT OF HIS SPEECH... HE SAID THINGS WAS **"JES' FINE"**.

I HAVE TO ADMIT THE **FORCE** AND **LOGIC** THAT SURGE ALONG BEHIND SUCH STIRRING **ELOQUENCE**... MIND YOU, **I'M** NOT FAULTING HIM ON ***THINK-TYPE THOUGHT THERE.***

NO... AND I BELIEVE WE CAN COVER UP THE FACT THAT HE'S A CANNIBAL... ER.. I MEAN, HAS STRANGE DIETARY HABITS...

BUT **HOW ARE WE GONNA FACE** THE **ROYAL LADIES OF THE FLAG SOCIETY** WITH A **CANDIDATE BORN IN A BOX OF** ***POPCORN?***
WE COULD SAY IT WAS A **FOURTH OF JULY** BOX... THAT'D BE NICE.

NO NEWS IS GOOD

NEWSLIFE, THE NATIONAL NEWS MAGAZINE OF TOGETHERHEID, POURED ITS POWERFUL POLITICAL TEAM INTO THE OKEFENOKEE THIS WEEK.

PENCILS AT THE READY, KEEN BRAINS AGLEAM BEHIND INTELLIGENT HORN RIMS, THESE EXPERTS SPREAD OUT TO RAVEL THE LOOSE ENDS OF WHITE-HOUSING, WEB-SPINNING SPIDERS FOR FREMOUNT.
RAVEL?

RAVEL
YOU MEAN UN-RAVEL.

LET'S LOOK AT THE NEWSLIFE STYLE BOOK ... CRISP, CURT, CLEAR ... IT SAYS USE TIDY-UP, TRIM-UP, POLICE-UP.
NEATIFY, CODIFY AND SYNTAGMATIZE.
WHAT HAPPENED TO RAVEL AND UNRAVEL?

AS WEEK'S END NEARED, A NEAT, SHARP-STYLED WRITER FOR NEWSLIFE, THE NATIONAL NEWS MAGAZINE FOR TOGETHERHEID, GATHERED HIS WELL-OILED WITS.
YOU EVER TAKE UP CAMERA WORK?

DMITRI, THE UNEDUCATED QUESTION PRESUPPOSES A SHORT, BALDING BRAIN ... THE PHOTO IS A ONE-EYED MAN IN THE KINGDOM OF THE WORD ... SHAFTS OF LIGHT IN CONSONANTAL AND VOWELED TONE ILLUMINATE PIERCING THOUGHT.
YOU SOUND LIKE A DARK-ROOM MAN.

RICH IN ORGAN NOTES ARE THE WORDS OF THE WINGED MIND... NEW TIMES, NEW STYLES, NEW POLITICAL MAKESHIFTS DEMAND NEW WORDS... ONE POSSIBILITY AT WEEK'S CLOSE WAS...
WAS WHAT?

OMITRI, THE UNERRING ACCURACY OF THE BLUNT THUMB HAS LED YOU TO THE CRUX... WHAT'S THE WORD? NEW, BITTER, BITING? HEAVEN, AT PRESS TIME, NO ONE KNOWS BUT.
YOU SURE YOU WOULDN'T RATHER PUT THIS ALL ON FILM?

BEIN' A POLL-TAKER CAN BE PRETTY UN-REWARDIN'... NOBODY ROUND HERE WANTS HIS POLL TOOK.

WELL, WELL! WHOM DO WE HAVE HERE? A MEMBER OF THE KLOO KLUCK-HEADED KLOWNS?
NOSSIR.. THAT THERE IS FREMOUNT HISSELF WITH A BAG OVER HIS HEAD FOR THE HICCUPS.
HIC HIC

HUM... WELL, I'M A PULSE TAKER OF THE PUBLIC ...AND...
IF YOU WANT FREMOUNT'S PULSE, ALL I CAN TELL YOU IS HE'S HICCIN' AT A STEADY 89 PER MINUTE.
HIC HIC

IS FREMOUNT GONNA LEAVE THAT BAG OVER HIS HEAD IF HE'S ELECTED?
IT MIGHT PAY... BUT WE'LL CROSS THAT BRIDGE WHEN WE COME TO IT.
HIC HIC

ALL'S I CAN SAY IS BEIN' A POLL TAKER IS HARD ENOUGH WITHOUT I GOTTA TAKE THE POLL OF A MAN WITH A BAG OVER HIS HEAD.
BUT HE SOMEHOW GOTTA GET CURED OF THEM HICCUPS.
HIC

WHY DON'T I JES' KINDA LIFT A CORNER OF THE BAG AN' SLIP A QUICK QUESTION UNDER THERE?
HIC
YOU WON'T GET BUT ONE ANSWER OR T'OTHER... HE MIGHT SAY "JES' FINE"...

AN' THE OTHER ONE WOULD BE...
HIC

I KNOW THE OTHER ONE... I GOT IT RIGHT IN THE EYE...
OH, HE'S A TIGER WHEN IT COME TO HICCUPPIN'.
HIC

PHOTO OF THE WEEK: EX-CANDIDATE, POGO, BASKS IN SLEEPY SWAMP. HIS FIRST WORD AN INQUIRING "HELLO?"
IS THAT POGO...? HE'S AGED.
I'M NOT POGO... WHO ARE YOU TWO?
HIC

AT START OF WEEK A DEAD-PAN DENIAL OF IDENTITY FROM POGO STARTLED A SUN-BESET OKEFENOKEE... WHERE'S THE REAL CANDIDATE WAS ONE IMMEDIATE QUESTION.
FREMOUNT? THE CANDIDATE'S IN THE BAG.
ALREADY?
HIC
HIC

YOU GOT ME WRONG, FRIEND, I'M A POLL-TAKER... NOT A 'POSSUM.
AND WHICH WAY POLLS THE SWAMP?

A LANDSLIDE FOR FREMOUNT, A TIDAL WAVE... A SURGE.
A GRASS ROOTS WILD-FIRE, WOULD YOU SAY?

NOT SO SURE IF IT RATES THAT YET, BUT IT'S UP THERE... A ROCKET BLAST.
WOULD YOU SAY IT WAS AN AVALANCHE OF DEEP DOWN SENTIMENT?

WELL, YES... THO' I'VE ONLY POLLED THREE PEOPLE... TWO FOR AND ONE ON THE FENCE.
AS NEWSLIFE FIGURES IT, THAT'D BE 2½ PEOPLE FOR... THAT OTHER IS HALF WAY THERE.

OUT OF A GRAVE SITUATION

FREMOUNT, THE BOY BUG, LIKES RUNNIN' FOR PRESIDENT... HE FOUND OUT ABOUT KISSIN' BABIES.
HE'S KINDA OF A INFANT HISSELF.

HE'S KISSIN' ONLY GIRL TYPE TADS.
THAT FEMALE VOTE IS POWERFUL.

CHURCHY TOLE ME THERE'S A PALLBEARER AROUND WANTS TO BURY SOMEBODY.
POLL TAKER... AN' HE DON'T WANT TO BURY ANYBODY.. HE WANTS TO DIG UP SOMETHIN'.

POLL TAKER... PALLBEARER... DIG IT UP... BURY IT... SIX OF ONE AND HALF A DOZEN OF THE OTHER.

THE PROPOSAL OF THE PROPOSAL

I THINK NEWSLIFE, THE NEWS MAGAZINE OF TOGETHERHEID, WOULD LIKE TO ENTER A BANG-UP, NEWSWORTHY, NEWSLIVELY DEAL WITH YOU, MRS. BEETLE.
THERE'S ONE NOW, GRUNION.
HIC HIC HIC
FINE

YES, INDEED.. AT WEEK'S END OUR EDITORIAL BOARD MEETS.
A WATCHMAKER CARRYING HIS WARES... ASK HIM IF YOU CAN SEE THE TICKER, BELMORE.
SIR... OH, SIR!
HIC HIC

CAN YOU WHAT?... OH? NO, THIS IS NOT A WATCH TICKING, SONNY.
A MAD BOMBER!
HIC HIC HIC

HMM.. CURIOUS! AS I WAS SAYING, AT WIT'S END... I MEAN AT WEEK'S END OUR EDITORIAL BOARD WILL.. UM.. MEET...
EVACUATE!

UP-COMING THIS WEEK IS A PROPOSAL FROM ME TO YOU, MRS. BEETLE.
OH, MISTER NEWSLIFE. SO SUDDEN!
HIC HIC

THE WEB OF WEDDING I SPIN NOT, MADAM.. SAVE IN THE PROXY.... BUT WHAT WOULD YOU THINK OF MARRYING FREMOUNT?
MARRY MY OWN CHILD?
HIC HIC

I DON'T MEAN **YOU**.. I MEAN TO MARRY HIM TO SOMEONE **ALREADY** IN THE WHITE HOUSE TO INSURE **HE GOES IN**... (HEREDITY-WISE.)
WELL ... UM ... MRS. DAVIS IS TOOK BY JEFF... AN'... UM...
HIC

YOU CAN LEAVE THAT DETAIL TO ME, MRS. BEETLE... I'LL ARRANGE ALL IN EXCHANGE FOR EXCLUSIVE PICTURES.
MM.. WELL, I GOT A EXCLUSIVE PICTURE ... ME AN' UNCLE FROD AN' ONE OF MY MA'S HEN HOUSE AN'... UM...
HIC

IN THE BAG MAY BE THE **NEXT CHIEF**.. A WEDDING TO ONE OF OFFICIALDOM'S FAMILY WILL ASSURE CERTAINTY.
I ALLUS HOPED FREMOUNT WOULD HAVE A **BIG WEDDING**.
HIC HIC

AN UP-JUMP POLL-WISE FROM LOCAL ACCLAIM TO NATION-WIDE, WORLDWIDE AFFECTION WOULD BE **MAIN RESULT** OF ROMANCE.
IT MAKES ME THINK.
HIC

FOR EXCLUSIVE PICTURE RIGHTS, TRIP TO HONEY-MOON ISLE (FREE) WE CAN ARRANGE ALL.
MMM... ***CANDY!***

STOP! YOU'LL EAT THE KID!
WHAT?! AN' CATCH THE HICCUPS...? **NOT ME!**
HIC HIC HIC HIC HIC HIC HIC

THE CONFOUNDING

A PUBLIC OFFICE IS A PUBLIC TRUST··· HOW CAN THE PUBLIC TRUST A MAN WHAT EATS THEM? IT'S DECEITFUL!
YOU SAID HE'D CHANGE.

MAJOR FRUMMY'S BUG ATLAS SAYS THE ANT LION LARVA CHANGES INTO A WINGED FLY ··· BUT IT STILL EATS OTHER BUGS.
I GUESS YOU DEVELOP A SWEET TOOTH THAT WAY, IT'S HARD TO BREAK.

THING IS THE PARTY··· OUR REPUTATION IS AT STAKE··· LATER WE CAN SAY FREMOUNT'S A CHANGED MAN AND, BEIN' THE FIRST NOMINEE WITH BONA FIDE WINGS, HE'LL BE A AVIATION EXPERT.
BUT HE'LL DEVOUR THE COUNTRY.
BUG ATLAS

ONE THING AT A TIME··· FIRST WE'LL SAVE THE PARTY ···THEN WE'LL GIVE THE COUNTRY SOME ATTENTION.

NOW, MY PLAN··· THAT IS, NEWSLIFE'S PLAN, WILL BE TO MARRY FREMOUNT OFF TO A MEMBER OF THE ROYAL, THAT IS, OFFICIAL FAMILY···
THAT'LL BE NICE.

I B'LEEVE DEACON MUSHRAT WILL BE GLAD TO READ THE CEREMONY.
OH, ONE DETAIL TO BE PINPOINTED: NEWSLIFE PLANS TO SIGN THE BIG BOY AT THE TOP TO SPLICE THE HAPPY BUG-EYED COUPLE.

WHAT? THE ONE THAT'S OVER THE WHOLE··UH···
YES, TO MAKE IT OFFICIAL··· NOTHING'S OFFICIAL UNLESS WE GIVE IT THE NEWSLIFE OKAY AS HARD NEWS.
HIC

LAND! YOU MEAN YOU CAN GET ··· YOU CAN GET···? MY!
OH, INDEED···RIGHT AFTER THE BOSS PUTS THE BOOK TO BED HE'LL COME DOWN FROM THE 267th FLOOR READY TO READ THE ··· YES ··· WHAT?
I SAID: HEY, THERE!

AT MIDWEEK THE CANDIDATE'S BAG-BOUND, CONGERSMAN.
WE BEEN BAGGED, ···THAT'S WHO! TURNS OUT HE AIN'T NO BEETLE··· HE'S A ANT LION.
HIC

WHAT DO YOU KNOW ABOUT THAT, MRS. BEETLE? IT DOESN'T CHECK WITH NEWSLIFE'S HIGHLY EXPENSIVE RESEARCH.
OH, DEAR, IT'S TRUE··· IT'S TRUE··· LI'L FREMOUNT IS A FOUNDLIN'.
HIC

NEWSLIFE HAS BEEN LED ASTRAY, A SACRILEGE··· NO SON OF BEETLE, HE.
I FOUND FREMOUNT IN A BOX OF POPCORN··· LIKE A SORT OF PRIZE, KINDA.
HIC

THIS IS A SERIOUS BREACH OF CONTRACT, MRS. BEETLE··· I'M DISAPPOINTED.
SO WAS I··· I WAS HOPIN' FOR A DIAMOND RING OR ANYWAYS A PITCH PIPE.
A PEACH PIE?

AN APPETITE FOR ONE'S FELLOW MAN

ALL OF A SUDDEN BOTH OF YOU IS WORRIED 'BOUT FREMOUNT BEIN' A CANNIBAL... IS HE EVER ET ANYBODY YOU KNOW?
FOR ALL YOU KNOW, NONE OF US MAY BE SAFE...

HE AIN'T NO MORE'N ME OR YOU A CANNIBAL... HE'S A GOOD LI'L' SCAPER.
THE ROAD TO HADES IS PAVED WITH GOOD LI'L' SCAPERS.

HE'S A ANT LION AND, AS SUCH, EATS ANTS... THINK OF THE SHORTAGE THERE MAY BE IN ANTS IF HE HAS HIS WAY... YOU'LL HAFTA TAKE YOUR OWN TO A PICNIC AN', WITH HELP SO HIGH, THINK OF INFLATION.

BUT MAYBE HE DON'T PRACTICE CANNIBALISM.
PRACTICE?! CANNIBALS EITHER DOES OR DON'T ...THEY DON'T NEED NO PRACTICE... NOT ON ME.

I'M AGAINST PEOPLE WHAT EATS OTHER PEOPLE...

BUT EVERYBODY EATS SOMEBODY ... YOU EATS HAM AN' EGGS ... WHERE D'YOU S'POSE HAM COMES FROM? WHERE DO EGGS COME FROM?
WELL.. UM...

I ALWAYS CONSIDERED EGGS TO BE VEGETABLES.
YOU? ARE YOU A VEGETARIAN?

WHAT I IS DON'T MATTER. RELIGION AND POLITICS IS TWO DIFFER'NT THINGS.

ALL'S I CAN SAY IS IF FREMOUNT'S A CANNIBAL SO IS EVERYBODY.
NOT ME

WHAT D'YA MEAN? YOU EATS EGGS... AN' MANY A OWL IS STARTED OUT AS A EGG.
OH, I WOULDN'T EAT OWL EGGS.

GACK... NEITHER WOULD I!

YOU KNOW, IT'S CLEARHEADED, STRONG-MINDED, INTELLIGENT, COURAGEOUS OBSERVATIONS LIKE THAT WHAT STAMPS THE TRUE LEADER.

WHY ARE YOU TRYING TO DROWN POOR OWL?
I'M NOT... HE FELL OVERBOARD OF HIS OWN FREEHAND WILL.
YEH

MATTER OF FACT, POGO JUS' MADE A MOST STATESMANLIKE REMARK... HE SAID HE WOULDN'T THINK OF EATIN' A OWL EGG ... ISN'T THAT FINE?

THINK OF IT? I WOULDN'T EVEN GO DREAM ABOUT IT.
ANOTHER CLEAR THINKER.

NOT UNLESS I WANTED THE NIGHTMARES.
'COURSE HE AIN'T AS STATESMANLIKE AS YOU.

PERSON'LY, I THINK ANYBODY WHAT COMES RIGHT OUT AND SWEARS OFF OWL EGGS IS GOT BONA FIDE PERSPICACITY.

WE GOT ENOUGH BUGS IN GOVERNMENT ... WHY GO FOR FREMOUNT, THE CANNIBAL ANT LION? I LIKE YOU TWO, WHO WON'T EAT OWL EGGS, FOR THE TOP JOBS.

I WOULDN'T EVEN EAT A OWL ... UGH!
UGH?

WHAT'S SO ALL FIRED UGH ABOUT IT? MAYBE THE COUNTRY DON'T NEED YOU.
ALL RIGHT... I WOULD EAT A OWL, THEN...
ENOUGH! ENOUGH!

WHAT'S WRONG WITH OWL'S IDEA.. I'LL BE VICE-PRESIDENT... YOU BE PRESIDENT?
UM...

YOU FORGETS THE CARES OF OFFICE.
DON'T EVERYBODY?

IT'S YOUR PATRIOTIC DUTY TO RUN... YOU DIN'T GET ELECTED EITHER TIME BEFORE, DID YOU?
WULL... NO....

WHAT ARE YOU AFRAID OF THEN? WITH THAT KIND OF LUCK YOU CAN DO IT AGAIN.

THE COLD PEACE

WHAT YOU GOTTA DO AS A PRESS CHIEF FOR THE CANDIDATE IS SEND UP A TRIAL BALLOON.
SUCH as?

WELL... HOW ABOUT...
JES' FINE

JES' FINE

Dangerous WORK THEM LEAD ONES---
PIP

I DUNNO... USUALLY IN THE POLITICAL WORD GAME THE BALLOONS ARE SO FULL OF HOT AIR THEY HAVE A KIND OF HOLIDAY BUOYANCY.

TICK TOCK IS CHEAP

WE OUGHT TO TALK THIS OUT MAN TO MAN.
IF WE ONLY HAD A **CAST.**

WE CAN'T ELECT **FREMOUNT,** THE FREE-LOADIN' ANT LION... .. HE'LL EAT EVERY ANT IN THE COUNTRY... ***NOSSIR!*** THE JOB IS GOTTA BE ***YOURS.***
MINE? A JOB EATIN' ***ANTS?***

WHAT DO I WANT TO GO 'ROUND EATIN' ***ANTS*** FOR... WHEN THERE'S ANCHOVIES, PINKLES, LI'L' BUNS, AND RAISINS?
FOOBASH

YOU DON'T THINK THE PRESIDENT GOES 'ROUND DOIN' NOTHIN' BUT **EATIN'** ANTS AND OTHER CONDIMENTS, DO YOU?
HE **DON'T?**

C'MON WITH ME... I'LL SHOW YOU WHAT THE GRASS ROOTS IS SAYIN'... ***THEY*** AIN'T FOR FREMOUNT... ***THEY'RE*** FOR **POGO.**

HELLO THERE, GRASS ROOTS... IN THE BIG FAT CURRENT ELECTION RACE WHO IS YOU FOR? ***FREMOUNT,*** THE CANNIBAL, OR **POGO,** THE NATURAL-BORN CHARMIN' SON OF OUR BELOVED SWAMP?

I'M FOR ME... WIN, PLACE, SHOW OR WEASEL-OUT.

DID YOU EVER HEAR SUCH A SNAP JUDGEMENT IN ALL YOUR LIFE, POGO? ... UM?... POGO? HELLO?

I'M HERE TO TELL YOU I'M ALL IN FAVOR OF YOUR BIG IDEA ... WE'LL DUMP THAT FREMOUNT CANNIBAL AND RUN POGO FOR TOP DOG.

AND, DEAR OLD FRIEND, I GOT ANOTHER GREAT IDEA ... GUESS WHO WE CAN RUN FOR VICE-PRESIDENT?

ME!

ER..UH... DID YOU SAY SOMETHING?

LOOK, LET'S BE SPORTS... WHO CARES WHO RUNS FOR V.P. WITH POGO LONG AS IT'S THE **BEST MAN**?
WHO CARES INDEED?

WE'LL START THE CAMPAIGN AND NOT GIVE A **HANG**...
WE'LL **POP** THE ***CHAMPAGNE*** WITH A SPLINTERING --

BANG

DAGNAB! DON'T YOU KNOW THEM **FIRE CRANKERS** IS ***UNLEGAL***?
OH, THAT'S JUST **GRUNDOON**... HE LEARNT A NEW WORD TO CELEBRATE FOURTH OF JULY WITH ... HOLLER IT AGAIN, GRUNDOON... 1..2..3...

HOW 'BOUT ALL THESE EXPERTS? **P.T. BRIDGEPORT, TAMMANANNY,** THAT **POLL-TAKIN' CAT**, THEM BOYS FROM **NEWSLIFE**.. ***IS THEY AGAINST POGO RUNNIN'***?

OHO! JUST THE OPPOSITE!
THEN THEY'S ***FOR*** IT?

WELL, NOT EGG-ZACKLY... THEY'S MORE OR LESS BIDIN' OF THEIR TIME.
BIDIN' THEIR TIME?

YEH... NONE OF 'EM IS HEARD OF IT YET.

NOW THERE GOES GOOD MATERIAL! THE KIND OF A MAN FOR SECRETARY OF STATE.

WHAT? HOW COULD HE TAKE OVER SUCH A OFFICE?

HOW WOULD MR. HERTER FEEL IF HE WAS FOLLOWED BY AN ALLIGATOR?

Y'KNOW, IN A LOT OF WAYS MR. HERTER MUST FEEL HE'S BEEN FOLLOWED BY AN ALLIGATOR FOR MANY A MOON.

SIGNS ON THE DOTTY LINE

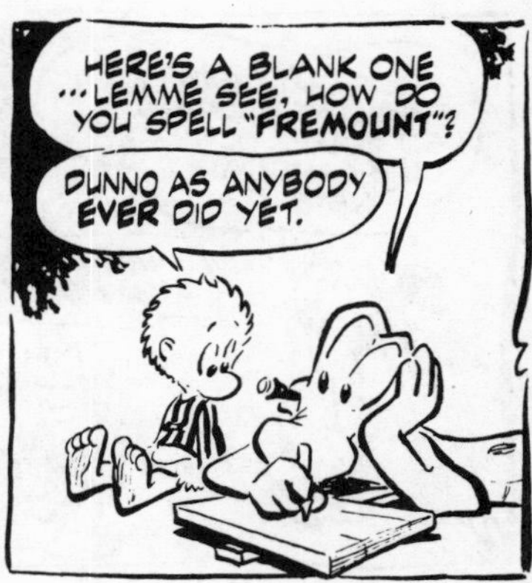

THERE'S NO TIME NOW TO RELETTER ALL THESE SIGNS FROM '52 AND '56... THERE'S JUS' ONE THING TO DO...
Z
I GO POGO
POGO

POGO, IT'S YOUR DUTY TO RUN FOR PRESIDENT.... YOU CAN'T LET ALL THESE SIGNS GO WASTE... CONGRATULATIONS, MISTER CANDIDATE!
I GO POGO

I HEAR THAT THEY'S CALLIN' FREMOUNT A CANNIBAL SO YOU'RE GONNA BE THE CANDIDATE INSTEAD...
HIP! HIP!
I GO POGO
WHY? WE NEVER HAD A CANNIBAL CANDIDATE!

... WE GOT ALL THESE OLD POGO SIGNS LEFT OVER FROM 1952 AND 1956... ALL WE NEED NOW IS A SLOGAN... A CALL TO COLORS!

A RALLYIN' CRY... A REBEL YELL SORTA... SOMETHIN' TO TELL THE RASCALS YOU'RE COMIN' THROUGH! FULLA FIRE!

HOW 'BOUT "FORE" ?

MUCH ADIEU

COME ON! IT'S ON TO LOS ANGELES! WE'LL PUT POGO ACROSS ON THE FIRST BALLOT.
PACK EVERYTHING WE NEED.

WHICH CONVENTION IS THE ONE AT LOS ANGELES? WHICH PARTY?

IT'S ONE OR THE OTHER... ...WHO KNOWS? WE'LL GO TO 'EM ALL! GET POGO...LET'S GO! WHERE'S THE CANDIDATE?
YEAH..WHERE!? DO YOU S'POSE THE LI'L SWAB IS RUN OFF?
G'BYE
HELLO?

C'MON, HURRY IT UP! HURRY IT UP! FIND THE CANDIDATE! WE'LL MISS THE KEYNOTE SPEECH.
THE NO GOOD WEASEL IS RUN OUT ON US ... WE AIN'T GOT NO CANDIDATE.
WE'LL NEVER MAKE L.A.

WHAT!? WE'LL MAKE IT ON THE FIRST BALLOT WITH OR WITHOUT A CANDIDATE!
WOODYA MEAN, MAKE IT?

ON THREE WHEELS?
WELL... I'M NOT A MECHANICAL GENIUS, TOO, Y'KNOW.
G'BYE GOOD-BYE

HERE'S A WHEEL TO TAKE THE PLACE OF THE MISSIN' ONE! DO I GOTTA DO EVERYTHING?
POGO! COME ON! THE CONVENTION CAN'T WAIT!
LOS ANGELES OR BUST
GOOD-BYE

NOW TO GET BACK AN' GIVE A SHOVE TO START HER.

WAIT! WAIT! WAIT! WHERE'S THE STEERIN' WHEEL?
STEER WITH THE PLIERS...WHAT DO YOU THINK I REPLACED THAT MISSIN' WHEEL WITH?
POGO! POGO!
THE CARTER
LOS ANGELES OR BUST
GOOD-BYE GOOD-BYE

IF YOU COULD GIVE US ANOTHER SHOVE I THINK I GOT THE HANG OF STEERIN' WITH THE PLIERS... I'LL POINT HER IN THE DIRECTION OF LOS ANGELES.
NOTHIN' DOIN'! THAT ENGINE AIN'T CATCHIN'... A CYLINDER MUST BE MISSIN'...
GOOD-BYE GOOD-BYE
LOS ANGELES OR BUST

THE WHOLE ENGINE IS MISSIN'.
THE CARTER
GOOD-BYE GOOD-BYE

MORE AND/OR LESS ADIEU

I NEVER SAW SUCH A BUNCH!
HELP! ALBERT PACKED ME IN BY MISTAKE! HELP!

NOW WE HAVE TO START OVER!
HELP HELP

WODDYA S'POSE HAPPENED TO POGO?
DUNNO, BUT HE MISSED A VERY FINE LEAVE-TAKIN'.
WELL! WHERE HAVE YOU BEEN?
G'BYE G'BYE
© 1960 WALT KELLY

FOOMPH
G'BYE G'BYE

CHANGING COURSES IN MIDSTREAM

DON'T WORRY, KIDDO, YOU'LL BE A SHOO-IN AT THE NEXT CONVENTION ··· I'M WRITIN' A CAMPAIGN SONG FOR YOU.
BUT I'M NOT RUNNIN'.

YOU'LL RUN WHEN YOU HEAR THIS.
YOU AIN'T FOOLIN'.

WHO ROARS FOR POGO, WHO ROARS FOR HIS BROWN EYES OF BLUE, WHO ROARS TO GO GO, HOOROARS FOR THE RED, WHITE AND BLUE!

WHO EVER HEARD OF RHYMIN' BLUE WITH BLUE?
YEH··· THAT ONE PART DON'T MAKE MUCH SENSE, DO IT?

IT WON'T STUMP ME.

I HEAR THE EXPEDITION TO LOS ANGELES GOT RAINED OUT
SWAMPED WE WAS... NEARLY DROWNT THE CANDIDATE.

THE NEW CAMPAIGN SONG GOT BUGS IN IT... LISTEN:
WHO ROARS FOR POGO,
WHO ROARS FOR HIS BROWN EYES OF BLUE,
WHO ROARS TO GO GO
HOOROARS FOR THE RED, WHITE AN' BLUE.

SOMETHIN'S WRONG... WHAT PART DON'T YOU LIKE?
MOSTLY LISTENIN' TO IT... WHY NOT SUBSTITUTE THE WORD "TWO" FOR BLUE?

THE RED, WHITE AND TWO? THAT DON'T MAKE SENSE EITHER.
THAT AIN'T WHAT I MEANT, BUT NOW I KNOW YOU IS TRYIN' TO MAKE SENSE I'LL THINK OF SOME-THIN' ELSE.

MOOMPH MOOMPH

NOW THAT YOU IS FED YO' CAMPAIGN MANAGERS LET'S GO FIND SOME WAY TO GET 'EM TO CHICAGO... THEY DROWNED THE AUTO.
BUT...

BUT I DON'T WANT NOBODY CAMPAIGNIN' FOR ME.
WOULDN'T YOU RATHER HAVE 'EM DO IT OUT OF TOWN THAN 'ROUND HERE WHERE THEY'S UNDERFOOT?

TROUBLE WITH YOU MODERN YOUTHS IS YOU'RE TOO APATHETIC... LEASTWISE THAT'S WHAT ALL THEM SAYS WHAT GETS DOWNWIND OF THE YOUNG THESE DAYS.

SHUCKS! WE AIN'T APATHETIC ... WE'RE JUS' SETTIN' TIGHT WAITIN' TO SEE WHICH WAY WE'LL HAFTA JUMP.

HELLO, FRIENDS, WE'RE STILL TRYIN' TO THINK OF A PRESS RELEASE.
BUT WE MUST INTERVIEW ☆THE CANDIDATE!☆ Where is he? WHERE'S ⇨ FLYMOCK?
FREMOUNT AIN'T THE CANDIDATE NO MORE.

OWL AN' THE OTHERS CLAIM FREMOUNT IS A ANT LION WHO EATS ANTS.... SO THEY'RE BACKIN' POGO AGAIN.
BUT I AIN'T.

OH, WELL, NOW WE HAVE A STORY! TAKE A PRESS Release TAMMANNANY~~~
EXTRA
P. T. BRIDGEPORT NAMES NEW MAN
BULLETIN
CAPITOL QUIET
SENATORS GO HOME
HOUSE DISBANDS
SAGE LEADER CHOOSES POGO
"A SAFE MAN TO LOSE WITH" SAYS POLITICAL BOSS
BELOVED P. T.

WE COME OVER TO SEE IF YOU STILL HAVE THAT OL' CIRCUS TRAIN, P.T., SO'S THE DELEGATES CAN GO TO CHICAGO.
BUT OF COURSE! PRAY STEP BEHIND this COPSE

YOU AIN'T GOT MUCH TRACK, P.T.
NO, BUT WE HAVE ONE WHALE OF A LOT of ENGINE
OLD 5+2 G.F.R.R. CO.
GRIZZLY FLATS

PERSON'LY I DON'T THINK IT'LL EVER GET OFF THE GROUND...

A RENDEZVOUS WITH FATE

WHERE'S POGO?
HEY.. WHAT DO YOU THINK I...

SORRY, MA'M, I AIN'T GOT TIME TO THINK... THE CANDIDATE'S MISSING.

EGADS! THERE'S ONE NOW, HUMBERT.

ONE WHAT?
RUN! RUN! SHE'LL BEWITCH US!

HAVE YOU SEEN POGO? THE TRAIN'S READY FOR CHICAGO... CAN'T LEAVE WITHOUT HIM.
POGO? OF COURSE... HERE, HOLD THIS.

I'LL GET HIM FOR YOU IN AN EYE-FLASH...QUICK-THINKING JOURNALISTIC ACUMEN LEAPT READILY TO THE RESCUE THIS WEEK AS...
HUP HUP

HOLD IT... HOLD IT! A SHOT OF YOU CAPTURIN' A WILD ANIMAL WILL GET ME THE PULITZER.
THOUGHT SO... KEEN-TRAINED BRAIN, RAZOR-HONED, SPOTS FUGITIVE.

GREAT!
CLICK
GOTCHA

POGO! YOU'RE WANTED!
I AIN'T POGO... LEGGO!

DON'T TELL NEWSLIFE WHO YOU ARE, PAL...
HOLD IT...IT'S A GREAT INTERVIEW SHOT.

SHALL I TELL THE HEAD OFFICE YOU'RE SITTIN' ON THE STORY?
I GOT IT TIED UP WITH MY FOULARD.

I STILL THINK YOU'D OF MADE A GOOD DARK-ROOM MAN.
THE CANDIDATE THIS WEEK WAS NOT ONLY DRAFTED BUT DRUGGED UNWILLING BUT ABLE TO A RENDEZVOUS WITH FATE.
WOOF

PURBLIND LOVE

THE JIG AND THE STEAM IS UP

THAT was A mighty PERTY engine, TAMMANNANY
HOLD EVERYTHING... AT START OF WEEK, EAGER-EYED REPORTERS RUSHED TO PARTY LEADERS. THEY HAD ONE DEMAND: HOLD THAT FLYER... STOP THAT TRAIN!

DID THE FLYER TAKE OFF?
IN A MANNER OF SPEAKING, YES...

PARTS OF IT ARE STILL IN ORBIT... TOO BAD YOU MISSED IT.
YOU, TOO?
U what? CARE, SIR, would be prudent.

A WASTED DAY... A WASTED DAY.
WHAT'S WASTED ABOUT IT? I USED UP 426 ROLLS OF FILM AND AIN'T EVEN TOOK THE LENS CAP OFF YET.
WHAT, pray tell, IS THIS?
BETTING IS TWO TO ONE AS MIDWEEK NEARS, THAT TOP WISEACRES ARE CALLING IT POGO.

POGO! This isn't a possum-- THIS, SIR, IS A SKUNK!

CLEAR IT WAS, AS SMOKE CLEARED, BIG BRASS POLITICOS WERE IN STATE OF SHOCK. EPITHETS ROLLED IN ROUND TERMS AS P. T. BRIDGEPOT CALLED POGO A SKUNK. HIS MAN HAD MISSED THE BOAT.
THAT'S BRIDGEPORT and it was a TRAIN!

MONSTER RALLY!

NOW'S OUR TIME... THEM OTHER PARTIES HAVE BLOWN THEIR CHANCE... WE CAN NOMINATE POGO... OR (HEH HEH) SOMEONE OF OUR OWN CHOICE.
A FREE CON-VENTION.
WE OWLS AN' DOGS CAN DO IT NOW... WE WAS GONNA HAVE A RALLY ANYWAYS.
Y'SAY FREMOUNT IS IN LOVE WITH A INVISIBLE BUG?
THEY SEES EYE TO EYE.
MONSTER RALLY
ALASKA

EVERYBODY CAN BE A KEYNOTER... EVERYBODY CAN BE CHAIRMAN... EVERYBODY CAN VOTE.
HOW COME YOU TOLE ME TO HOLD ALL THEM MOPS AN' ALL?
I FIGGERED IN CASE ANYBODY OFFERED YOU THE PRESIDENCY, YOU COULD SAY YOU HAD YOUR HANDS FULL.
THAT SUITS US BUGS EH, WASP?
ESKIMO?
MONST RALLY
GEORGIA
ALASKA

STEP FORWARD AN' CAST YO' BALLOTS FOR THE NOMINEE.
HERE COME FREMOUNT ESCORTIN' HIS INVISIBLE BUG FRIEND, MISS EM'LY.

I'LL BE DOGNABBED... WE GOT FOURTEEN DELEGATES WITH FOURTEEN VOTES AND WE IS SELECTED FOURTEEN CANDIDATES... WHAT A COINCIDENCE!
I VOTED FOR YOU.
YOU WASTED IT.. I VOTED FOR YOU.
PLUS ONE INVISIBLE VOTE FOR MISS EM'LY.

THE PARTY OF THE LAST PART

QUITE A PARTY, THAT CELEBRATION OF EVERYBODY'S NOMINATION.
YUP
YOU STILL INSIST THIS IS POGO?
AT PRESS TIME DOUBT ENTERS MIND AS TO NEWSLIFE RESEARCH?
RIGHT

DOUBT, DEBT and DOOM LOOM
BAZZ FAZZ
WELL, IF YOU DON'T WANT EXPERT OPINION IT'S GOOD-BYE.
AN' NONE TOO SOON

ONE THING FILLS ME WITH CONFIDENCE FOR THE COUNTRY'S FUTURE.
WHAT?

NONE OF US WILL GET ELECTED.
IT IS COMFORTIN'.